CAN I COME HOME NOW?

A True Story of Childhood Trauma

by

Barbara Godin

While every precaution has been taken in the preparation of this book, the publisher assumes no responsibility for errors or omissions, or for damages resulting from the use of the information contained herein.

CAN I COME HOME NOW?

First edition. October 1, 2022.

Copyright © 2022 Barbara Godin.

ISBN: 979-8215271780

Written by Barbara Godin.

Table of Contents

This book is written in memory of my sister Mary and for all the children who thought they were the only ones!

Acknowledgments

A special thank you for the support and encouragement of the following people.

Ed for convincing me that my story needed to be told.

Brenda Missen for helping to create the first draft, a long time ago in 1988.

Stan, my husband, for reading and rereading my manuscript.

Madison for her supportive words, reminding me that "it is my story to tell."

Barbara Lehtiniemi for providing exceptional editing and proofreading skills.

My readers, especially Tina Laurelli and Megan McCauley, I couldn't have done it without your contributions.

Prologue

When people learn about the events of my life, their reaction is always the same—"How did you survive?" "Why aren't you selling yourself on the street corner?" "You must have had years of therapy." Even as a child, I can remember acquaintances who knew our family whispering things like, "There's Millie's daughter, the poor girl. When she grows up she'll hate her mother for the life she's had."

By the time I was 16 years old, I'd been to thirteen schools and lived in as many homes, including two stays at the Ontario Training School for Girls, and one year at The Inn, a halfway home for girls in Windsor. Even marriage, at seventeen, didn't bring the security and happiness I so badly craved. My husband, insecure himself, physically and mentally abused me. We were two emotionally disturbed people who were not able to give each other the encouragement and caring we both needed.

For most of those years, I couldn't laugh. I can remember sitting in a room watching television with other people, and if someone on the television said something funny, everyone would laugh. But I just sat there. I wasn't able to feel anything, except my constant inner pain. I didn't know how to enjoy life or get pleasure out of everyday things like going for a walk or enjoying the company of friends. I had no idea of what it felt like to trust; I was always on guard, wondering when I was going to get hurt again.

Books that changed my life. I began reading books on how to change your thinking and how to change your attitude. I learned I didn't have to be a victim. I learned how to love myself and forgive my mother. I could change my life just by changing the way I thought. This was my motivation for writing this book. If my book can help one person find their way through the pain, then it was all worth it.

After ten years of marriage, I took my daughter Lisa, left my husband, and began to make a life for myself. I enrolled in college and, after 2 years, earned my diploma as a Library Technician. Shortly before I was to graduate, I met Ed, and my life changed forever. Ed convinced me that I was lovable, worthy, and strong. I began to believe in myself. I went to university and earned my BA in English, and began writing my way through the trauma of my childhood.

This is my story.

This story is true, some of the names have been changed to prevent identification.

Chapter 1

My earliest memory was of living with Mom, John (Mom's boyfriend), and my three siblings. As it turned out, this would be the last time we would all live together. When John came to live with us, my oldest brother, Lyle, seemed to resent his presence the most. The two of them began fighting on the first day, and the fights soon became physical. The night John kicked Lyle out of the house was an evening that Lyle had been left in charge of Mary and me, while Mom and John went out for the evening. Jeanne, who was fourteen, was usually the babysitter, but she was at a friend's house.

Lyle invited a few of his buddies over, and then a few more. Eventually, it turned into a party, and Mary and I, who were five and four years old, spent the evening trying to stay out of the way of the drunken teenagers. We were so glad to see Mom and John come home. When John spotted Lyle, slumped semi-conscious in a chair, he reached down, grabbed him by the shirt, and pulled him to his feet.

"What the hell is going on here?" John's huge eyes were black with anger. Mary and I hid behind Mom. Lyle looked confused. He tried to focus on John's face.

"Answer me, you goddamn idiot!"

Mom tried to pull John's hands off Lyle. "Leave him alone, John. He doesn't understand what you're saying."

"You keep your nose out of this. I pay the bills around here, not this hoodlum son of yours."

Still holding Lyle, John yelled at the others. "You'd better all get the hell out of here before I call the police."

Mom came over and clutched Mary and me tightly in her arms. John's voice was scary, and we were glad to be somewhere safe. The house emptied in minutes.

Lyle was sobering up quickly; he tried to pull away from John. "Leave me alone!" Lyle hollered.

John was not much taller than Lyle, but he lifted weights and was a street fighter, while Lyle was still a lanky 18-year-old.

"Sure, kid, I'll leave you alone." He dragged Lyle to the back door. Lyle managed to shake him off, but John grabbed him again, this time getting a better grip.

Mom, who had let Mary and me go, was screaming at John. "Let him go, you're going to hurt him!"

John ignored her and pushed Lyle out the back door. "Don't you ever come back, or you'll wish you hadn't," he hollered at Lyle while slamming the door and locking it.

Lyle banged at the door. "Ma, let me in, please, Ma!"

Mom moved to open the door.

"Millie, if you touch that door, I'll leave and never come back."

"But he's my son, I can't just leave him out there."

I couldn't bear to see the tears streaming down her face.

"You heard what I said, it's him or me."

Mom turned away from the door and ran to the bathroom. We could hear her sobbing until Lyle stopped banging. Then an awful silence descended.

John went to the bathroom and tried to turn the handle. "Come on, Millie, open the door." His voice was cajoling now. When he heard the click of the lock, he opened the door and gathered Mom into his arms.

"Cheer up, we did the best thing. That boy has got to grow up, he'll thank us for this one day."

Mom gave in to John's caresses.

Tears filled my eyes as I thought about my brother and wondered if he would ever be back.

In the 1950s, it was the law that if a separated woman was living with a man she was not married to, her ex-husband did not have to pay child support. Dad had stopped paying child support as soon as he had found out about John. Unfortunately, the welfare office also clued in and cut off the monthly payments, leaving us dependent on John. I remember him putting a padlock on the pantry door and rationing food. After he went to work, Mom would get the key from the top cupboard and take out some snacks for us.

When I was five, Mom registered Mary and me at King Edward Public School. Mary was a year older than I, but had not started school the previous year because kindergarten was not mandatory. Now she was put into grade one, while I went into kindergarten. Mary didn't like going to school and didn't see why she had to go all day when I only had to go in the morning. Every day after lunch, she yelled and stomped her feet until Mom let her stay home. On the days Mom was strong and made her go back, Mary often came home after school with soiled underwear.

One day, when Mary and I came home after school, John noticed Mary's odd way of walking and called her over. She started towards him, but he grabbed her hand and pulled her into the living room. Then he called the rest of us in.

"You might all learn something," he said as he began to take off Mary's clothing. He took the pants that were full of feces and rubbed them all over her naked body. I watched in shock. I could see Mary's shoulders quivering. I wanted to yell at John to stop, but I was afraid. He made her stand in the corner covered in feces, with the rest of us reluctantly watching.

Our older sister Jeanne ignored John's threats and ran out of the house and phoned Grandma. The next day, Grandma and Grandpa came down and took Mary away to live with them on their farm, just outside Windsor. Mary had always been Grandma's favorite. She had spent many holidays and weekends with Grandma, Grandpa, and Mom's only sibling,

Uncle Jack, who still lived at home. Aside from her stubbornness, Mary was a quiet, content girl whom Grandma and Grandpa could manage even at their age.

Mom didn't seem to put up much fuss as she packed Mary's clothes into cardboard boxes. Mary watched, not saying a word. I didn't want Mary to leave, but I held back my tears, fearing Mary would start crying if I did.

"I wish you could stay here, Mary."

"I don't want to anyway, because of what John did to me."

We hugged tightly and kissed goodbye. I gave her one of my school pictures to take with her. She promised to bring one for me the next time she came to visit. I was quickly getting the message not to cross John, or I might be the next to go.

It was Jeanne who left next. She moved in with Dad when she couldn't take the fighting between Mom and John anymore. There were just three of us, and the house felt empty. I wished everyone would come back home. If I asked Mom when Mary was coming back, she always said the same thing: "Someday, dear, someday we will all be together again."

We lived in the east end of Windsor, just before a viaduct on Douillard Road, a street well known as one of the tougher areas of Windsor. The house, a bungalow, had been painted at one time, but now it was just old wood that was cracked and weathered. Outside was a big backyard, where John parked his car. The weeds grew wildly around it. The front of the house was surrounded by a hedge that was almost as high as the roof. John wouldn't trim the hedge; he said it gave us privacy.

Each window in the house had a green roll-up blind covering it, all of them, under John's orders, were to be kept pulled down. Sometimes during the day, Mom opened them. It felt wonderful to see the sun beaming in for a few hours.

John had many other rules that Mom and I had to obey. We were not allowed to answer the door. If someone knocked, John would go into the front bedroom and peek out through the edge of the blind to see who was there. If he did not recognize the person, which was most of the time, he would tell Mom and me to stay perfectly still and not move a muscle until the knocking stopped. When I asked John why we had to do this, he laughed nervously. He always laughed when people asked him a question.

The phone was the same. He let it ring, maybe ten times, and then he would pick up the receiver. He would not say anything until the other person spoke. If he recognized the voice, he spoke, if not, he hung up.

Gradually, I learned to keep out of John's way and do what he wanted. I forced myself to eat all my vegetables and everything else on my plate. I tried not to talk back to him or Mom. I didn't answer the door or the phone. The worst thing I had to do was sit on his lap and let him tickle me. If

I did all these things, we would get along fine. Sometimes he would give me a pocket full of coins to spend on whatever I wanted. I began to even like him and see him as a father.

After Jeanne and Mary left, John and Mom began fighting more often. I hated the screaming and the things that were thrown. I could not stand to see John hitting Mom. I cried and screamed at John, but he just ordered me to my room. I hated spending time in my room. I never went there until I absolutely had to at bedtime. It was always dark because of the pulled-down blinds, and Mom could not convince me there weren't monsters in the closet. Every corner had a dark, moving shadow. I squeezed my eyes shut so I wouldn't see them. When the shouting got louder and closer, I took refuge under Mary's old bed. I folded my hands in prayer the way Grandma had shown me while keeping my eyes tightly shut. Because it was so dark, I couldn't tell when it was time for bed. Eventually, I fell asleep under the bed with my clothes on.

The mornings after were always the same. When I got up, sore from the hard floor, the house was a mess of broken glass. John had gone to work, and Mom was silently cleaning up. Her eyes were red and swollen, and her wrists were red from John's grip. We didn't say anything to each other; I went around and picked up the larger pieces of debris, careful not to cut myself until it was time for school.

Often on the weekends, I was sent to stay with John's Uncle George and Aunt Alice. They had no children of their own, and I liked going to their apartment since they had two small dogs. At some point during the summer holidays between grades one and two, Mom arranged for me to spend a few weeks with Dad and Jeanne. I hardly knew Dad. The only previous contact I could remember was when Jeanne was still living at home, and I used to tag along when she met with Dad for dinner on Friday nights. I thought he was a nice-looking man. He often wore a hat and a white shirt, as well as dark pants held up by suspenders. His skin was pale, and his eyes a soft blue. He wasn't very tall. He had fallen arches and had to have his shoes specially made, so they were always the same style: black or brown lace-up oxfords.

Dad and Jeanne were living on the upper floor of a small building that housed four two-bedroom apartments. The apartment had all the necessary furniture, yet it still felt empty; there were no pictures on the walls or shelves of knick-knacks like at Mom's place. Jeanne was eighteen now and working in a nearby store as a cashier. She was dating a fellow named Ray, who eventually became her husband. I enjoyed my visits but looked forward to going home to Mom. I was devastated one Friday night when it was about time for me to leave, and Jeanne and Dad said that I would be staying with them for a while. I was confused and asked if I could call Mom, but Jeanne told me Mom would call me the next day. Mom didn't call. I had no choice but to resign myself to a long stay and wait for Mom to call. Since Dad lived in the same school district as Mom, I was able to attend the same school and keep the same friends.

CAN I COME HOME NOW?

After about a month, I became anxious to see Mom. I hadn't heard a word from her, and Dad and Jeanne rarely spoke of her. One night at dinner, I got up the courage to tell Dad how I felt.

"Daddy, I want to call Mom and see if I can come home yet, okay?"

My question took him by surprise. He stopped eating and gave me a stunned look.

"Please, Daddy, I really miss her."

"Okay, Babs," (a nickname he had given me), "we'll see what we can do." I immediately felt better.

The next afternoon, while Dad was at work, Jeanne and I tried to phone my mom, but the number had been disconnected. We searched through the phone book but there were no listings under either mom's name or John's.

I became hysterical. "What if Mom has died? I know that's what's happened. I'll never be able to see her again!"

"Stop it! Stop it!" Jeanne shouted. "Mom has not died. She probably just doesn't have a phone. Tomorrow, when I get home from work, I'll take you over to see her, okay?"

I felt somewhat relieved, but my relief was short-lived: someone else was living in our old house on Drouillard Road. I began thinking horrible things had happened to Mom and started crying.

"Stop this right now!" Jeanne yelled, but I could see she was upset too. "Mom is not dead. If she had died, someone would have told us. You just have to face it, Barbara, she doesn't care about us—otherwise, she would have told us where she'd moved."

"Why doesn't she care?" I didn't believe her. It couldn't be true.

"John has a lot to do with it. When you're older, you'll understand more. But don't forget we've still got Dad."

I didn't feel connected to Dad. I never knew what to talk to him about, or even how to act around him. He worked, as he had since he was eighteen, at Ford Motor Company as a lift truck driver. When he wasn't on the evening shift, he fell asleep in front of the TV, his breath so heavy with the smell of liquor I could smell it across the room. When I gave him a good night peck on the cheek, the smell made my stomach queasy.

He was not very demonstrative with either Jeanne or me. His main gesture of affection was to walk by me, put one hand on my head, then hit it with the other and laugh.

I missed Mom's hugs.

One night, I woke up to find Dad sitting on my bed with his arm around me.

"It's okay, Babs," he murmured, "It's okay."

I didn't know what was okay, but I enjoyed his arm around me in the darkness.

In the morning, he told me I'd been screaming and crying in my sleep and must have been having a nightmare. It came back to me then: I'd been dreaming about Mom—I kept reaching for her, but she moved farther and farther away. I didn't tell Dad or Jeanne about my dream, but I had it many times and often woke to find Dad at my bedside.

Jeanne, being a typical teenager, found it a burden to babysit me, especially when I interfered with her social life. Occasionally, she vented her frustration at Dad.

> "She's not my kid, why should I have to take care of her?"

"I'm sorry," Dad pleaded.

I felt more and more as though I didn't belong there. When Jeanne's friends were over, I was not allowed to stay in the same room as them.

"If you don't get out of here right now," Jeanne threatened, I'll tell Dad not to buy you anything on Friday."

I left, although I knew Dad would still buy me anything I wanted. Friday evenings or Saturday mornings, depending on his shift, marked our shopping expeditions to the market downtown.

I looked forward to this time. There was always so much happening. It was fun to see all the different farmers trying to sell their produce. On the way home, Dad went into a store by himself, making me stand around the corner. He said children were not allowed in these stores. He came out with a brown paper bag that he tried to hide under his arm.

"What's that, Daddy?"

"Oh, never mind. It's nothing for you to concern yourself with." He clutched my hand and held his head high, as I often saw him do, his eyes focused straight ahead.

When we got home, and he had gone into another room, I peeked into the bag to see the bottle of whiskey. I wondered why he kept it a secret. Mom and John never hid their bottles.

I had never stopped thinking about Mom. I knew she would want me back if only I could find her. I missed her more and more each day. It had been almost a year since I had seen Mom. I was scared that maybe she was dead, and nobody wanted to tell me. If I asked Dad or Jeanne about her, they made vague replies and changed the subject.

Finally, the day I had longed for came. Grandma and Grandpa called to say they would be coming to visit. When they arrived, they took us out to dinner and told us Mom wanted to see us. Jeanne didn't see why we should be bothered with her, but I grabbed the piece of paper with the address on it, and the next afternoon, after school went to find Mom. I didn't tell Jeanne or Dad, afraid they wouldn't let me go.

Mom and John had moved into a smaller house, just two streets over from Drouillard Road on the same street as my friend from school. I walked up the laneway and knocked on the door. I hoped Grandma had given me the correct house number. I knocked and knocked. Finally, I saw the blind move and the door quickly opened. At last, I felt my mother's arms around me.

"Oh, my Barbara, I have missed you so much."

I couldn't stop crying. I couldn't say anything. I just wanted to stay in her arms forever.

After we calmed ourselves, Mom gave me cookies and milk and invited me to stay for supper. In the meantime, John had come home and seemed happy to see me.

After supper, I helped Mom clean up the kitchen. "Do you want John to drive you home now?" she asked, glancing at the clock.

Tears filled my eyes. "I don't want to go; I want to stay here with you."

Mom was silent. Then she put her arms around me. "Barbara, I want you to stay too, honey, but I don't have any room."

"I'll sleep on the floor, please Mom." Her eyes softened.

We went to a phone booth to call Dad. Jeanne answered, furious when she heard it was Mom. I could hear her voice even from where I was standing. “I had a feeling she was with you. The least you could have done was call us; we were worried sick. Bring her home right now."

"Barbara doesn't want to stay with you and your father; she wants to live with me." Mom's words sounded mean, and it wasn't true that I didn't want to live with them; it was just that I wanted to live with Mom.

I began grade three at the same school, but from yet another home. I had forgotten about Mom and John's fights when I'd been away, but I was soon reacquainted. What was worse than the fighting was when the door was locked when I arrived after school, and no one was home. Usually, it was dark by the time they got home, and I was so relieved to see them that I'd forget to be angry.

One evening Mom and John were going out and said I could sleep in their bed until they got home. I loved sleeping in Mom's bed. I felt warm and secure. I crawled into the bed and wrapped the covers tightly around myself. About an hour later, John came back, having forgotten something. When he turned on the light in the kitchen, it shone in the bedroom. I wasn't asleep, although my eyes were closed. I could feel John standing nearby. I pulled the covers down from my face and saw him there, staring at me with a silly look on his face.

"Not sleeping yet, eh?" He sat on the side of the bed. "You're such a pretty girl, you know that? You're almost as pretty as your mother."

I smiled, as everyone had always said how pretty Mom was. He rubbed the side of my face for a few moments, then left. I felt funny.

On Thursdays, I rushed home from school to see Grandma and Grandpa, who came to visit every other week because Grandma belonged to a bridge club in Windsor. Mary came with them if she had a holiday from school. It seemed as if every time I saw Grandma, she made the same comment: "You are so wild, Barbara, your mother must have gone to a circus when she was pregnant with you."

I tried to be like Mary while Grandma was visiting. I tried to sit still and be quiet, but it was hard.

Grandma was a beautiful woman, her skin smooth and unlined. She wore a fur coat, which felt soft when she hugged me. Her cheeks were rosy from a touch of rouge, and her lips were a soft red. She wore no other makeup. I loved the smell of her perfume, and sometimes she would put a dab on my wrist. I tried to avoid washing that spot until every trace of the scent had vanished.

Grandpa was the typical strong, silent male. He was a handsome man, with pronounced cheekbones and a thick head of red hair, which Mom and I had inherited. His voice was gruff and hard for me to understand. Grandma, however, was ever ready to interpret his words. Often

Grandma brought me hand-me-downs from Mary, and sometimes she gave me money or candy. For Mom, she brought homemade jams and fruit. Then she would start on Mom about John.

"I don't know why you're staying here with that man. He's no better than your husband. You should bring all the children to live with your father and me. We'll keep you together as a family."

"Ma, I have to live my own life."

"Mildred, stop thinking of yourself and do something for the sake of your children—they need a home."

Mom invariably became upset and began to cry. I went to her and put my arm around her shoulder. She held my other hand tightly.

"Okay, okay, I'll think about it," she said to Grandma.

Even though I got mad at Grandma for making Mom cry, I secretly hoped we could go to live at Grandma and Grandpa's, and all be together.

I am not sure why (I may have blocked it out), but by the beginning of the next school year, I had been sent to stay with Uncle George and Aunt Alice. I didn't protest too much because Mom said it was only for a short stay, and I loved the dogs.

Eventually, I came to see Uncle George as a father figure, since he seemed to occupy a big presence in my life. Uncle George was in his fifties and didn't have much hair left. When he smiled, I could see the few stubby teeth that remained. He had never married before he met Aunt Alice; they had been together ten years now. He was playful and spry for his age and his size—he had an enormous stomach. From the time I was quite young—when we used to visit before I lived there—he chased me around the yard and, when he caught me, threw me on the ground and tickled me. I loved being with Uncle George—he was fun, and he didn't look at me and laugh in the strange way that John sometimes had.

With Aunt Alice, I was less comfortable. I think it was because Mom didn't like her. I felt I would be betraying Mom if I liked Aunt Alice too much. She was a large-framed and fair-skinned woman of German ancestry, although she rarely talked about her background. She was only in her mid-fifties, but her hair had been completely white for almost as long as I can remember. She wore no make-up except for ruby red lipstick and was forever licking her lips. Aunt Alice had been in one other marriage. On her dresser was a picture of a baby boy, her only child, who had died in infancy. When I asked her about the picture, her voice became unusually soft, and I could see the sadness in her eyes.

She seemed to have two different personalities: one for company and one for home. When she was with others, she was friendly and laughed at everything that was remotely funny. At home, she was serious and miserable. I hardly ever saw her laugh; mostly, she barked out orders for Uncle George and spent the rest of the time criticizing me. I tried to stay out of her way as much as possible. After months of living with them, I was getting anxious to go back to mom.

"Aunt Alice, when do you think I'll be able to go home?" I asked while on the drive home from school. Standing in the backseat of the car, I dangled my arms over the front, in the space between Aunt Alice and Uncle George. I saw a look pass between them. As if they knew something I didn't.

"Well, I don't know, Barbara. It may take your mother and John a long time to work out their problems."

"But it's already been a long time. What kind of problems do they have anyway?"

"It hasn't been that long, just a few months," Aunt Alice replied. She spoke carefully as if to keep impatience out of her voice. "Anyway, I thought you liked living with us."

"I do, but I still miss my mom."

There was a pause. Uncle George's eyes were fixed on the long highway ahead. Aunt Alice, too, avoided my eyes. "I wonder if Candy is ready to have her pups yet. What do you think, George?"

I threw myself back on the seat. I hated it when they changed the subject, which they seemed to do whenever I talked about Mom. I was sure they were hiding something from me. At the time there were many good things about living with Uncle George and Aunt Alice. They had moved to the country on the banks of the Ruscom River and were building a two-bedroom bungalow. It wasn't finished, which created some practical problems, but still, I had my own room, all the food I could ever want, and my own dog, a black poodle named Gypsy. Unfortunately, this would prove to be one of the worst homes I had lived in.

Chapter 2

I loved sitting on the dock Uncle George had built. If I were still and quiet, I could see the fish swimming by. We had an enormous yard with lots of different kinds of trees; my favorite was the weeping willows. My friends and I would cut out the center branches and put lawn chairs inside, pretending it was our house. Although the neighbors were quite a distance away, there were a couple of girls my age that I played with.

Aunt Alice bred cockapoos, a cross between a cocker spaniel and a French poodle. We often had as many as eighteen dogs at a time. I taught them tricks and, on sweltering summer days, bathed them with pails of water I filled from the river. The only problem was that I inevitably got attached to certain ones and was heartbroken when they were sold.

Because the house was still unfinished, the only running water was in the kitchen, and Aunt Alice would not let us use this for anything except drinking, because it had to be put through an expensive conditioner. We kept a bucket of water beside the toilet for flushing, and each time someone used the pail, they had to go to the river to fill it up again.

The drain in the bathtub was hooked up even though the taps were not, so we heated pails of water from the river on the stove and Uncle George poured them into the tub alternately with pails of cold water. I bathed first, and then

Uncle George bathed in my water—much to Aunt Alice's disgust. By the time we were finished, the water on the stove would be hot enough for her bath.

The interior walls were not finished so Uncle George nailed up pieces of plywood between the rooms for privacy. The floors were also sheets of heavy plywood. A small heater in the center of the house provided warmth in the winter. On cold nights, the smaller dogs huddled up around it.

On the second September I was with them. Uncle George started a job in a small nearby town. I began grade five in the French language school in our district. Aunt Alice and Uncle George said I would have to register as Barbara Belanger, explaining it would be easier if my name were the same as theirs. I didn't want to go by their name but felt I had no choice. I was enrolled in St. Ambroise School in St. Joachim, a small French community nearby. The thought of starting yet another new school and again having to make new friends depressed me. I could not speak a word of French, but there were no English Catholic schools nearby. Mother Marion gave me a catechism book to read while she taught the rest of the class their lessons in French. If there was enough time, she went through my English lessons with me, but often, I was sent home to figure out my lessons on my own.

My appeal to Aunt Alice for help only made her angrier.

"Why can't you understand your lesson?"

"No one showed me how to do it. Mother Marion was too busy with the French lessons."

"Then why didn't you ask her for help after school or during your lunch?"

"I couldn't, I had to catch the bus, and when we go on lunch, so do the teachers."

"Well, you're just going to have to find a way," Aunt Alice said sternly.

"But how can I?" Tears of frustration sprang up in my eyes.

My tears seemed only to provoke her more. "Stop that, Barbara. I don't want to hear any more excuses; I want you to finish those lessons."

I banged my books shut and stomped off to my room. I could not seem to do anything the way Aunt Alice wanted me to. She always found something wrong, even with the way I did my chores around the house. We fought more and more often.

With Uncle George, it was the complete opposite. He was easygoing and fun. We joked and teased and tickled each other until Aunt Alice yelled at us.

"Will you two stop acting like babies!"

Uncle George stood in front of her and brought his hand to his forehead in salute. I tried to repress a giggle. Aunt Alice looked at us in exasperation. Her disapproval only had the effect of drawing Uncle George and me closer together. We became great buddies. When Aunt Alice picked on me, he came to my rescue. Every evening when he came to get me from the babysitter's, he brought me an Oh Henry chocolate bar. I had to eat it fast before we picked up Aunt Alice, who didn't like me eating sweets—I'd had nine cavities filled at my last visit to the dentist, and Aunt Alice was complaining about the expense of fixing my teeth.

Uncle George took me everywhere with him, even to the junkyard on Sunday mornings, and we spent Saturdays together while Aunt Alice was at work. I tried to do some of the house cleaning for Aunt Alice so she wouldn't have as much to do on Sunday. Sometimes Uncle George helped, but usually, he worked in the yard. Afterward, we watched the Saturday afternoon wrestling on TV. I didn't like wrestling, but Uncle George insisted I sit and watch it with him. Often, he offered me a dime to scratch his back. Aunt Alice said this was a disgusting thing to do, so we never did it in front of her.

I still missed Mom terribly. It had been a year now since I'd moved in with Aunt Alice and Uncle George. I got tired of waiting for Mom to come and get me, so I wrote her a letter. Every day I checked the mailbox, waiting for her reply. Then I trooped dejectedly up to the house to give Aunt Alice the mail. But I never gave up hope that the next day would bring a letter from Mom.

CAN I COME HOME NOW?

The day I saw the familiar handwriting on an envelope addressed to me I was ecstatic. I took the letter down to the dock to read it privately, then raced up to the house.

"Aunt Alice, Aunt Alice, Mom says I can come home soon!"

Aunt Alice shot me her most disgusted look.

I waved the letter at her. "Mom wrote to me. She says I can come home soon."

Aunt Alice's face tightened in anger. "I'll believe that when I see it."

"What do you mean?" I asked angrily.

She ignored my tone. "You're better off without her, Barbara. She isn't a good mother to you."

My stomach instantly went into a knot. I hated it when she talked like that. "Please don't say that, please."

"Well, you may as well face the facts. Why do you think you're here with us?"

I ran away to find Uncle George.

He wiped the tears away from my face. "Don't mind Alice, honey. She's just jealous of your mom."

I didn't understand why she should be jealous, why she didn't want me to be with my mother. I continued writing to Mom, begging her to come up and see me. I was careful not to let Aunt Alice see my letters.

Finally, months later, Mom wrote saying she would come the following Sunday. Aunt Alice pursed her lips and said nothing. I counted the days anxiously.

On Sunday morning, I got up, dressed early, and went out to sit on the huge rock at the end of the driveway to wait. I ignored Aunt Alice's calls to come in for lunch and dinner. When it got dark, Uncle George came out to bring me inside.

My eyes burned with tears, and I could hardly see the gravel beneath my feet as we walked up the drive. "I wonder what happened?"

Uncle George put a comforting arm around me. "Oh, maybe the car broke down or something."

Mom did this again and again, and Aunt Alice never failed to point out what a bad mother she truly was.

As my second Christmas with Aunt Alice and Uncle George approached, I desperately hoped this year I would be able to see my family, especially Mom. I continued to make my daily trips to the mailbox. Finally, three weeks before Christmas, I received a letter.

I ran up to the house to find Aunt Alice. She was in the kitchen. I hesitated. I didn't want to hear her scoff and say she'd heard that one before.

She looked at me and the letter in my hand. "Well?"

But her voice was not as harsh as usual.

"Mom says she and John are coming on Boxing Day." I looked at her defiantly, as if she were the one who kept breaking her word.

Aunt Alice turned away without saying a word. I was relieved.

I barely got excited about Christmas Day, although Aunt Alice and Uncle George gave me a wonderful new pair of figure skates. It was Boxing Day I was waiting for. I got up extra early to be ready for Mom. I knew this time she would come. I hoped we would have some time alone. I had secret hopes she would take me home with her.

When I saw John's familiar old black car pull up the drive, I let out a big sigh of relief. Still, I was nervous about how Aunt Alice and Mom would be with each other.

But Aunt Alice. had on her friendly "company" personality and, to my great joy, insisted Mom and John stay for dinner. I sat nervously through the meal, hardly able to eat, afraid something would go wrong. Dinner was perfect; there was no tension between Mom and Aunt Alice, or between Aunt Alice and me. After we finished, Aunt Alice even offered to do the dishes so Mom and I could visit.

We went for a walk in the bright afternoon, the sun reflecting off the snow. I didn't hesitate to ask my question. "Mom, when can I come home?"

Mom looked at me in surprise. "Don't you like it here?"

"No, it's not that. I just really miss you."

She grabbed my hand but didn't say anything.

"Please Mom, can I come home now? Why did I have to come here anyway?"

She hesitated for a moment and then stopped to face me.

"I'm sorry, but now just isn't the right time. But soon. I promise soon we will all be together again."

I tried to hide my disappointment, barely listening to her chatter about the family. "Lyle is working in a factory and living on his own. I haven't seen Jeanne, but I heard she's getting married.

"What about Mary?" I asked. "Have you seen her?"

"Oh yes dear, Grandma and Grandpa bring her in quite often when they come to town. They still come in on Thursdays."

I felt a pang of envy for Mary being able to see Mom so often and being able to live with Grandma and Grandpa. Mostly I missed her.

Darkness was beginning to fall as we headed back to the house. Once inside John looked at Mom impatiently and I knew he wanted to get going. I didn't want Mom to leave; I didn't know when I'd see her again. I ran to my room, trying not to cry, but the tears burst out, and I buried my face in my pillow. A knock came at the door. I ignored it.

"Barbara, it's Mom. Can I come in?"

"I guess," I mumbled without raising my head.

Mom sat down on the bed; she put her hands on my shoulders to turn me towards her, then hugged me tightly. I clutched onto her.

"Please Mom, take me with you. I won't be any trouble, please, Mom, I'll be good." I couldn't control my shaking body.

Mom pulled away; I could see the tears in her eyes. "Come on, where's my brave girl?" she said. "You know you're special to me, don't you?"

I nodded. I knew she was going to say I couldn't come home, and I wouldn't be able to change her mind.

"Then you know as soon as I can take you home, I will."

I wiped away my tears and lifted my head. I would be brave; I would be what Mom wanted me to be.

We went out into the hall. I kissed John goodbye. I watched out the kitchen window until the red taillights vanished in the distance. When I turned from the window, Aunt Alice was stretched back in her La-Z-Boy chair, looking smug. I raced past her to my room.

Within days of Christmas, I received a Christmas card — "love Jeanne and Dad."

When the Christmas rush was out of the way, and all that seemed to be ahead was a long, cold winter, Uncle George said he had something special in mind for us. He went out weekly to assess the ice on the river. When it was frozen solid enough, he promised to teach me to skate. He had some old skates that looked like they were antiques. I could hardly wait to try my new ones. Finally, the ice was hard enough. I carried my skates strung over my shoulder down to the dock. Uncle George laced my skates up for me, then led me onto the ice. The dogs followed us, and I laughed to see them trying to run but not getting any traction.

Uncle George glided around effortlessly, but when I tried it myself, I found it wasn't so easy. Uncle George picked me up every time I fell.

I went down to the ice every chance I got, Uncle George accompanying me.

"You're lucky to have such strong ankles, Barbara, " he said one afternoon as he bandaged up one of the many blisters on my heels.

"Lots of people can't skate because they have weak ankles."

Since November, Aunt Alice had been talking about having surgery on the varicose veins in her legs. She had put it off for several years and was just waiting for the doctor to phone with an opening. Finally, one afternoon in late January, he called her at work to say they would be able to take her the next week.

I went shopping with Aunt Alice to get new nightclothes and other toiletries she would need. She said I could come up with Uncle George to visit her at the hospital.

The morning she was to go in, she took me aside. "I'm leaving the responsibility for feeding the dogs with you, Barbara," she said. "Uncle George will help with the cleaning and cooking if you ask him. You know he would do anything for you."

"I'll miss you," I said, hugging her tightly. I didn't mind feeding the dogs; I loved them.

That evening, Uncle George said I could stay up until nine if I promised not to tell Aunt Alice (my usual bedtime was eight thirty). I felt privileged to be able to stay up so late and was careful not to go past nine o'clock. When I went to bed, I put on an extra blanket. I could hear the wind whistling around my bedroom window.

Uncle George stuck his head in the doorway. "Are you warm enough Barbara? Would you like another blanket?"

"No, I'll be alright. But can you turn the heat up?"

"It's up as high as it'll go, I'm afraid. It's a cold one tonight."

I wrapped the blankets around myself tightly and was soon asleep.

The next night, when we got home, Uncle George called the hospital to see how the operation had gone. The nurse assured him everything was fine; Aunt Alice was resting. He asked her to tell Aunt Alice we would be up to see her the next evening.

I was again allowed to stay up until nine o'clock. It was another frosty night, and I put on my flannelette pajamas and piled the blankets on my bed. Uncle George said he was tired and going to bed too. Again, as he passed my room, he stuck in his head.

"It's colder than last night—you can crawl into bed with me if you want. You'll be much warmer that way. It's supposed to be a chilly one tonight."

I crawled into bed with Uncle George.

He hugged me closely. I felt warm and secure. Suddenly, his hands began touching me everywhere. I felt funny.

"Stop doing that," I said and pushed his hands away. He stopped, but only for a moment. I sat up. "I'm going back to my bed."

"Please Barbara, I didn't mean anything, I'm sorry." He hung on tightly to the back of my pajama top. "Come on back where it's warm."

I lay back down. I wondered if he did this to Aunt Alice. Maybe that was why she slept on the sofa and not with him.

The next morning at breakfast, Uncle George gave me a peculiar look. "I want to talk to you about something, Barbara. But not now, there isn't enough time. When we get home tonight."

I spent the day wondering what he wanted to talk to me about. I had never seen that look on his face before.

He chattered away about work while we ate supper, but afterward, I saw that peculiar look again, and I knew he was going to bring up whatever it was he wanted to say.

"Barbara," he began, "why were you touching me last night?"

I stared at him. "What are you talking about?"

"Barbara, you were touching my privates last night. When I pushed your hand away, you wouldn't stop."

I felt my face grow hot from his words. I didn't know what to do or say. I tried hard to recall the night before. I could only remember Uncle George touching me. Finally, I blurted out, "I didn't do it to you! You did it to me!"

He kept insisting; I kept denying. Tears rolled uncontrollably down my face. He came close and put his arm around me. I stiffened, but he didn't seem to notice.

"Don't get so upset. Maybe you did it in your sleep. It's okay, it's okay."

But I couldn't think about anything else. How could I have done something like that and not remembered? I felt scared. I wanted to talk to someone.

On the drive to see Aunt Alice that evening, I told Uncle George how I felt. "I wish I could talk to someone."

Uncle George looked alarmed. "Don't tell anyone, Barbara."

"What about Aunt Alice? Shouldn't I tell her?"

"No, Barbara, not Aunt Alice for sure. She would get very mad at you."

"Why?"

"Because you were sleeping with me, and you're not supposed to do that."

I looked away from him in confusion.

"I'll tell you what," Uncle George said, putting a hand on my knee. "We'll just wait and see if it ever happens again. Then we will decide what to do about it. How's that? Now cheer up," he added with a wide smile that showed his darkened teeth.

Aunt Alice looked the same as she always did. I was happy to see her, glad she was coming home soon. But I found it hard to meet her eyes. She chattered away, confident about the operation, seemingly oblivious to my silence.

During the rest of the week, Uncle George kept inviting me to sleep with him. I shook my head each time, confused. Why did he keep asking me when he knew it was wrong?

Aunt Alice's homecoming did not bring relief. She was not the kind of person to sit around and do nothing, and, impatient to be up and around, she vented her frustration on Uncle George and me. We were glad when she was finally able to go back to work.

I was in my second semester of grade five at St. Ambroise school. The language difference was an added barrier to my shyness when it came to making friends, but there was one girl, Corinna, who could speak English almost as well as French, and we began to hang out at recess and lunch.

My schoolwork absorbed me, Aunt Alice was back to normal, and I soon put the events with Uncle George out of my mind briefly.

One morning while Uncle George and I were eating breakfast, he reached over and touched my arm. I turned to look at him. He had that peculiar look on his face, which brought the knot back to my stomach.

"I have to talk to you," he whispered. "Later, okay?"

My heart thumping in my chest, I nodded. I tried to remember the previous night. Had I done anything in my sleep? All I could remember was going to sleep.

"Good morning, Barbara." Aunt Alice's voice interrupted my thoughts. "You'd better hurry up and eat, or you'll be late for school."

At school, I couldn't concentrate on my work.

"Barbara, are you with us today?" Mother Marion tapped her ruler on my desk, bringing me back with a jolt.

When Uncle George picked me up at the sitter's, he began to tell me what I didn't want to hear.

"You came into my room last night, Barbara. You did the same thing you did before. I tried to push you away, but you wouldn't go. You were in my room for about twenty minutes."

Tears fell on my trembling hands. I tried to talk, but no words came out.

"Don't start that now," Uncle George ordered. "Alice will wonder why you were crying, and we must never tell her about this." He paused for a moment. Then, in a harsh tone, "All right?"

I still couldn't speak but gestured my agreement and tried to stop my tears.

"We'll have to do something about this if it continues," he went on more calmly. "I don't know what we can do, but we'll figure something out."

Every minute of every day my thoughts were consumed with this terrible thing I was doing—doing and not knowing I was doing it.

It was impossible to act as though nothing had happened. Corinna asked me what was wrong. I desperately wanted to tell her.

Aunt Alice and I were arguing more and more. Mom hardly ever wrote to me, and I never heard from Dad. Grandma and Grandpa wrote occasionally, enclosing pictures of Mary, Uncle Jack, and themselves. The pictures made me cry.

I tried to imagine myself touching Uncle George in the way he'd said I had. Even thinking of it confused me. At night, before I went to sleep, I lay in bed and told myself I wasn't going to do it tonight, that I wouldn't go into Uncle George's room. Many nights, I woke up crying, drenched in sweat. When Aunt Alice came in to see what was wrong, I made up a story about having a bad dream.

Every morning when I got up, I looked at Uncle George's face. He gave me either a nod or a shake of his head. The fate of my day depended on this morning's gesture. If he shook his head "no," I felt encouraged. If he nodded "yes," I felt horrible. I was able to conceal my tears from Aunt Alice, determined not to make her suspicious. According to Uncle George, I was coming into his room more and more often, almost weekly now.

"Last night you came into my room, and I couldn't get you off," he said to me one day when he picked me up at the babysitter's. "You're keeping me up half the night—I can hardly stay awake at work. We have to do something about this."

"I'll try not to do it again! I promise I'll try!"

"Barbara, stop this crying, now stop it." I had never seen Uncle George angry before. For the first time, I was frightened of him.

The school called Aunt Alice. My marks had slipped so much it was doubtful I would pass the year. Aunt Alice came to me, concerned.

"I don't understand it, Barbara. You were doing so well. What happened?"

I wanted so badly to tell her, but I could only shrug my shoulders.

She misinterpreted my silence. "Well, if you don't care..." She sighed. "Well, when you grow up you can get married and become a housewife. That doesn't require brains, and you obviously haven't got any."

I ran to my room to cry out my pain and frustration.

I expected Aunt Alice to continue nagging me about my marks, but once she had decided I just wasn't intelligent, she left me alone.

To my surprise, as it got near my birthday in the spring, she came to ask me if I wanted to have a party. I forgot all about Uncle George and my "problem." I phoned Corinna, who got as excited as I was.

"This is great—you can invite all our friends.

"Yeah—and maybe we can play games and get some of the kids to bring records so we can dance."

"Aunt Alice said she'll make a cake and we can have hot dogs and French fries."

The next day at school, Corinna told everyone about my party. Suddenly, I was the center of attention, overcome with a group of friends again. Kids who had shunned me the day before were begging me to join them. It felt good to be liked—even if it was just for my party.

My happiness carried me through the day, but one look at Uncle George the next morning and my world came crashing down again. He was nodding his head, yes.

I held back my tears and ran to my room, to the corner on the other side of the bed. Anger at myself welled up inside. I gritted my teeth and grabbed my hair close to the scalp, squeezing hard. My brain was spinning. How could I do this? What was wrong with me?

There was a knock on the door.

"What do you want?" I screamed.

"I just wanted to tell you it's time to get dressed for school," Aunt Alice's voice came through the door. "But if you're in that kind of mood maybe you should go back to bed and get up on the other side." Her voice was joking, but nothing was funny to me.

That afternoon, when Uncle George came to pick me up, I braced myself to hear the usual words.

"You're keeping me up all night. I'm so tired now at work. Alice is going to catch us. We have to do something about this soon." I wished I could turn his voice off.

"I'm going to talk to the priest at the church in town tomorrow."

I jerked my head up to look at him. "I thought we weren't supposed to tell anyone."

"A priest is different." Uncle George reached out and put an arm around me. "They're supposed to help people."

Relief flooded through me. A priest would help. He would know what to do.

At school, Corinna and the other girls were still talking about my party.

"What kind of cake are you having?"

"Have you got some fast songs for dancing?"

"Are you inviting boys?"

I answered their questions, happy for the attention, but my mind kept wandering. Finally, I was on the bus to my sitter's. Two more hours until Uncle George picks me up.

The minute I got into the car, I burst out, "Did you talk to Father? What did he say?"

"Slow down, just a minute."

I sat quietly and waited for him to tell me.

"I went to a priest, but not the priest at the church we go to. I thought it would be better if I went to a church where we're not known." I nodded.

"Father gave me a letter to give you, " he continued. "You know I can't read, so he told me what it said."

"What does it say?" I asked anxiously.

"There isn't enough time to read it now, so in the morning when I drive Alice to the bus station, I'll leave the letter on your dresser for you."

"Can't you just tell me what it says?"

"No, I can't. Father told me to let you read it by yourself."

"Okay."

"Oh, another thing," Uncle George added. "Father agreed with me that we shouldn't tell anyone about this. Remember when I told you it was wrong for you to sleep with me, well Father agreed."

I looked down at my fidgeting hands.

The next morning, as soon as I heard the car pull out of the driveway, I opened the folded piece of paper Uncle George had left on my dresser.

"Dear Barbara," it began, "I understand you are quite upset with this problem you are having...." I skimmed down the page until I came to the last paragraph.

> *The things that we do in our sleep are the things that we really want to do when we are awake. The only way to stop doing this in your sleep is to do it when you are awake. I know you don't want to, but this is the only way to cure yourself, Barbara. So please try.*

There was no signature.

I tried to swallow but couldn't because of the lump in my throat. My face felt hot. The bedroom began spinning. When Uncle George came back, I couldn't say anything. We drove to the babysitter's without exchanging a word.

At school, everyone kept asking me what was wrong. I said I wasn't feeling well and went to the school nurse. Lying on the sofa in the lounge, all I could think about was the letter. How could I do what it said? I didn't even know how to do "IT."

When Uncle George came to pick me up at the babysitter's, he broke the silence.

"What do you think about the letter, Barbara?"

"I can't do what it says! I can't do that while I'm awake, I just can't!"

Uncle George spoke calmly, ignoring my outburst. "I know you don't want to do it, but we have to do something. Alice is going to catch you coming into my room, and then we're both going to be in trouble."

I felt instantly chastised and sorry for Uncle George. I hated myself. I felt ashamed and confused. I didn't want to do these things with Uncle George, asleep or awake. I pushed it aside—I didn't want to think about it.

It was almost the middle of March, a few weeks before my birthday. One evening after supper, Uncle George took Aunt Alice and me into town to buy invitations for my birthday party. When we got home, I began writing them out. I couldn't put off asking any more:

"Aunt Alice, can I invite boys?" I held my breath waiting for her response.

"Sure, as long as there's no funny stuff." She laughed.

My spirits lifted. I was the only girl allowed to have boys at her party. I decided to invite three boys and five girls. The girls were so excited when I told them about the boys.

For a week now, I have been successful at avoiding Uncle George. When he picked me up after school, I talked constantly so he wouldn't have a chance to say anything. I never came out of my bedroom for breakfast until after he had gone to drive Aunt Alice to the bus station. But I couldn't keep this up forever.

A week before my tenth birthday party, when Uncle George picked me up from the sitter's, he confronted me.

"Barbara, we have to talk about this. You were in my room every night last week. I was so tired I could hardly work. If Alice catches us, who knows what will happen. You can't go back home because your mother doesn't want you, and I don't know what would happen to me."

My heart began pounding. I knew I had to do something. It wasn't fair to keep Uncle George awake like that. I took a deep breath.

"Okay, I'll do it." Then I burst into tears.

Uncle George continued talking as I tried to get control of myself. "The best time is Saturday when Alice is working. Don't worry, Barbara," he said, patting my knee. "Just this once, and you'll be all cured. You'll never have to do it again."

I repeated this to myself for the rest of the week: "Just this once. You'll never have to do it again. You'll be cured."

When Saturday came, I was frightened. I didn't want to go through with it.

Aunt Alice left early in the morning. When I walked into the kitchen, Uncle George was making us bacon and eggs for breakfast. I hardly touched mine; my stomach was quivering. While Uncle George cleaned up the table afterward, I tried to sneak away, hoping he wouldn't notice; maybe he'd forgotten.

"Barbara," he called after me, "are you ready?"

My stomach felt sick.

"I don't know what to do?" I pleaded.

"Go into your bedroom, take off your clothes, and put your housecoat on."

He said this naturally, as if he were telling me to get ready for bed. It made it easier to be told what to do.

I wrapped my housecoat tightly around myself and came out for further instructions.

"That's good," said Uncle George. "Now go back into your room and lie on the bed and put this towel under you. I'll be there in a minute."

I did as he said.

Within seconds, he came into my room, I zoned out, I felt nothing, my mind went black.

Uncle George's words jolted me back to reality. "Now go into the kitchen and wash."

Again, I obeyed, like an automaton. Relief spread through me: it was over, and I was cured.

When we picked up Aunt Alice that evening, a part of me felt closer to her. Another part of me felt dirty and loathsome.

April sixth, my birthday, arrived. Despite everything, I was excited. Aunt Alice was just finishing icing the cake when my first guest arrived. The rest seemed to come in a bunch, and we stuffed ourselves with hot dogs, French fries, chips, homemade cookies, ice cream, and cake. We played games and put on records to dance. Aunt Alice didn't leave the party for one minute.

I felt shy and self-conscious around the boys. It was different having them in my house from having them in my class. The other girls danced with them, but I didn't want to touch them or even be close to them. I sat on a chair almost in the corner, watching Corinna and Jeff, the boy she liked, dance and giggle together. I felt different from the other girls because of the secret Uncle George, and I had.

After everyone was gone, Aunt Alice commented to Uncle George, "Barbara didn't dance once with any of the boys."

Uncle George gave me an approving look.

One morning, a few weeks after my birthday, I got up, as usual, to go down to the kitchen for breakfast. When I sat down at the table and looked up to Uncle George to say good morning, I felt the familiar sick feeling in my stomach. Across his face was that dreadfully familiar look.

"I have to talk to you later," he whispered in my ear.

Chapter 3

I was supposed to be asleep, but I could hear Aunt Alice and Uncle George through the thin plywood partitions.

"I wonder what's wrong with that girl."

"Aw, don't worry about it Alice. She'll outgrow it."

There was silence, then Aunt Alice's voice again. "It could be puberty. Although she's still pretty young for that. Why don't you talk to her, George? She seems to be closer to you."

"Okay, maybe I'll take her for a drive or something."

I closed my eyes and saw myself being sucked into a black hole.

When I woke up in the morning, I wanted to go back to sleep. I hated waking up. I hated seeing Uncle George's face. I hated going to school and hearing my classmates' laughter. I hated Aunt Alice trying to rush me along. But most of all I hated Saturdays—not every Saturday, just the Saturdays when I had to do that horrible thing with Uncle George. I hated hearing his words:

"Maybe this time you'll be cured, Barbara." I didn't even think about that possibility anymore. I just lay there, holding his body away from mine until I thought my arms would break.

Aunt Alice began to ask me what the matter was. "Why are you so miserable, Barbara? What's wrong with you?"

"Nothing. There's nothing wrong with me. Is there something wrong with you?" I answered sarcastically. I was tired of hearing that question.

"Don't you talk to me with that tone of voice, young lady."

"What tone of voice?" I screamed.

That was how our arguments began. They ended with me running to my room screaming, "Leave me alone. I hate you so much!"

"Come back here, right now!"

I banged the door behind me, still screaming to drown out her voice.

When I finally stopped, my head hurt so much I was sure it was going to split down the middle. Aunt Alice burst through my bedroom door. I crawled under the bed trying to get away from her. The pain in my head was excruciating. I hated myself. I punched my head and banged it against the floor, only making the pain worse. Aunt Alice grabbed for me under the bed.

"Let go or I'll scream again."

Still, she clung to me.

I screamed louder and louder, the pain in my head unbearable.

Finally, Aunt Alice let go and got to her feet. "See what your wonderful mother has done to you," she said as she left the room. "Now you're crazy."

Sometimes Uncle George would have to break up our fights. Exhausted when they were over, I crawled up into a ball and cried myself to sleep. When I woke up a short time later, my face would be red and splotchy but the pain in my head was more tolerable now.

For days after these outbursts, I was withdrawn and wouldn't speak to anyone, afraid I would provoke an argument if I said anything.

Uncle George was at me every available opportunity, in the car on the way to the store or, more often, on the way to the sitters in the morning. "Barbara, we have to do something. You are in my room every night."

I hung my head and listened to his horrible words.

"Alice is going to catch us," he persisted. "We have to do it this Saturday."

"But it doesn't help. Why do I have to keep doing it?"

"It'll work as long as we keep doing it. I talked to the Father at church again. He said one day you'll stop doing it. But we must keep doing it while you're awake. After we do it you don't come into my room for a few weeks, sometimes even a month. So, it must be helping."

"I guess so."

"How about this Saturday."

"I can't, I have to go to my friend's. Her father is going to pick me up and we're going to work on a school project."

"I don't want you making plans anymore without asking me first."

I could tell he was angry by the look on his face. It scared me.

"But Aunt Alice said it was okay," I protested.

"Well, next time you ask me first."

I nodded reluctantly.

Finally, it was the last day of school. You could feel the excitement and anticipation in the class as everyone waited to receive their marks, restless to be out for the summer. I was halfheartedly anxious to find out if I'd passed. Mother Marion was making her way around the room, handing out the report cards. When she reached my desk, she gently lifted my face, forcing me to look into her eyes. This was something I had become uncomfortable doing—meeting anyone's eyes.

"Put a smile on that somber face—you passed."

I smiled. Aunt Alice would be happy.

Once school was out, instead of going to the sitters all day, I went to work with Aunt Alice. I didn't care where I went as long as I wasn't alone with Uncle George.

I had been doing this for about two weeks when one evening after supper, Grandma called to ask me if I could spend a week with them.

I went running to Aunt Alice, ecstatic. "Can I go, can I go?"

Aunt Alice didn't hesitate. "Sure, it would be a nice vacation for you."

Grandma and Grandpa were busy with the farm for the next couple of weeks, but they would come for me after that. I felt as if I were dreaming. I would finally get to be with some of my family. I would get to see Mary. And best of all, Uncle George would have some peace and quiet, without me to keep him awake and I wouldn't have to do "it." I couldn't wait to tell him; I knew he would be relieved that I was going.

"What do you want to go to an old farm for anyway?" he grumbled. "We got everything you want right here."

"But I thought...."

But he just gave me a dark look and turned his attention back to the TV. Aunt Alice looked on in confusion.

Even this didn't dampen my enthusiasm. I began counting the days. Uncle George said I was coming into his room more and more and insisted we do it again while I was awake, that it might be the last time, that I might finally be cured. I reluctantly agreed. I didn't cry anymore, I just stared up at the unfinished ceiling and zoned out.

When Grandma and Grandpa finally came to get me, I had been packed for days. I was playing with the dogs and saying goodbye to Gypsy when the car pulled in.

Grandma hugged me and Grandpa said "Howdy" in his usual gruff voice. Mary got out of the back seat, and we greeted one another with an awkward "hi." I couldn't believe it; I was taller than she was. But she still had long braids and was as cute as I remembered.

I took Grandma and Grandpa in to see Aunt Alice and Uncle George while I got my suitcase. To my relief, they declined the coffee Aunt Alice offered: I was anxious for us to be on our way.

Mary and I sat in the back seat, me chattering away, her listening and giggling shyly, all during the hour-long journey to Kingsville. The old farmhouse was bigger than I remembered. I hadn't remembered there being any houses nearby, but now I noticed a sprawling brick ranch to the left. On the other side, new crops were springing up in the field, and behind the house was a hilly landscape as far as you could see. I took a deep breath. I wanted so badly to roll down the green hills.

As we got out of the car, we were greeted by a black shaggy cocker spaniel, barking half from excitement, half from surprise at seeing a stranger.

"Quiet down, Pepper. This is Barbara. Don't you remember her?"

I didn't mind. I didn't remember him either. Despite his barking, I bent down and let him smell my hand. Before long, he was licking me. I was accepted. I loved it here already and hadn't even gone into the house yet.

A wooden box sat along one side of the house. Inside were eight of the cutest kittens I had ever seen, meowing at the top of their lungs. I picked one up and discovered kittens aren't as easy to hold as puppies.

Grandma came up beside me as I was trying to pry the tiny claws out of my shirt. "Put the kittens down, for now, Barbara. Let's go in and get your things put away." She gently took the kitten from my arms.

Once inside the house, it felt familiar. I watched Mary take off her shoes and put them neatly on the newspaper in the corner of the pantry.

"You can put your shoes over there, Barbara," Grandma said, pointing to a spot beside Mary's. As I untied my laces, I looked around the pantry. There were canned goods carefully placed on shelves that lined the clean white walls. Along the opposite wall, a big freezer was barely squeezed in. A small table with two chairs on either side sat in a corner. I learned that early in the morning before anyone else was up, Grandpa sat here to have his breakfast, followed by a coffee and a Pall Mall cigarette.

I followed Grandma upstairs to Mary's room. "You can just put your suitcase on Mary's cedar chest for now."

The room reminded me of a princess. Mary had a pink bedspread and curtains, and a vanity with an attached round mirror and matching stool. In the bottom of the wardrobe were stacks and stacks of games: Monopoly, Clue, Sorry, and all kinds of Colorforms.

Grandma set up the roll-away bed in a corner of the dining room where it was quiet. Seldom used, the dining room was the center of the house. On one side was Grandma and Grandpa's bedroom. French doors on the other side led to the living room, in which a beautiful cabinet-style television sat in the corner.

During the evenings, everyone gathered around the television set, Grandma and Grandpa side by side on the chesterfield, Uncle Earl—Grandpa's brother—in the straight-back chair, and occasionally Uncle Jack in the recliner. Mary and I sat on the floor in front of the TV. I tried hard to be quiet, but every time I thought of something, I wanted to say it before I forgot it. Grandma kept putting her finger up to her mouth. I envied Mary for being able to sit so still.

At seven-thirty, Grandma gave us some milk and cookies and ran our baths before bed. After my bath, I kissed everyone good night. Mary thought I was crazy and turned her head away to avoid my kiss.

It was dark in the dining room. The buffet and table, with its twelve surrounding chairs, created large shadows. I felt a little anxious that I was going to go into one of the men's rooms as I had Uncle George's, but I drifted off to sleep quickly, lulled by the faint sounds of the television in the next room.

Grandma was so good to us. Every morning, she made us bacon and eggs for breakfast. We also had to take vitamins and brush our teeth three times a day.

Grandma was very orderly; her favorite saying was "There's a time and place for everything." Sometimes I found her ways restricting; I wasn't used to everything being so organized.

Everyday Mary and I did something different. The land felt so good under my feet. I loved walking through the tall grass up and down the hills. We searched most of the day, finding wonderful places to explore, stopping only to spread the blanket and eat our sandwiches, which Grandma had cut into four and wrapped in waxed paper, with the ends folded neatly, like a present. By supper time, we were worn out

We heard Grandma's voice in the distance. "Mary Rose, Barbara," she called. "Yoo-hoo, girls, it's supper time."

Suppers were wonderful. The six of us gathered every evening in the main kitchen for a wonderful homemade meal. Grandpa and Uncle Earl discussed the farm work, and Uncle Jack rambled on about the weather. Grandma kept track of all the conversations. Mary and I just sat and listened, occasionally giggling to each other about whatever adventure we were having that day. Every evening we had a homemade dessert: cake, pie, or fresh fruit.

I grew to love it more and more at Grandma's. It felt so good to be with my own family. I became less withdrawn and never had temper tantrums. I felt happier than I had in a long time. I didn't have to worry about bothering Uncle George in his sleep, and I had soon lost my anxiety that I was going to go into one of the men's rooms here.

I became attached to Mary, although at first, it seemed one-sided. I felt possessive of her when her friends came over. I wanted to run around, wrestle, and get dirty and sweaty. They were content to sit in Mary's room and color, do crossword puzzles, or read books. At first, they let me play with them, but eventually, they became annoyed and chased me away.

As the end of my visit approached, I realized I didn't want to go back to Uncle George and Aunt Alice's. I wanted to stay here where I felt I belonged.

Mom and John came out to visit and spent the whole day. I couldn't sit close enough to Mom; just her touch made me feel good. Mary was not affectionate with Mom, and she wouldn't go near John at all.

Mom kept saying, "I wish things had turned out differently." I smiled when she said this, although I wasn't sure what she meant.

Sometimes I liked just to look at Mom, she was so pretty. She seemed to be deep in thought most of the time.

"Come on, dear," she said to Mary. "Come and sit on this side of Mom." Mary came over hesitantly and sat down on the couch about a foot away from Mom.

"Oh, come on, I won't bite." Mom put an arm around each of us and squeezed tight. She smelled like cigarettes and perfume.

I had been away from her so long now that even though I wanted to be with her I was able to control my feelings better when it came time for her to leave. I knew she loved me, and I believed that she wanted us to be back together. I felt it was as hard on her as it was on me to be apart.

Mary and I sat in the living room, lamenting the fact that there were only two days left before the end of my visit.

"Why don't we ask Grandma if you can stay longer?" Mary suggested hesitantly.

I looked at her, brightening. "Do you think she would let me?"

Mary shrugged, but I could tell she wanted me to ask.

"You stay here, I'll go ask her."

I rushed to the kitchen where Grandma was baking a pie.

"Grandma, do you think I could stay a little while longer, ple-e-ease?"

She laughed softly and said she would discuss it with Grandpa. I raced back to the living room.

"She's going to talk it over with Grandpa. Wouldn't it be great if I could live here all the time? We could go to school together and play together. We should ask."

"Maybe we should wait and see what Grandma says about you staying a little longer first."

I nodded. Mary was right; I was getting ahead of myself again.

During dinner the next evening, Grandma announced that she had talked it over with Grandpa and Aunt Alice. I could stay for the rest of the summer. Mary and I were in heaven. We ran up to her room and sat on the floor, impatiently discussing everything we would do for the rest of the summer.

Grandma said that one day, before I went back to the Belanger's, we would go to Windsor to see Mom and Dad, and Jeanne and Ray, who had gotten married while I was at the Belanger's and were expecting their first baby.

"Do you know your mother didn't go to her own daughter's wedding?"

This didn't strike me as strange—I remembered how they used to fight when we lived on Drouillard Road.

We made plans to go to Windsor that Friday afternoon. Grandma called everyone to make sure they would be home. We hadn't seen Dad for a long time, or Jeanne for that matter. When I asked about Lyle, it seemed no one knew what had happened to him.

Despite our excitement, we had a productive week helping Grandpa pick vegetables. Afterward, he built a vegetable stand to set by the roadside, and Mary and I had fun selling fresh vegetables.

Grandpa was always very tired by the time he came in for dinner. He was in his seventies, and the farm was a lot of work. Periodically, Grandma brought up the idea of selling the farm and buying a small place closer to town. Grandpa just grumbled something under his breath.

Mary liked the idea. "That would be great. Then I would be closer to my friends who live in town."

To me, it seemed like an awful idea. I loved it at the farm. But I didn't say anything.

When Friday arrived, we drove to Windsor, stopping first at Jeanne and Ray's apartment, where we had lunch. Mom and John were living in a little apartment on the top floor of a duplex on Drouillard Road. John was at work, and Grandma began lecturing Mom almost the minute we walked in the door. "Mildred, you should leave that man and come home with Dad and me. You can raise the two girls and have a good life."

"It's not that easy, Ma. John loves me and wants to take care of me. Soon I'll be too old to get a man."

"Never mind about men. You should be taking care of your children. Your father and I are getting too old to take care of Mary. And what about poor Barbara, stuck with strangers?"

"The Belanger's aren't strangers. They're good to Barbara—aren't they, sweetheart?"

I nodded, wishing they would stop arguing. Eventually, Grandma stopped, and Mary and I were able to have a short visit with Mom before Grandma and Grandpa dropped us off at Dad's.

I knew Dad better than Mary did and felt more at ease. She sat on the couch, not saying more than yes or no. Dad asked us all the typical questions.

"How's school?"

"Good," I said. Mary shyly nodded her head in agreement.

"What grade are you two in now?"

"I'm going into six."

"What about you, Mary?"

"Seven," she said, her voice cracking from nervousness.

Dad turned his head toward the television. The room fell silent.

"How do you like it with the Belanger's, Babs?"

"It's okay. I like the dogs the best."

"They're fine people, and you're lucky to be able to stay with them."

"Yeah, I guess so," I said rather hesitantly.

Dad made more small talk until Grandpa came to pick us up. An hour seems a long time when you don't have much to say. Before we left, Dad gave us ten dollars each; he usually went out of his way to give us money and extravagant gifts. When I went to kiss him as we were leaving, he turned and gave me his cheek.

When we arrived home, a note lay on the table in Uncle Jack's handwriting: "AT HOSPITAL LEAMINGTON GENERAL UNCLE EARL HAD A STROKE. COME AS SOON AS YOU CAN, JACK."

We rushed back out to the car. By the time we got to the hospital, Uncle Earl was dead. Grandma and Mary cried. Grandpa walked away to be alone. Uncle Jack started to babble that he'd done the best he could. I just watched everyone, feeling a bit out of place. I didn't know Uncle Earl well.

Slowly, things returned to normal. The four weeks passed too quickly. I was enjoying myself and fantasizing about living here.

A few days before I was to leave, Grandma took me aside.

"Barbara, how would you like to come and live here with us?"

I just stared at her; I couldn't believe my ears. There was no question about what my answer would be.

Grandma worked out the details with Aunt Alice. I don't know what was said, but when I went to pick up my things, Aunt Alice was cold and distant. I tried to avoid being alone with Uncle George, but he managed to corner me.

"Barbara, you aren't going to tell anyone about what happened here, are you? If you do, you'll get into big trouble. That was a bad thing you did."

> I held back my tears. I knew I wouldn't be able to explain to the others why I was crying. "No, I won't tell anyone."

Chapter 4

During the year I lived at Grandma and Grandpa's, it became clear to everyone just how different Mary and I were. Mary was extremely shy, while I was more outgoing. I became withdrawn only in new or unfamiliar situations. Mary could sit in her bedroom for hours reading. I had to be outside running around, climbing trees, and being active.

Grandma never tired of pointing out our differences. "Barbara, why can't you keep your clothes clean like Mary? Didn't anyone ever teach you how to cut your meat properly? Watch how Mary does it, Barbara. Why don't you stop jumping around and go read a book like your sister?"

I tried hard to be what Grandma wanted me to be. I went to Mary's room to pick a book from her collection and took it back to my room—Uncle Earl's old room. After the first page, I realized I had no idea what I had just read. I began again. My eyes read the words, but my mind wandered. First to Mom, then to Uncle George. At least now he would be getting enough sleep without me bothering him. When I came back to the words in front of me the number at the bottom of the page said ten, but I could not remember a word I had read. I tried selecting different books—books Mary said were interesting: *Black Beauty*, *Little Women,* and *Nancy Drew Mysteries*. But it was always the same: I couldn't get past the first few pages, and if I did, I had no idea what they were about.

"Mary, how can you read so much? It's so boring."

"I don't think it's boring."

Despite our differences, we were happy to be together - there was a bond between us.

When September came, we were bused to a regional district school. I received a lot of attention the first day since most of Mary's friends didn't know she had a sister. When the bell rang at nine o'clock for school to begin, I didn't want to leave Mary, but she shooed me away. I found the other sixth graders and lined up with them. I was the new kid again, an uncomfortably familiar feeling. As school progressed, it became clear that scholastics was yet another way Mary and I were different. While I got Cs on my tests, Mary brought home A's.

"Barbara," Grandma said, "if you would pay attention in class, your marks would be as good as your sister's."

"But I do pay attention, Grandma. I just can't do any better."

"I bet you are daydreaming about climbing trees and running around like a tomboy instead of listening to the teacher."

It was useless to try to explain to her why I couldn't concentrate and the way my mind wandered off whenever it wanted to. I did manage to pass into grade seven that year.

That summer, Grandma planned for Mary and me to spend the summer with the family in Windsor. They had finally decided to sell the farm and buy a smaller house closer to town. Grandma thought Mary and I would just be in the way during the move, which was planned for early July.

Our first visit was with Jeanne and Ray. Jeanne greeted us at the door with a beautiful baby girl cradled in her arms. We were thrilled to finally meet our niece. We took her for walks in the stroller until Jeanne said, "That's enough, girls."

Then we were off to Dad's. This would be the first time Mary had stayed with Dad for longer than a few hours.

"What if he doesn't like me?" she whispered to me.

"Of course, he'll like you, he's your father," I whispered back. She accepted my reasoning.

Dad had moved into a two-bedroom apartment that was in a small building of eight apartments. He went to work during the day, leaving us on our own. We felt grown up. In the spare bedroom where we were sleeping was a large jar filled with pennies. Dad said we could use them if we needed any money while he was out. We bought a lot of penny candy during our stay. I thought of how disapproving Aunt Alice would be if she knew I was eating all that candy.

In the evening, Dad cooked for us or ordered take-out, usually from the Tunnel Barbecue. More often, he left money for us to send out for food ourselves, while he went out drinking after work. Although he stumbled in late in the evening, smelling of liquor and looking at us through bloodshot eyes, Mary and I didn't mind his drinking—it made him more relaxed and talkative, that is until he passed out. For a few evenings, he stayed home with us and sat in his La-Z-Boy chair in front of the TV, and we sat on the sofa.

"What would you girls like to watch tonight?"

We shrugged, unable to decide, even when he read us the programs from the TV Guide. We knew he would pick either a horror movie or a comedy. Tonight, it was a horror movie. He got a kick out of watching us get scared.

"Let's turn the lights out."

"No, Dad, please..." Mary and I begged, clutching each other.

The only lamp in the small living room clicked off.

"O-O-O-O-O-O!" came a deep, scary voice.

When he stopped, we sat in complete silence, gripped by the movie. Suddenly, a strange noise made us jump. We looked over to see that Dad had fallen asleep and was snoring loudly, his index finger resting on his temple to hold the weight of his head. When his head fell back too far, he woke abruptly, his surprised face sending Mary and me into a fit of laughter.

During the day, left on our own, we began to hang out with kids our age who lived in, or near our building. Most of them smoked, and occasionally we took a puff of their cigarettes.

When it was time to leave, Dad called a taxi to take us to Mom's. We waited on the curb, giving Dad the usual goodbye peck on the cheek. In turn, he handed us the usual ten dollars. I wanted to say, "I love you, Dad," but the words got stuck somewhere inside.

The taxi couldn't get us to Mom's fast enough for me. They still lived in the same one-bedroom apartment. I could not believe my long-awaited visit was finally here.

Mom conducted her life exactly the opposite way Grandma did. While Grandma was very orderly, Mom seemed to do whatever struck her fancy at any moment. We had no set rules; there were no regular meals. We could come and go as we pleased, and if we were hungry, we made ourselves something to eat—although, as we soon discovered, the choices were limited. It seemed neither Mom nor John bought much food.

Aside from the lack of food, Mary and I thought this life was great. We could stay out as long as we wanted and sleep in the next day until noon or even later. When Grandma called to see if we were homesick, we avoided answering her.

During the first week, Mom spent the days with us. We talked or went window shopping, and I was in heaven.

"Lyle got married a while ago," she chatted one day as we sat around the table drinking glasses of Double Cola. "And his wife is pregnant—you're going to be aunts again. They live not too far from here; I'll take you to see them."

I tried to remember Lyle's face, but I couldn't.

The next week Mom did not spend any time with us at all but went about her life as if we weren't there. Mary and I set about finding other ways to amuse ourselves. One day, when I was on my way to the corner store, I ran into Wayne and Ronnie, whom I remembered from when I had lived with Mom and John.

"Hey, are you back in the neighborhood?"

"My sister and I are staying at my mom's."

"Well, why don't you bring her around tonight?"

We began hanging around with them. They took Mary and me under their wing. They treated us as if we were important to them. We felt an intense sense of belonging, of being a part of something important, and we wanted more than anything to belong.

We began smoking because everyone else did. After a few days of pleading, Mom agreed to let us smoke in the apartment. We hung around the street corners with the boys till late at night. Neither John nor Mom asked where we had been. Most nights, they were amid an argument anyway, and our return went unnoticed.

Summer was ending, and we did not want to go back to Grandma's; we were having too much fun. We begged Mom to let us stay with her.

"This may be our last chance to live with you," I pleaded with her. "We'll be a family again." I nudged Mary to indicate it was her turn to say something.

"Please Mom, Grandma, and Grandpa are getting too old. I have been there for so long. I want to stay with you." Mary told me many times she felt over-protected by Grandma and Grandpa. She said when she was sixteen, she was going to move out on her own.

Mom's face went soft. Her eyes were saying yes, but her mouth had not said the word yet. After moments of silence, I began again.

"We won't be any trouble. We'll help around the apartment." Finally, she spoke. "Well, John and I would have to get a larger place."

Mary and I looked at each other. "Does that mean we can stay?"

"I guess so. I'll have to talk to John first, but I'm sure I can convince him."

We hugged Mom. Mary and I thought we were the luckiest two girls in the world.

The next day, Mom called Grandma. "Ma, it's Mildred. How are you and Daddy?" After Grandma's long answer, Mom's voice changed, becoming almost defiant.

"I don't know how you are going to take this, but the girls want to stay and live here with me. John and I'll get a bigger place and take good care of them."

Mary and I were sitting on the floor with our fingers crossed.

"Mom, these are my girls... Yes, I know, Ma, but I still have custody."

Mom handed the phone to Mary, gesturing that Grandma wanted to talk to her.

"No Grandma, I want to stay here with Mom and Barb."

She handed the receiver to me.

"Barbara, was this your idea?"

I didn't know what to say. After a brief pause, I heard Grandma's angry voice. "That's what I thought."

I handed the phone to Mom and ran into the living room, throwing myself on the sofa. Grandma's words hurt. I wondered why she blamed me.

The following weekend, we went to pick up our clothes. Grandma hardly spoke to us. Her mouth was held in a tight line. I had seen that angry face before, but not very often.

All our clothes had been packed into cardboard boxes, stacked near the back door. I felt empty inside. I loved being at Grandma's; it had been a happy time. Now the atmosphere was tense and somber. Part of me wished I wasn't leaving. But I had been waiting so long to be able to live with Mom. I was scared this might be my last chance.

While Mary put the last box into John's car, Grandma reached for her. "Please Mary, don't leave us. This is your home." Tears were filling her eyes.

Mary pulled away. She walked out the door without turning back. As usual, I was amazed at her ability to be so distant when the need arose. I was the one who wanted to cry, but Grandma didn't have a hug for me.

When we officially moved in, Mom phoned Social Services and applied for an increase in her welfare benefits. But first, she talked with us. "I suppose you girls are wondering why John doesn't keep his clothes here?"

"Well, kind of."

"It's because I'm receiving welfare payments. If the people at the welfare office were to find out that John is living here, they would stop sending money to us."

Mary and I were confused. We didn't remember this happening when we were younger.

> "I guess it's too complicated for you two to understand," said Mom, looking at our faces. "All you girls have to remember is not to tell anyone

> that John lives here. Not your friends, not the school, no one. If anyone asks, say John is a friend of your mother's and he visits us occasionally."

I was confused but eager to do what Mom wanted so I could stay.

Each month our case worker, Ms. Jones, came to visit. She was a middle-aged matronly-looking woman. We could tell by her wandering eyes that she was searching for signs that a man was staying with us. She talked briefly with Mom and then slowly walked through each room in the apartment. She looked under Mom and John's bed; she even opened the drawers. She looked in the medicine cabinet and the linen closet. Each time she found nothing until her one unannounced visit.

She arrived early one morning and burst through the closed bedroom door to find John in bed sleeping.

"And who is this, Mrs. Bennett?" she demanded.

John opened his eyes and grasped the blanket, pulling the covers up to his neck. His face changed quickly from shock to anger.

"Who the hell are you?" John said sternly.

Mary and I backed away, scared of what would happen next.

"I'm Ms. Jones, from the Department of Social Services, Welfare Department."

John was silent.

"We're just friends; he doesn't live with us," Mom protested, but her words were ignored.

Ms. Jones walked out of the house, lips compressed but a look of satisfaction in her eyes.

We were immediately cut off from welfare. Money became an additional source of problems and arguments between Mom and John. John was working at a low-paying factory job, while Mom was doing a little sewing and babysitting. There was barely enough to make ends meet. Moving to a bigger place was out of the question now. We had to make do with our one-bedroom apartment. Mom and John slept in the bedroom, and Mary and I put blankets and pillows on the kitchen floor each night and made ourselves a bed. Many nights while I lay on the floor listening to Mom and John arguing I wished I were back with Grandma and Grandpa.

Chapter 5

In our desperate need to belong, Mary and I did everything our friends wanted us to. The only thing we cared about was belonging. We became pros at stealing candy from neighborhood stores and harassing people on the street. We yelled obscenities at young and old. I could see fear in the eyes of the older women and outrage in the men's faces. We were angry young girls who felt the world was not a fair place.

One evening, Mary was hanging out with a guy who liked her. I felt like a third wheel, so I came home early. John was sitting alone at the kitchen table, rolling a homemade cigarette, a gin and seven-up half empty in front of him.

"Where's Mom?"

"She's at a friend's," John replied, his face brightening when he saw me. "Sit down here and talk to me." He patted the chair beside him.

Flattered by the attention, I sat down. He often invited me to join him, telling me things I didn't always understand at 12 years old. Sometimes rambling on for what seemed like hours, about various injustices in the world. Occasionally, he talked about Mom. Tonight, however, his conversation focused on me.

"What were you doing tonight?"

"Oh, nothing really."

"You must have been doing something."

"No, just hanging around."

"With who?"

"Friends."

"Boyfriends."

"No."

"Do you like boys, Barbara?" he asked, frank curiosity in his voice.

"Some boys," I replied cautiously.

"I bet the boys like you." He laughed.

I could feel my face redden.

"What's growing there?" He pointed to my breasts and laughed again. His big circular eyes seemed to peer through my clothes. I crossed my arms over my chest. I felt uncomfortable, ashamed of my arriving physical maturity.

A few days later, Mom took me out shopping for my first bra. I tried on training bras until I found one that fit: a white 28 AAA.

"Here, try this one on, Barbara," Mom said, handing a bra through the change room door.

I looked at it in horror: it was a black padded bra. Under protest, I tried it on. Mom looked at me with satisfaction. "That's the one we'll take."

"But I hate it."

"You'll get used to it." She tried to sound convincing.

I wasn't convinced.

"Oh, it looks nice, dear," Mom said when I tried it on again at home.

"I feel funny." I pointed at my breasts through my shirt. "They look so big."

"Go show John and see if he notices."

"No!" I protested.

"Go, Barbara." She pushed me into the living room, where John was watching TV. He glanced up at me but didn't say anything.

Mom called from behind, "John, do you notice anything different about Barbara?"

Completely embarrassed, I tried to cover myself.

"Stand up straight, Barbara," Mom called from behind me.

John looked at my breasts and began to snicker. I ran out of the room and took off the bra. I never wore it again, but instead wore Mary's old ones until I could buy my own.

On the first day of school, Mary and I slept late. When we got up at ten o'clock, Mom didn't seem concerned. She spent the next hour doing her hair and make-up. Mary and I looked on, envying her obvious beauty. Since it was too late to go to school, we stayed home the whole day. Some of our friends came to pick us up later that evening.

"Don't be too late tonight, girls," Mom called to us on our way out the door. "Remember you've got school tomorrow."

We came in at ten o'clock, but no one was home, so we went back out. At eleven, there was still no sign of Mom or John.

"Maybe we'd better stay in," Mary said. "They'll probably be home soon, and we got to get up early tomorrow." Mary was always the voice of reason. We made our beds on the floor and fell asleep.

Mom and John came in later that night and argued till the wee hours. The next morning, we dragged ourselves out of bed for school. I immediately felt out of place; everyone had paired up and formed their groups the day before. Every face was a stranger. I was accustomed to being the new kid since Gordon McGregor was my fifth school, and I was only in grade seven. I couldn't get to sleep that night, thinking about the day at school. It wasn't unusual for me to lie awake at night. Since living at the Belanger's. I had never been able to fall asleep easily, my mind always anxious and restless. I was forever analyzing things I did or things other people did. I had an intense curiosity to understand why things happened and why people did the things they did.

I could hear the TV in the living room—John always stayed up late watching. I got up and joined him in the living room, curling up on the sofa with my head resting on my hands under my cheek to watch the TV. Soon I became conscious that John was looking at me. When I looked over at him in the chair, I saw his pants were open and his hand had disappeared inside them. I looked at his face, trying to figure out what he was doing. His eyes were on me, but they seemed glazed over.

"What are you doing?" I asked in confusion.

"Nothing, just keep watching the TV." His voice was different, deeper. I didn't know what to do or where to look.

"Why are you doing that?"

"What's the matter with you, you know why I'm doing this." His voice seemed to be coming from some hollow place within his body. It scared me. I sat perfectly still, afraid to move my eyes from the television set. Still, I couldn't avoid seeing his moving hand out of the corner of my eye. After what seemed an eternity, I got up the courage to get up and go back to my bed on the kitchen floor.

After that, each time we were alone, or if everyone else was asleep, John did something similar. I got to the point where I could almost ignore him until one evening, as we sat in the living room, he said to me, "Here touch it, Barbara."

I looked over at him in disgust.

"Come on, Barbara, it feels nice."

"No."

He reached over and grabbed my hand. "Here, touch it with your finger."

I turned my face away while he guided my hand where he wanted it to go.

"See, it didn't feel too bad, eh?"

I didn't answer. My stomach turned, and I felt like I was going to throw up.

John now treated me differently during the day. He talked to me more often and in a different way: he treated me like an adult. He told me good things about myself. "You're special, Barbara. You're better than the other kids in your family."

I grew to depend on his reassuring words, but I knew something wasn't right.

"When you grow up you will make something of yourself. Always remember how special you are."

To hear these comforting words seemed well worth the price I had to pay for them.

When I didn't go into the living room with him, he stopped saying nice things to me. I desperately needed to hear his words.

Mom was a very quiet person. She spent many hours a day sewing. A lot of the work she did was making outfits for overweight women. There was a scary side to Mom when she got angry. Rather than tell us to do the dishes or sweep the floor, she would ask us, and given the choice, of course, we always chose not to do as she asked. Then she would become angry and begin yelling and swearing at us.

One night, after a lot of drinking, Mom came storming into the kitchen, wielding one of John's belts. Mary and I were in our beds on the kitchen floor, she hit us over and over with the belt, all the while screaming, "You girls don't listen to me, I know you don't care about me."

"Stop it! Stop it!" I screamed. "I love you, Mom. I love you."

Abruptly she stopped and left the room, never explaining, never mentioning the incident.

When she had extra time, Mom remade old clothes into something nice for Mary and me. Winter was approaching, and I didn't have a coat. Mom sent me across the street to the Salvation Army. For seventy-five cents, I found a large green coat that she was able to remake into a smaller jacket for me. Sometimes when I woke up in the early morning to go to the bathroom, I could hear the whirr of her sewing machine. I followed the sound into the living room. Mom was hunched over, her long red hair almost completely covering her face, as she guided the material through the machine. Her glasses sat on the tip of her nose, ready to fall off if she made a sudden movement. No matter how quiet I tried to be, she always heard me.

"Hi sweetheart, can't sleep?"

I sat down beside her, and she put her arm around me. At that moment, I felt loved.

One of the older guys in the neighborhood became interested in Mary and came over and asked her to go for a walk with him. By now, I was used to being passed over for Mary and went home. When I got to the door of our apartment, I found the door locked. I looked through my pockets, but then remembered Mary had the key. I could see light under the door. I looked through the keyhole. Mom was sitting at the table. I called her, but she didn't answer. I knocked on the door. She still didn't answer. I kept trying but couldn't get her to respond.

Feeling confused and alone, I sat down beside the door. It made me sad that things weren't working out with Mom. She wasn't as I'd remembered her. I had hoped our family life would be like it was at Grandma's.

When I thought about what was happening with John, I felt disgusted. I didn't fit in at school, and Mary, who was the closest person to me, had other interests. I felt alone but didn't know where to turn. I knew there was no one I could talk to about what was happening. I began to shiver from the chill of the night air. The dresser where Mary and I kept our clothes stood in the hallway because there wasn't any room for it in the apartment. As I searched through it for a sweater, a razor blade lying on the bottom of one of the drawers caught my eye. I picked it up. Without hesitating or thinking, I started to cut my arm along the forearm. When I saw blood, I got scared and ran outside. Mary was walking up the sidewalk.

I called her, "Don't bother coming home, Mom won't let us in."

> "But I have the key." She searched her pockets, but it wasn't there. She looked at me. "What happened to your arm?"

"Oh, I cut it, it's nothing."

We walked the streets aimlessly. Feeling scared and lonely.

"Isn't it kind of late for you girls to be out?" The man's voice seemed to come out of nowhere. We turned and saw the black and white of a police car moving slowly alongside us.

My heart thumped in my chest, and I blurted out, "Our house is locked, and our mother won't let us in."

"Let's go see about that." The officer seemed concerned, and without fear, we got into the back seat and told him our address. I felt like I was in a taxi with the voice crackling over the radio at an almost steady pace. I felt safer in the car with him than I had on the streets.

As we neared the apartment door, I could see there was no longer any light shining under the door. The police officer pounded and pounded on the door, but no one answered.

"Well, you girls will have to come to the station until we can locate your mother." He smiled reassuringly.

The station was dimly lit and seemed even darker with its moss-green walls. The officer handed us over to a woman in a navy-blue uniform. She took us into a small office and asked us all kinds of questions: what were our names, what was our mother's name, how old were we, where did we live, and had we ever been locked out of the house before? Everything we said was written down. Then we were left sitting beside a desk in the main lobby.

It was now about two in the morning. For the next couple of hours, we saw all kinds of people coming and going. It all felt unreal. My body and eyes felt heavy, and I wished I could lie down. At about four a.m., a policeman—a different one—came to take us home.

"Hi girls, I'm Officer Grey. You must be the Bennett girls?"

He was much older than the first officer. He had white hair, and I could see his dark-colored shirt stretching between the buttons to cover his protruding belly. But like the other one, he too seemed understanding of our situation. He didn't seem angry at us at all. When we arrived, the door was open, and Mom was sitting at the table.

She angrily looked at us. "Where were you, girls? I've been sick with worry."

Officer Grey took off his hat. "An officer was here earlier, Mrs. Bennett, and no one was home. We took the girls to the station until we could locate you. I would suggest that if you are not going to be home, you make arrangements so your girls will not be walking the streets. It can be very dangerous for girls this age to be out late at night."

Mom was silent.

Officer Grey turned to Mary and me. "Well, good-day girls." He put on his hat and left.

"Mom," I said, "why didn't you let me in? I saw you through the keyhole."

"Oh no, you're wrong. I was out looking for you girls, and John is still out looking."

"But I saw the light under the door. You were—"

"I don't want to talk about this anymore." She ran into the bathroom.

Exhausted, Mary and I got into our bed on the floor and slept late the next day.

I began to take an interest in boys, and a few even seemed to notice me. I began to resent John. I hated having to do those things to him late at night. I hated myself. Rage built up inside me, a fit of anger ready to explode. I began to feel the same way I felt at the Belanger's. Mary was always asking me what was wrong and why I was so mad. I even got angry with my friends.

Mary had limited interaction with John. They seemed indifferent to each other. I sometimes thought about that horrible thing that John did to Mary, and I wondered if she still thought about it. We never discussed it until many years later.

I was losing interest in school and often pretending to be sick, so I didn't have to go. I persuaded Mary to play sick with me. We convinced Mom we were sick, and she wrote notes for us. On the days we were home, we discovered Mom didn't stay home as we had assumed, but she didn't tell us where she was going.

Before long, Mom became suspicious of our numerous sick days. If we didn't have a fever or some other obvious symptom, she sent us off to school. But we didn't go. We hid out in an alley or a store until someone became suspicious and asked us why we weren't in school. Then we quickly disappeared to another hiding spot and went home when we knew Mom was gone. We began forging notes for ourselves. We felt out of place at school and had no friends. It was easier to hang out in the alley all day.

Eventually, the school principal sent the truancy officer out looking for us. Since Mom went out every day between ten and two, she was never home when he came around. Eventually, we got to know what the truant officer looked like and became pretty good at avoiding him.

As the fall days became colder, Mary and I were in more of a rush to get back into the apartment and were arriving home earlier each day. One morning, we arrived a little before ten. As we were on our way up the stairs to our apartment, we heard Mom's voice and a man's. Instinctively, we both turned and ran.

We hid in the backyard until we saw Mom and a man we'd never seen before get into a car that was parked in front of the house. Mom got in the front seat and slid over close to the man. Mary and I looked at each other, not knowing what to think.

Later that evening, when John came home, he asked Mom what she had done that day.

"Oh, nothing. I stayed home and did some cleaning and ironing."

Mary and I knew she was lying.

The next time I was alone with Mom, I got up my courage. "Who was that man you were with this morning?"

"What man? And when did you see me with a man during the day when you were supposed to be in school?"

I didn't say anything. She had caught us. I waited for her to yell, but she said nothing about missing school.

"As for what I do during the day, that is none of your business."

But somehow, Mary and I got involved in her deceitful game. Openly letting us stay home now, she started giving us notes to take to the bar down the street to give to Lionel, the man she was seeing. He was waiting out front.

"Barbara?" He looked questioningly at me.

I nodded. "Yes."

"I recognized you by your red hair. I'm Lionel."

I was surprised by his appearance. He looked as old as Grandpa. Tall and thin, his hair was completely white, and he wore thick glasses that made his eyes look extremely small. After handing him the note, we hung around outside the bar while he went in to write his reply. He gave us a couple of dollars to take his note back to Mom. Often, a bottle of liquor for Mom accompanied it.

We had no problem getting Mom to write us notes for school anymore.

Despite what was going on between John and me, we still had our conversations. He was the only person who would sit down and talk to me. We rarely heard from anyone else in the family except Grandma and Grandpa when they came into town. I needed to hear John's words. He still told me how special I was. We talked about what I could be when I grew up. He tried to give me pointers on how to handle certain problems I would encounter. I didn't always understand what he said, but I listened. And he listened to me. A few times he asked vague questions about Uncle George, almost like he knew something. I felt awkward and changed the subject.

Lately, John's conversations were focusing on Mom.

"Where does your mom go during the day?" he asked casually one evening.

I shrugged and tried to look like I didn't know anything.

"Do you know where she gets all the money? —She seems to have an endless supply of booze these days."

"I don't know," I said defensively. "I don't know what she does during the day. Do you want a bologna sandwich?"

John dropped the subject.

The truant officer eventually caught up with us and marched us back to school. We were given a crushing load of schoolwork to catch up on, plus a month's worth of detentions.

"How are we ever going to catch up—we're so far behind," Mary sighed when we walked home after our first detention.

I shrugged. Never having done well in school and faced with the impossible prospect of trying to catch up, I was tempted to give up altogether. "Let's quit," I said to Mary.

"But we're too young; they'll make us go back."

I ignored her words. I was becoming more and more resolved. It didn't take too much to convince Mary that with all the work we'd have to do to catch up, quitting was the better option. We called the school to tell them we were quitting, unaware that we couldn't legally quit school.

The school sent a social worker, Mr. LaFave, to our house to talk to us. It was a waste of time. Mom also made superficial attempts at convincing us of the importance of school.

Mary and I went out searching for jobs, with, of course, no luck. We soon found out you can't just quit school at ages 12 and 13.

Just after the new year, Mom received a subpoena summoning us to family court. The date was set for January 18, at ten o'clock.

Mom seemed unconcerned. "I won't let anything happen to you girls, don't worry." She slurred her words and poured herself the last drink out of the bottle.

During the early part of January, while we waited for our court date, Mom began seeing more and more of Lionel. She even had him come to the apartment during the day.

One day, while Mom and Lionel were sharing a bottle at the kitchen table, John walked in the door. He looked at Mom as if he was going to kill her. Without saying a word, he grabbed Lionel and pushed him out the door.

"Leave him alone!" Mom screamed, rising unsteadily to her feet. John ignored her. "Get out of here, old man." He shoved Lionel roughly down the stairs at the end of the hallway; Lionel almost lost his balance on the stairs.

"John, stop it!"

Mary and I rushed into the living room and sat side by side on the sofa, listening to the angry voices through the half-closed living room door.

John came back into the apartment. He walked calmly past Mom into the bedroom and began to pack his clothes.

Mom followed him. John turned and hit Mom hard across the face. "I'll be back later for my clothes," he said to no one in particular and walked out.

Mom was hysterical.

"Mom, it's okay, he'll be back. I tried to put my arms around her.

"Get out of here! Leave me alone, both of you!" Frightened, Mary and I grabbed our coats and left. We had never seen Mom this upset before.

When we came back a few hours later, John and Mom were sitting at the table. Something was wrong. Mom's head was resting on the table.

"What's wrong with her?" I asked John.

"Your mother took some pills," he replied calmly.

"Mom! Mom!" I shook her, but she wouldn't move. I lifted her head; her mouth was hanging open. "Do something!" I screamed. "She's going to die! Do something John!"

"What can I do?"

"Get an ambulance." I was shocked by his apparent indifference.

Mary hovered in the background, looking terrified.

John lifted Mom's lifeless head and pinched her cheeks a few times. She didn't even wince. He picked her up and put her on the couch. We could see that she had wet herself.

John pulled on his winter jacket. "I'm going to find help," he said and rushed out the door.

I sat on the edge of the couch where Mom was lying down. I gently touched her face as she used to touch mine when I was a little girl. She looked so peaceful. I loved her so much, I prayed she wouldn't die.

John finally returned with two policemen and two ambulance attendants with a stretcher. They took Mom to the hospital and pumped her stomach. She was admitted to the psychiatric ward but signed herself out a week later. During her hospital stay, John changed his mind about leaving.

The day of our court date arrived. I couldn't believe it; we had all overslept: it was 9:30. I knew we couldn't make it down to the courthouse in half an hour.

"Just stay in bed, I'll go and use the phone downstairs to call Mr. LaFave," Mom said, pulling on her housecoat. Mary and I pulled ourselves and our beds closer to the stairway so we could hear Mom talking on the phone.

"I'm sorry, the girls and I won't be able to make it today. I've got a very sore back." There was a pause, "What? I can't."

We pushed ourselves back from the door as we heard Mom stomping up the stairs.

"Get dressed, a car will be here in ten minutes. We have to go; we can't postpone it."

As I folded my blankets, I could feel my heart thumping in my chest. I was scared.

"What if we get sent to reform school?" I whispered to Mary.

"We won't, but I bet we'll have to go back to school." She seemed very sure about things. I, on the other hand, was expecting the worst.

When we entered the large stone building, Mr. LaFave was standing outside the double doors, the words FAMILY COURT printed in gold on a plaque just above them.

The room was small and informal, not at all like the courtrooms I'd seen in movies on TV. I was surprised to see Dad seated in a chair on the opposite side of the room. He was wearing a dark suit and was holding his hat in his hands. He made no movement or gesture towards us; his eyes looked straight ahead. I sensed he was not too pleased with having to be here.

I looked down at my black stretch pants and felt out of place. Mom had said it didn't matter what we wore, but as she walked up to the stand with her red skin-tight pants, I knew she was wrong.

Her words echoed in my mind. "I can't manage them. I tried to tell them to go to school, but they wouldn't listen. They treat me awful. They call me horrible names." She looked helplessly at the judge. I could feel anger rise in me as her words sank in. Mom had betrayed us. She seemed to want us to go to reform school or wherever they might send us. When she stepped down, she avoided looking at us. Mary and I were called up to the judge.

"Why won't you girls go to school?"

We hung our heads and shrugged our shoulders. The judge told us to sit down. A few minutes later, he left the courtroom. We all sat like statues, Dad still looking straight ahead, Mary fidgeting with her hands, and Mom looking at the floor. Every so often, she touched her hair to make sure it was still in place. All the love and yearning I had felt for her disappeared at that moment. I looked around the room, wishing I could escape before the judge got back.

Everyone stood up as he walked back in. Mary and I looked at each other. I could see she was just as scared. As the judge spoke, my mind was racing and I could hardly hear him.

"You girls have left me no recourse; I have to send you to the Ontario Training School for Girls."

I swallowed hard.

"You can go and wait with Mrs. Coulter," he said. Someone will come to take you to the Ontario Training School for Girls, Galt Reception Center, immediately."

Chapter 6

I sat on the hard mattress trying to ignore the gnawing pain. I felt as if I had a big empty cavity somewhere in the center of my body. If I could only fill it up, the pain would stop. When I grasped myself tight and squeezed, it seemed to stop for a short time. But the second I let go, I could feel my insides pull apart and immediately begin to ache again.

So much had happened since the morning. It seemed like another lifetime or a bad dream. We hadn't been allowed to go home but had been sent into a small room to wait for our ride to Galt. Mom had been brief and evasive when she'd said goodbye. As I looked at her, she seemed far away, her words faint, as from a great distance. She seemed like someone in a dream who you know is supposed to be your mother, but isn't like a mother at all. After she left the room, Dad gave us one of his rare smiles; it was a tender smile, full of compassion. He patted each of us on the shoulder awkwardly. I wanted to cling to him.

Mrs. Gold, the social worker, came into the room, and Dad left. Mrs. Gold was young and attractive. She looked more like a fashion model than a social worker. She made attempts at friendly conversation, but Mary and I were too flooded with anxiety to respond.

After what seemed like hours and hours of driving on Highway 401 with a brief stop in a restaurant where Mary and I barely touched our food, we saw the sign for Galt.

Almost immediately, we turned off the highway into a driveway that seemed to go on forever. We were greeted by a large sign: "Ontario Training School for Girls." Beyond that were three large brick buildings with bars on the windows, each building surrounded by a fenced-in area. I couldn't believe it. This was just like the jails I had seen on television.

Mrs. Gold drove to the first building. A plaque beside the door read, "Galt Reception Centre." Mary and I got out of the car and silently reached out to each other with our eyes. We were met at the door by two middle-aged women. Mary went with one, and I with the other. I was taken into a small room where I had to turn over all my possessions—a small locket, a ring, which I had to tug to get off and had left my finger green, a flip-top silver-colored lighter, a package of Rothman's cigarettes, some coins, and a two-dollar bill. The lady sitting behind a desk wrote down on a card everything I had given her, then presented the card to me to read and sign. She put everything into a manila envelope. I felt as though a part of myself was being locked into the envelope.

Back out in the hall, the woman I was with finally introduced herself. "I'm Mrs. Hardy. Just follow me, and we'll get you all the things you will need for your stay with us."

Her face was colorless, with no make-up or lipstick, and she wore glasses the same grey as her hair, which made her face blend into nothingness. She held a large circular key ring tightly in her hand, and when she walked, the keys jingled slightly. I trailed close behind. I could see she wasn't much taller than me. I felt indifferent to her. I followed her to a room in the basement. The walls were lined floor to ceiling with shelves of neatly folded clothes. She handed me three pairs of underpants, three pairs of socks, two bras, three moo-moo's, one sweater, one nightgown, and a pair of brown lace-up shoes. The moo-moo's looked like nightgowns.

I looked at my black leather buckle-up shoes. "Can I keep my shoes? They're new."

Mrs. Hardy shook her head firmly. "All the girls must wear the same outfits."

As I held the clothes in my arms, I noticed each piece had the letters O.T.S. written on it with black marker. I realized they stood for Ontario Training School. I hadn't seen any other girls yet. I asked Mrs. Hardy where they were.

"The other girls are in school."

"Where do they go to school?"

"There are classrooms down there." She pointed in the opposite direction. "Let's go and get your bath now."

We went back upstairs and walked through a room that looked like a living room. It had a sofa, several chairs, a television, and a record player with records lying neatly on top. We walked through another doorway and down a long corridor. One side was lined with twelve or thirteen wide-open metal doors, the other side with large windows, covered in bars that fragmented my view of the outside world.

Mrs. Hardy led me to the second door. "This is your room while you are here, Barbara."

"How long do you think I'll be here?"

"I have no idea; that will depend entirely upon you."

My room was about six feet by eight feet. Along one wall stood a long, narrow bed with a mattress no more than two inches thick on top of a heavy board. Beside the head of the bed was a sink, with what looked like a pulpit on wheels next to it. The pulpit slid away to reveal a toilet. A wardrobe with drawers for clothing stood against the opposite wall. I laid my clothes on the bed and looked for the light switch but there wasn't one, although there was a light fixture on the ceiling. The light from the hallway gave just enough light to give the room a cellar-like appearance. I learned later that the staff had a master switch for the lights in the rooms, and that they were turned on only at certain times.

Mrs. Hardy picked up one of the moo-moos and clean underwear and handed them to me. "Come with me."

I dragged behind. She stopped at a small closet at the end of the hall and took out a towel, a washcloth, and a bar of soap. "These are your things; you can keep them in your room. Once a week they will be collected and washed."

At the far end of the hall was a cubbyhole just big enough to contain a bathtub, with a stool beside it. There was no door.

"Start running the water the way you like it and then get in."

When I turned around, Mrs. Hardy was sitting on the stool. I looked questioningly at her.

"I have to stay and watch. Our girls are not allowed to bathe by themselves."

I could feel my eyes starting to burn with tears. I was so humiliated. I couldn't stop the tears.

"Oh, come on, you haven't got anything I haven't seen before." Mrs. Hardy's voice was harsh.

I had no choice. I undressed very carefully, trying to cover myself. I could taste the salt from my tears as they ran into my mouth. I got in the tub, wishing the water were right up to my neck. I slid the soap over my arms.

"You're not doing that right. Put the soap on the washcloth and scrub hard."

The soap kept slipping awkwardly out of my hand under Mrs. Hardy's examining eyes. It was hard to find it through the blur of my tears. Finally, I got it onto the washcloth and ran the cloth over my arms and legs.

"Do your legs again, you haven't done them properly."

I washed my limbs over and over until Mrs. Hardy was satisfied I had done a proper job. At last, she handed me the towel, and I held it tight around myself. It wasn't very big, but it was such a relief to have something covering me. To my further relief, Mrs. Hardy left the room to take my clothes away, leaving me to dress in one of the moo-moos. It felt odd as if I were wearing a nightgown.

When Mrs. Hardy came back, she took me to a nurse's office where I had to take off the moo-moo and put on a big hospital gown. The visiting doctor was coldly professional.

After the standard medical, he said to me, "Have you ever had an internal examination before?"

My eyes widened as I shook my head. I didn't know what one was. I shut my eyes and pretended the pain and probing weren't happening. Discovering I was underweight, the doctor put me on a list that allowed me to go up for seconds at mealtimes. He also informed me I had a bad case of tonsillitis and a mouthful of cavities. I had never thought about my sore throats; they came and went; I took them for granted. I'd had a lot of toothaches but hadn't told anyone because I was afraid to go to the dentist. The doctor said my tonsils would have to come out, and he told the nurse to put my name on the list to see the dentist on his next visit to the school.

After my medical, Mrs. Hardy brought me back to my room. "You will have to be locked in your room for forty-eight hours. Your meals will be brought to you."

I looked at her in horror. "You mean I can't come out at all?"

"No, you can't, but don't feel too bad, it used to be seventy-two hours." She pushed the door shut behind her, and it closed with a metal clang. I could hear her locking it with one of her many keys and then her steps echoing as she walked down the empty hall to the living room.

I went to the door and looked through the thick glass facing out into the hall. There was no one in sight. I felt so scared, so alone. I sat down on the hard bed, and the tears streamed down my face. I hugged myself tightly again, wishing the aching inside would stop. I tried to think of the reasons why I hadn't wanted to go to school, but couldn't think of any. I wished I had gone to school.

I wondered if Mary was feeling the same way. I wished I could see her. I knew I would feel better if I could just talk to Mary. I would feel connected again. I thought about all the things Mom had said about us in court. I hated myself. I was so bad. I really must deserve to be here in this horrible place.

After what seemed like an eternity, I heard voices in the hallway. I looked out the window and saw four or five girls walking down the hall toward my room. They were dressed in colorful moo-moos, like mine.

"We must have a new girl, a door is shut," one of them said. They pushed and shoved each other trying to get a peek through the small window in my door.

"What's your name?"

"Barbara Bennett."

"I'm Mary," a dark-eyed girl said. The others repeated their names, but I couldn't catch them all.

They drifted away from the door. In parting, Mary said, "Get ready for a long stay."

Her words made me angry. I didn't belong here. I wanted to go home now. I wasn't like them. I had learned my lesson. I would never skip school again.

Another new face brought my supper. This was a softer, younger-looking face.

"Hi, I'm Mrs. Jones. I've brought your dinner. If you would just pull the pulpit over, you can sit on your bed and set your dinner on the bottom ledge."

"Where's Mrs. Hardy?" I asked.

"She's gone home for the day; she'll be back tomorrow. Is there anything you need?"

"How long do I have to stay here?" I blurted out, hoping she would have a different answer from Mrs. Hardy's.

"Well, this is just a reception center. You'll be here for approximately three weeks, and then you will be sent to the appropriate training school. It's hard to say how long your stay will be. That will depend on how well you behave.

That wasn't the answer I wanted either. I sat down on my bed to begin my dinner, but couldn't eat.

When Mrs. Jones came back to get my tray, she saw the food hadn't been touched. "You must eat all your food, or you will get an orange and a glass of milk at your next meal."

"I can't eat. I don't feel very good."

"Okay, I'll let it go this time because it's your first day. But keep in mind that you must eat your meals from now on, okay?"

I promised I would.

She left, locking the door behind her. I could hear the girls in the lounge talking throughout the evening. Occasionally, one of them got up to go back to her room, stopping on the way to peer at me through my window. I felt like a dog in a pet store.

Each time I thought I had a grip on my pain, it started again. I wanted so desperately to get away from here. It was as if the training school and everyone in it were on another planet. Somehow, I had been brought along by mistake. Someone would have to come and save me soon.

There was nothing in my room to keep my mind occupied except a Bible, strategically placed on the pulpit. Eventually, I gave in and began reading. "In the beginning God created...." But my mind wandered off to another time—not a better or worse time—just another time.

I must have fallen asleep. The next thing I knew, Mrs. Jones was tapping my shoulder.

"Barbara, it's time to wash up and brush your teeth. The lights will be turned out at nine-thirty."

There was no mirror in the room, but I could feel my eyes were swollen. I wet the washcloth with cold water and held it against them. A moment later the lights went out, and a girl began singing.

That fateful night

The car was stalled

Upon the railroad tracks

I pulled you out and we were saved

But you went running back.

Teen Angel, can you hear me?

Teen Angel, can you see me?

Are you somewhere up above?

And am I still your own true love?

What was it you were looking for

That took your life that night?

They said they found my high school

Ring clutched in your fingers tight.

Teen Angel, can you hear me?

Teen Angel, can you see me?

I had never really listened to the lyrics before. The girl's soft, melodic voice, along with the words of the song, made me feel hollow and alone. The pillow was wet with tears long before I fell asleep.

I was awakened from a restless sleep by the sound of jangling keys unlocking metal doors. I opened my eyes and realized I hadn't been dreaming; I really was here in this awful place. A familiar voice was coming closer and closer to my room.

"Wake up, girls, time to clean your rooms."

I could hear girls grumbling. "Leave me alone. Turn the lights out."

Mrs. Hardy came into my room with clean linen in her arms. She instructed me on how to take the top sheet off and put it on the bottom, then put on a clean top sheet and pillowcase. Next, she took me down to a cupboard at the end of the hall near where the bathtub was and unlocked the door with one of her keys. Inside I saw about eight or nine dust mops, brooms, and dustpans arranged in neat rows along the back wall. Spray bottles and white cloths sat on shelves. Along another wall stood mops and pails. Mrs. Hardy grabbed one of everything and handed the broom and mop to me to carry. After I was finished cleaning, my door was locked again.

The times between meals were long, lonely hours filled with tears and remorse. I thought about Uncle George and Aunt Alice. I wondered if they knew I was in here. I wondered if Uncle George would think I deserved to be in here because of what I did to him.

My days were briefly interrupted for written I.Q. and psychological tests. I also talked to psychiatrists and other professionals. They asked me droves of questions.

"How do you feel about your mother?"

"I miss her."

"How do you feel about your father?"

"I don't know?"

"Do you miss your sister?"

"Yes, can I see her please?"

"Whose idea was it to play hooky from school?"

"I'm not sure."

My forty-eight hours of confinement were finally up, and I could come out of my room. I walked with my arms crossed in front of me as if to protect myself. I found it difficult to speak to anyone and never initiated a conversation, speaking only if someone spoke to me. I also found it difficult to look into anyone's eyes. It was easier to sit by myself, much less painful. I spent a lot of time alone, although Mrs. Hardy and Mrs. Jones were always trying to get me involved in activities.

Everything about this place seemed unreal. Even *I* seemed unreal. How could this be me? Was I this bad person who had to be made right again? I began to feel detached from everyone and everything.

In the evening, I sat with the other girls watching TV. During the day while the other girls were at school, I did cleaning, laundry, or went to the sewing room. I spotted Mary sitting at one of the sewing tables, cutting material. A wave of relief spread over me. Reality returned. Mrs. Hardy introduced me to the sewing teacher, Mrs. Peterson, and said she'd be back to pick me up in an hour. While the two women talked, I snuck over to Mary's side.

"Hi," I whispered. Her shining face reflected my own.

"Hi," she whispered back.

We weren't sure if we should be talking, but I ventured in a low voice, "I hate it here. What about you?"

Mary nodded cautiously, looking around. All eyes in the room seemed to be on us.

A tall dark-haired girl called to us. "Hey, do you two know each other?"

"We're sisters," I replied.

The girls all turned to look at us.

"Wow, sisters, that's a first."

We were allowed one parcel a month. There was a list of items we could and couldn't receive. We were allowed half a pound of candy a month, cream deodorant—not roll-on, toothpaste, face cream, and talcum powder. If you didn't get these items from home, the school would provide them, but the quality wasn't good. The face cream was watered down and seemed to dry your skin instead of moisturizing it. And the school didn't give out toothpaste—only toothpowder, which was awkward to use. Parcels were very important to everyone.

Each Sunday, we had to write to our parents whether we wanted to or not. I had no trouble writing to Mom.

(These letters are unedited. My brother gave them to me after my mom passed; she had kept them all these years.

January 1966

Dear Mom,

How are you? We can only write letters on Sunday. I miss you very much. I am very sorry for what I did I will never do that again. I am trying to be good so I can go home. How are my mice? Mary and I are separated Mary is upstairs and I am downstairs. In sewing we are making a pajama bag which looks like a stuffed animal. How is everyone? There is one bedroom for every girl. On the way here Mrs Gold bought us something to eat. When I come back I am going to finish my schooling. I don't know how long I will be here. Some say 4 to 6 months. Yesterday we saw a show The Moon Spinners.

Are you coming down here to see us? You'll get a letter saying when you can visit. I can't think of too much more to say so I'll close for now.

Love

Barbara

xoxoxoxoxo and lots more

Two weeks later, Mary and I were sent to a training school in Lindsay, Ontario, a five-hour drive from Windsor. The Lindsay building was newer than the ones at Galt. From the outside, it looked like a hospital or university campus. There were no bars on the windows, but small blocks were nailed on the inside of the window frames to stop the windows from opening more than two inches. The building had four wings, two for the dormitories or "houses" of the girls, one for the administration offices, and one for the school, which went from grade 7 to grade 12. The few girls who were in grade 13 went to the regular high school in town, but they were chaperoned very carefully.

There were four houses, one upstairs and one downstairs, in two of the wings. Here, we were not locked in our rooms, only locked in the house. The houses were each named after a nearby lake. I was in "Catchecoma" house, and Mary was in "Cameron." The other two were Crystal and Chemong. You could tell which house a girl belonged to because of the colour of her clothes: my house wore blue, and Mary's wore grey. Chemong House wore brown clothes, and in Crystal, you get to wear your own clothes; this was the house where girls lived just before they went home.

Each girl was assigned a social worker. If there were problems or if you just wanted to talk, you were to fill out a request form and give it to your housemother, who would get you an appointment.

Mary and I were both assigned the same social worker, Mrs. Smith. She had short dark hair and was slightly overweight. I answered her brief questions but had no desire to share my thoughts with anyone. I had become guarded and unable to trust anyone. There were no support groups or real counselling services. We were simply contained until we conformed.

Lindsay housed approximately one hundred girls between the ages of twelve and sixteen. Again, I was the youngest. I felt as alone and isolated here as I had in Galt. I wondered if Mom or Dad would ever come to visit.

Feb 2, 1966

Lindsay Ontario

Dear Mom,

How are you? I am fine. I was just writing to tell you I have left Galt and I am in Lindsay. This building is very nice Mary is downstairs I am upstairs. The place where you eat is just like a restaurant. The room I am in has five beds; you have to be good then you get a room of your own. There was a girl here that got out in four months. Here you get brand new clothes. I miss you so very much. One of the ladies said that most of the girls don't go home, I want to. Some of them do. I love you so very much. Did you get my other letter? We got a letter from Lyle. I am going to be very good. Bye-Bye will write soon.

Love

Barbara

xoxoxoxoxoxo

P.S. I am about 130 miles from Galt

One day ran into the next until it became a week, then a month since I had arrived. I wanted to put time on rush speed, just until it was time to go home. Each day's routine was pretty much the same as the previous one.

I was enrolled in the grade 7 class. There were only four other girls in my class, and they were older because of repeated failures. Our teacher was a soft-spoken young woman named Mrs. Barrett, who seemed nervous a lot of the time. One girl, in particular, Sally, harassed her almost daily. Many times, Mrs. Barrett was in tears by the end of the day.

Sally was a hard, unfeeling girl with striking blue eyes, and blue-black hair that was cut into a bob. As soon as she came into the classroom, she rearranged the desks to her liking.

Everyone knew better than to argue with her. Her reputation of beating up on anyone who got in her way was well established. She caught me looking at her.

"Wha'd'ya looking at four eyes?"

My heartbeat was fast, and I fearfully looked away. She walked over to my desk and rested her elbow on the top.

"You didn't answer me, little girl."

She was so close to me I could feel her breath on my face, but I didn't dare move. I was angry but more scared of what she would do.

"Nothing," I finally answered.

"You had better keep it that way."

I sighed with relief when she walked away. After that, I did my best to stay out of her way.

Lunch was at noon in the cafeteria, after which we went back to our houses for half an hour. The girls sat around knitting or crocheting. As soon as I learned how, I too looked forward to doing crafts. We went back to school from one to four, then from four to five could listen to music, do crafts, or do our homework. Supper was from five to five-thirty, after which it was back to our houses once again.

At seven pm was something called "quiet time," and we had to go into our rooms and do our homework; we weren't allowed to talk or to do crafts. The only sound that could be heard was that of the staff walking up and down the hall, peering into our rooms.

At eight pm, we could watch television; we gathered the chairs and sofas into a semicircle around the set. Often, there were explosive arguments and fights among the girls. I remained detached and fearful of becoming involved. The staff chose the TV shows, but there weren't any we didn't enjoy. At nine o'clock, showers began.

On Saturdays, all the girls had to clean the entire building, including the school wing. Finally, Sunday was a free day.

Each day would have been unvarying if it weren't for the girls who ran away—they frequently attempted to sneak out the fire exits, setting off a barrage of alarms. There were also the girls who couldn't take it anymore and tried to kill themselves by slashing their wrists with stolen razor blades. Other girls were mentally disturbed and had to be sent away to psychiatric facilities. One girl sat in a rocking chair rocking back and forth all day; she refused to go to school or even speak to anyone. There was a problem with girls liking each other too much; they had to be kept apart. Many girls were filled with uncontrollable anger, which frequently got them sent to "the hole."

One evening during quiet time, I heard a loud smash and a girl's scream. We all rushed to our doorways, hoping to see what had happened. Mrs. Rogers was running down the hall, holding towels around the bleeding arms of a girl whose name was Adrian. Adrian was pulling away from Mrs. Rogers, screaming, "I hate it here! Let me go! Let me out of here!"

After they left, there was a noticeable trail of blood down the hall from her room. I never saw her again.

"Did you hear what is happening?" It was Marlene, the girl in the room next to me.

"No, what?"

"There's a riot upstairs in Chemong House. They've plugged up the toilets and barricaded themselves inside. The police are there, but they can't get through the doors—the girls have piled furniture in front of each door."

My first thought was relief that Mary wasn't in that house.

Mrs. Rogers came walking down the hall. "All right, break it up, girls. Come on, back to bed."

I got into bed and pulled the covers up to my chin. I was scared, yet all the activity was exciting. The revolving red light from the police cars parked out front lit up my room at regular intervals.

By morning, the excitement was over, and the story spread quickly throughout the school. Mrs. Moody had been taken out of the building on a stretcher. Three girls had been put into a police paddy wagon and taken away. We never found out where they went. The rest of the house's residents were confined to their quarters for a month. They were not allowed to participate in any activities, such as watching movies or going tobogganing, or even allowed to watch television or listen to the stereo.

I was relieved this hadn't happened in either Mary's or my house. I was scared by the whole thing. I couldn't imagine myself becoming involved in something like this. I was too withdrawn and uninterested in my surroundings. All I wanted to do was to put in my time and get out as soon as possible.

I learned almost immediately that the way out was to be completely submissive. If you showed even a hint of rebelliousness or independence, you were punished—or at the very least, a note was added to your file saying that you had displayed rebellious behaviour. This would be brought up at your three-month Review Board. This was a meeting with your social worker, a staff member, and the superintendent of the school. It was like a progress report.

At my first Review Board, they told me I wouldn't be going back to Mom's when I left the school, and that they would have to find me a foster home.

I spent as much time as possible in my room. The other girls didn't like the way I kept to myself.

One afternoon when I was doing my homework, I felt someone looking at me. I looked up and saw about six girls standing in my doorway.

"Hi, Barbara, why don't you come out to the lounge and watch TV?"

I was suspicious. I knew they didn't like me. "No," I replied, "I'm doing my homework."

Suddenly, someone said, "It's okay, get her."

One girl grabbed my arm from behind and twisted it. They dragged me out of the room.

"If you say anything, we'll kick your head in."

Scared, I went with them to the lounge. They all sat around me for a while, then disappeared. After a few minutes, I felt it was safe to go to my room. I couldn't believe what I saw. Everything was covered with talcum powder: the dresser, the floor, the bed.

There was only one thought in my mind—how was I going to get this cleaned up in time to get my marks? I didn't cry, I just started cleaning. I wanted one thing more than anything in the world: to get out of here. So, I cleaned and cleaned, trying not to let the staff see. I knew I would get in as much trouble as the other girls. The girls kept walking by my room, snickering. I ignored them. I had to make as many points as I could each day. I had to get out of here.

After approximately five months, Mary and I were called into the office by our social worker, Mrs. Smith. We were going to be put into Crystal House together. In Crystal House, there were no locked doors; you could come and go as you liked. You could also get day passes to go into town. You could wear makeup and your clothes from home. Mrs. Smith said she was going to try to find us a foster home. After a year or so, we might be able to go back to Mom.

> "Do you have any suggestions about where you might like to live?" Mrs. Smith asked us. Mary and I looked at each other. "What about Grandma's?"

"We already contacted your grandmother, Barbara. She doesn't feel she can handle both of you. She said she would take Mary but not you. But we turned her down. You and Mary are not to be separated again."

Mary and I smiled happily at each other.

"Well, tomorrow we'll move you down to Crystal house," finished Mrs. Smith, "and if either of you can think of anywhere you would like to live, let me know. Good luck, I'm sure you'll like it very much in Crystal."

I kept trying to think of where we could go. If I could find a place, we could get out of here.

A week later Mrs. Smith brought us back into the office and asked if we had any suggestions. She was finding it difficult to find foster parents who would be willing to take in two teenage girls.

I mentioned Aunt Alice and Uncle George, and she said she would investigate it. I didn't want to go there, but I wanted to get out. I told Mary all the good things about Aunt Alice and Uncle George. I convinced her that they were alright people and that we would like it there. I had put the incident with Uncle George out of my mind. It was all over, and I felt sure it would never happen again.

Soon, Mrs. Smith called us back into the office. "I contacted the Belanger's, girls, and they would be happy to have you girls live with them. A few more details still need to be worked out, but the chances are good that you'll be going there." I felt both happy and apprehensive, but it was the only way to get out of here. I tried to hide my feelings from Mary.

I wrote Mom and told her the news.

June 1966

Dear Mom,

How are you? I got your letter last Monday it was nice. Well this week I have something nice to tell you. I got moved to Crystal House. It is real nice down here we can go outside any time we like. We will be going to Aunt Alice's place to live for a while instead of a foster home. We will be able to visit you, don't worry. Next week our probation officer is coming to see us. She might tell us when we are leaving. My parcel is due today. When you get the pattern book get one with nice sweaters in it. We are going out on a barbecue tonight. I got a letter from Grandma. They are thinking about coming down. But I think it would be too long a drive for them to come. I wish you would come down soon. Well, I can't think of much more to say so I'll close.

With all my love Barbara

Write Soon xoxoxoxoxoxo and more

Mrs. Moen came to see us. She was tall and thin and wore her hair in a bun. She seemed quite pleasant.

"Well girls, the arrangements have all been made; you'll be leaving in four weeks."

Four weeks! Mary and I looked at each other, and our faces broke out into wide smiles. We were so happy that we barely listened to the rest of what Mrs. Moen was saying.

"I'll be visiting you once a month," she went on. "And if you have any problems, you shouldn't hesitate to tell me—I'm here to help. You'll be on probation until you're eighteen. You are now wards of the court."

This meant we would become wards of the court, financially and emotionally. In effect, the courts were to be our parents.

Mary and I each got a welcoming letter from Aunt Alice the following week. She said she had got a new double bed and fixed up a room for us.

"This will be a fresh start," I told myself. "And it'll only be for a year, then we can go home to Mom again."

When we arrived at Aunt Alice and Uncle George's, we were greeted by a colourful array of barking dogs. Aunt Alice rushed out the back door and put her arms around both Mary and me. She looked just the same, but I remembered her as being much taller than I. Now we were almost the same height. She wore a flowered summer dress that was gathered at the waist. As she hugged me, I could smell the distinct smell of her soap.

As I looked over Aunt Alice's shoulder, I could see Uncle George walking toward us. My first thought was "Why isn't he at work?" He took one quick puff of a half-smoked cigarette and then abruptly threw it to the ground.

He had gained weight. His large belly hung over his white, belted painter pants. The little bit of hair left on the top of his head had turned all white. His brown-framed glasses made him look older. He had hardly ever worn glasses in front of anyone before, but now he seemed comfortable in them. He looked very much like a little old man, not at all like the big, strong man I remembered. He reached his hand out first to Mrs. Moen, then to Mary, and finally to me. His hand was cool. I felt apprehensive as I looked into his eyes.

"We're glad to have you home, Barbara."

I smiled and slipped my hand out of his.

July 1966

CAN I COME HOME NOW?

Dear Mom

I got your letter just before we left training school. Oh Mom nobody in this whole world knows how much I miss and love you. I thought we would have to go to a foster home for a month but that's all, not all this time. Yeah, we sure did have a lot of plans. How is John? Good, I hope. We got our last parcels. I have started a doily, but it won't be too small I don't have a pattern for a small one like you would like but I will make one later O.K. We don't know if Jeanne can visit us yet. But I will write her when I find out. I can't wait until Mrs. Moen comes back then she will tell us when we can visit you. I can't wait till my radio comes. What was the matter with it, was it the tuning I forget? It seems so good to be able to write letters and no one reads them. Well, I guess that's all I can write for now so I'll close with all my love and even more.

Bye Bye

Barbara

xoxoxoxoxo and so many more I can't write them all.

Chapter 7

In the two years that I had been away from the Belanger's, many changes had taken place. Aunt Alice had resigned as manager of the dry cleaners and was boarding and breeding the cockapoos full-time. The dog kennel behind the house had been completed and was well stocked with cockapoo dogs and their pups. They were such a popular breed that Aunt Alice usually had the pups sold before they were born.

Uncle George was still doing his auto body work and was very much in demand. He told us how people came to the house asking him to do their car, but he was so busy at work and with the house, he didn't have time for moonlighting. I was amazed at the amount of work that had been done on the house. All the rooms were finished in various shades of wood paneling, which contrasted effectively with the white drop ceilings in each room. The makeshift shelves in the kitchen had been replaced with beautiful oak cupboards and white countertops. The plywood flooring had been covered with poured floors.

Aunt Alice looked proudly at the kitchen floor. "They came and poured a special liquid evenly all over the floor, and then we had to leave it for a few hours, and it dried to this hard, shiny finish. It never needs waxing."

"It looks great, Aunt Alice," I said. I could see how pleased she was with the kitchen.

"I've still got some finishing trim to put up; it's not done yet," Uncle George said. But I could see he was pleased too.

"Come on and see the bathroom," Aunt Alice said, motioning for us to follow.

I couldn't believe it was the same bathroom. The tub was surrounded by beautiful blue and white ceramic tiles. The sink had been installed, and the pail of water that had stood beside the toilet for flushing was gone.

I looked around in admiration. "Do you remember how we had to heat our bath water on the stove?"

Aunt Alice laughed, and Mary gave me a peculiar look.

"I'll tell you about it later," I said. We followed Aunt Alice down the hall.

"Here's your room. I hope you like it." Aunt Alice looked at us expectantly

Mary and I walked in tentatively. Aunt Alice had refinished the old dresser and roll-top desk that I had used before and bought a new double bed with a wooden headboard that almost exactly matched the dresser. A pink comforter lay on the bed, and matching curtains hung in the window. Although it was the same room, it gave me a much warmer feeling than before.

"It's really nice," I breathed.

Aunt Alice smiled at me, and I felt a rush of affection for her; she was trying to make us feel at home.

Next, we went into Aunt Alice and Uncle George's room. Aunt Alice had refinished their old chest of drawers too, and the double bed had been replaced with twin beds.

I felt uncomfortable being in the room. In my mind flashed a picture of the old bed, Uncle George lying on it, clutching a girl in his arms. I blinked my eyes quickly to erase the picture.

After we finished our tour, I went outside for a walk. The yard had been sodded and landscaped. It looked like a picture in a gardening book. I went down to the dock, weathered but still standing, and dangled my feet in the murky water. It had been so long since I'd been outside like this with no one watching over me.

Mary was very shy. She hardly spoke to Aunt Alice and Uncle George. In the beginning, they tried extra hard to draw her out, but eventually gave up. Her shyness seemed to intimidate Aunt Alice. She seemed almost afraid to assert her authority around Mary. It was easier to scold me because I was more outgoing. Consequently, I ended up getting blamed for everything, even if it wasn't my fault.

Aunt Alice began to sound like Grandma: "Why aren't you more like your sister? Don't you ever stop talking? Why don't you go read a book?"

Even Aunt Alice couldn't dampen my spirits. We were out of training school. It was great to be in a real house, not to have to rise at 6:30 and do exercises, to be able to go outside whenever I wanted, and not to have anyone read my mail.

The summer passed all too quickly, and as September approached, Aunt Alice took me to register at the public school in a nearby town. We also went with Mary to register at the regional district high school. I had thought I would be returning to St. Ambroise school, where I had done grade five. But they had since changed their policy and would accept only baptized Catholics.

I wasn't a baptized Catholic— I wasn't even baptized.

When it came time to buy clothes for school, we learned from Mrs. Moen that we had to order all our clothes through the Simpson-Sears catalog. We were to make a list of what we wanted and then send the order to the training school. They would attach a cheque and send it on to Simpson-Sears for processing. We could spend a maximum of one hundred and fifty dollars per year. We had made a promise that we would never tell anyone that we had been in training school.

This was the seventh school I had attended. It was a small country school, and the students were bused in from a large surrounding area. My teacher was Mrs. Rosedale, who was also the school principal.

I had always found it very difficult to make friends; I was so different when I was away from home. Although at home I talked nonstop, at school or anywhere outside of the home,

I barely spoke. I was afraid I would say the wrong thing, and people would laugh and make fun of me. I tried to get around this feeling by complimenting the girls in my class on their clothes and hair—even if I didn't like them. I was always willing to help my classmates. Anything to be liked.

During recess and lunch hour, I discovered I wasn't the only girl who sat alone. A dark-haired, chubby girl named Helen didn't seem to fit in any more than I did. I was immediately drawn to her. I wanted to talk to her, but wasn't sure how to approach her. Then one day, Mrs. Rosedale changed the seating arrangement of the class, and Helen and I found ourselves sitting side by side. Within weeks, we were best friends. We both felt intimidated by the other girls and became masters at avoiding them. We were inseparable. Unfortunately, we lived so far apart that we couldn't visit each other after school. Helen. was from a poor family of farmers and had seven brothers and sisters. I envied her for her large family. She envied me in my Simpson-Sears clothes. I didn't tell her about training school.

That year we had to stand up and give a three-minute speech in front of the class. Helen and I were sick about it. On the day it was my turn, I got stomach cramps. But that only postponed my turn until the end. Helen said hers and confessed, reassuringly, that it wasn't as bad as she had thought.

My ears were burning as I stood before the class, and what had taken me three minutes to rehearse at home took me only about a minute and a half. I couldn't tell if Mrs. Rosedale's smile at the end was encouragement or amusement; I felt only massive relief that it was over.

Early one morning, I got up before Mary and went into the kitchen to make breakfast for myself. Uncle George was already up, eating toast and jam.

"Morning," I said as I brushed past him. He didn't respond. I went to the counter to put a slice of bread in the toaster. Within seconds, I felt his hands come to rest heavily on my shoulders.

"We have to talk." His voice was harsh. I could feel his breath on my neck. Before I could turn around, his hands lifted from my shoulders, and I heard his footsteps as he walked away.

I tried to think, but my brain spun. Could it be happening again? I prayed desperately, oh please God, don't let it happen again. That evening, Uncle George confirmed my worst fears. I was coming into his room; I was doing those disgusting things again.

"You know what we have to do, Barbara," he said to me the following Sunday afternoon while we were alone in the car. I tried to ignore his words.

"Now, if you tell anyone about this, you'll be sent back to that school you just got out of."

Fear traveled through my body. That was the last place I ever wanted to be.

My temperament again began to change. I became short-tempered and ready to explode with the minimum of provocation.

"I don't know what's wrong with you, Barbara," Aunt Alice commented. "It's like you're waiting for someone to say the wrong word to you so you can jump all over them."

I folded my arms across my chest and sat in angry silence.

During Mrs. Moen's next visit, I overheard Aunt Alice discussing my behavior while they sat at the kitchen table. I stood frozen in my bedroom, straining my ears to hear their hushed voices.

"Barbara is having these terrible outbursts. I don't know what to do about them."

"Does she become violent?"

"Yes, she throws things and hits herself. Why once, she yelled at me to kill her because she would be better off dead."

"Is there anything that triggers them?"

Aunt Alice started to say something, but broke off as the door opened. I heard Mary saying a meek hello to Mrs. Moen, then she came down the hall to our room.

After visiting a while longer with Aunt Alice, Mrs. Moen knocked on our bedroom door.

"How would you girls like to go into town for a shake or a sundae?"

Mary and I climbed into the backseat of Mrs. Moen's Volkswagen. We liked Mrs. Moen and enjoyed these monthly outings. She asked the same questions each time. "Are you happy? Do you feel content? How's school? Any problems getting along with Aunt Alice or Uncle George?"

We gave the right answers. I was scared that if I said there were any problems, I would be sent back to training school.

This time, Mrs. Moen's questions were more probing.

"Do you feel comfortable here?"

"Yes."

"Does Mrs. Belanger talk to you girls?"

"Yeah."

"Is there anything about Mr. Belanger that bothers you?"

"No." I tried to sound indifferent.

She never came right out and mentioned my outbursts, but I knew they were behind her digging. I managed to keep up the facade that everything was fine.

When Mrs. Moen brought us back, she said she would like to talk to Aunt Alice alone. Mary and I went into our room. I stood with my ear to the slightly ajar door.

"What are you doing?" Mary asked.

"Shush!"

I could just hear Mrs. Moen's voice. "I questioned the girls, and there doesn't seem to be a problem with you or your husband. I'm wondering if Barbara's problem doesn't go back to her mother. She may feel resentful of you for trying to be a mother to her. I'm going to speak to Mrs. Bennett to see if we can't get her and Barbara into some sort of therapy together."

"I don't think her mother would agree."

Aunt Alice's voice trailed off as they walked out of my hearing range.

Now I felt worse; Mom was being blamed for this. My frustration increased.

After Mrs. Moen left, Aunt Alice came into my room." Mrs. Moen is going to try to get your mother and you into therapy together." She fixed her eyes on me and sighed. "Not that I think it'll do any good, but..." She shrugged and went back to the kitchen.

A few weeks later when she came to tell me that Mrs. Moen had called to say Mom wouldn't agree to see anyone, Aunt Alice couldn't seem to keep the triumph out of her voice.

> "See how much your mother loves you, she won't even help you."

Her smug look infuriated me. "I hate you! I hate you!"

Mary was beginning to wonder why I was getting so angry at everyone. "What is wrong with you, Barbara?"

"None of your business." I stormed out of the house and down to the river. The river was the only place that made me feel peaceful. I spent hours sitting on the dock watching the water flow gently but steadily to its destination, unhampered by any obstacles.

My final exams, as well as my grade 8 graduation, were rapidly approaching. I sat at the old roll-top desk in my room for hours and hours trying to study. But it was impossible to concentrate; my mind wandered away to everything except the War of 1812 or the parts of a flower. Sometimes I threw my books on the floor in sheer frustration. I began to wonder if I would pass and be able to go to high school with my classmates.

A couple of weeks before graduation, Aunt Alice mentioned getting me a new dress for the ceremony.

"I don't know why you're even bothering with a dress; I probably won't pass anyway."

"Barbara, will you stop being so negative? Of course you will pass."

This rare confidence in me from Aunt Alice stunned me. I wondered if she knew something I didn't.

"We'll go next Saturday into Windsor - Mary, you and me."

I couldn't take pleasure in the prospect even though I wanted to. Uncle George was increasingly pressuring me, and my brooding moods were escalating into raging temper tantrums. The least thing set me off. I became like an animal, screaming and yelling. I banged my head into the walls and wouldn't listen to anyone.

Finally, in utter exhaustion, I crawled into a closet or under a bed.

I couldn't believe it was all happening again. I wanted to erase it from my mind.

A few days before we were to go into Windsor I had a severe temper fit that ended, as usual, with me crawling under my bed exhausted.

Aunt Alice didn't say anything until the next day when I asked what time we were leaving for Windsor on Saturday.

"You won't be coming."

"What do you mean? Why can't I go? It's my graduation. I should be able to pick out my dress."

"No, Barbara, I discussed this with Uncle George, and he agrees that you must be punished for your behavior."

I wondered why Uncle George would say something like that. He was the one who usually defended me and argued with Aunt Alice on my behalf. Then it clicked. He had been telling me that I was coming into his room more and more often and that we had to do something.

At breakfast that Friday morning, Uncle George motioned for me to come out to the dog kennel with him.

"We should do it tomorrow morning, no one will be home."

I turned away from him.

"I am so tired at work we have to do something soon."

I took a deep breath, overcome by a feeling of nausea.

Saturday morning I opened my eyes and looked up at the ceiling. I looked over beside me; Mary was already up and gone. Maybe if I just lay here and sleep it would become Sunday. I didn't want to get out of bed. The door opened suddenly, and Uncle George came into the room. He must have been waiting at my door for me to wake up.

"Alice and Mary are on their way to Windsor. Do you want to get started?"

"What should I do?"

"Like we used to remember?" He left me to change.

Mechanically, I put on my housecoat, took off my underthings, and lay on the bed. A few minutes later Uncle George called from outside my bedroom door.

"Are you ready?"

"Yes," I called back, choking on the lump in my throat.

He walked in with just a T-shirt on. I closed my eyes to shut out the sight of him. He crawled on top of me.

"Open your legs, Barbara."

I tried to but they wouldn't move.

"I can't." I tried to sit up.

Uncle George pushed me down on the bed. I tried to move but couldn't. He pushed his knee between my stiff legs, forcing them open. His aggression scared me. He got my legs opened wide enough to lay his body between them.

"Relax Barbara, you know we have to do this."

"You're hurting me."

"Then quit fighting me, and I won't hurt you."

I looked at the ceiling, tears rushing from my eyes into my hair.

He began moving on top of me. His breathing became heavy, his face red. I looked at his eyes and they looked different like he was not behind them. I wondered who this mean-looking red-faced man lying on top of me was. Abruptly he stopped moving and lowered himself heavily onto me. I felt sick from the weight and tried to push him off.

"Just a minute," he said and lifted himself.

I went into the bathroom wishing I could wash the pain away from my hurt body. I spent the rest of the day cleaning the house until everything shone.

The day finally arrived when we would find out if we passed. Mrs. Rosedale asked me to come into her office. My heart sank into the pit of my stomach. This meant for sure I had failed, and she was going to tell me before I got my report card.

"Barbara, I know this year has been very hard for you. You have been pushed around a lot through your life, and I feel you will do better now that you have a stable home life. Your average this year was forty-nine percent, but I'm going to give you the passing mark of fifty percent. I know you will do well next year if you concentrate and try hard."

Relief spread through me. I looked at the floor. "Thank you so much."

My graduation dinner and dance went well. Aunt Alice, Uncle George, and Mary gave me a gold watch.

For the next few weeks after the episode in my room, Uncle George did not talk to me or take me on any trips to the store, although he still defended me if Aunt Alice was too hard on me. But within weeks of my graduation, he was making sure I came with him on his frequent trips to the store and was after me again. I was coming into his room every night, he said. He was tired at work. I sat in the car beside him, listening to his words, a rage boiling deep within yet not visible on the surface.

During the following days and weeks, I tried to notice if I was tired in the morning, or if I was sore like I had been that Saturday. I looked for any sign that I was doing what Uncle

George had said, but there was none. I wondered about his accusations but quickly dismissed any doubts. I knew Uncle George would not lie to me.

Uncle George kept creating situations where we would be alone. He used these opportunities to convince me that we must do it again and again. The time between these episodes seemed to be getting shorter and shorter.

One day, shortly after I began menstruating, Uncle George signaled for me to go out to the dog kennel with him. I waited for a few minutes before I followed so as not to look suspicious.

"Barbara, are you sick?"

"No, why?" I was confused.

"You're bleeding down there?"

I hung my head in embarrassment. I wondered how he knew. "You came into my room last night, and now there is blood all over my underwear. I had to throw them out before Alice saw them."

I ran out of the kennel and into the house.

"Shut the door, Barbara," Aunt Alice yelled after me as I tore down the hall.

Her words were just enough to set me off on another temper tantrum. An hour later, I found myself sitting in my closet wishing the pain in my head would go away.

That summer seemed to fly by. Mary and I spent our days outside with the animals, bike riding, swimming, or visiting friends. I was looking forward to going to high school with Mary that September. By now, I was used to going to new schools, and this was just one more.

Any illusions I might have had about having extra freedom once I got to high school quickly fell by the wayside. Aunt Alice was very strict. We were not allowed to join any extracurricular activities or go to school dances. She kept telling us we would be sure to get in trouble if we were out by ourselves. Mary, who had to abide by these rules the previous year, never pressed the issue, although she wanted to go and had friends who were allowed to go. As for me, I had no friends to go to these events with anyway, so Aunt Alice's rules were fine with me. I became even more withdrawn and spent my time at school alone, not trying to make any friends.

One fall evening, while I was in my room doing my homework, Uncle George came to my doorway and, without saying a word, motioned for me to come outside with him. I could feel my body tense up and my heart begin to pound. I followed him to his car. He opened the trunk and pulled out a newspaper, which he began unwrapping.

"I found this in the toilet late last night. I went in right after you."

I stared at what he held in his hand. It looked like a piece of bloody meat. I couldn't understand what it was supposed to be.

"This is a baby. It must have come out of you when you went to the bathroom."

I could feel my stomach turning. I thought I was going to throw up. Anger rose in me and I snarled at him. "What are you talking about?"

I couldn't hear his words anymore. My head was spinning. I felt dizzy. Uncle George was becoming smaller and smaller.

"What if Alice had found this? Barbara! Barbara, are you listening to me?"

I ran into the house and into my room, throwing myself on the bed. A few minutes later, a shuffling noise outside my window distracted my empty thoughts. I went to the window. Uncle George was out in the field digging a hole. I watched him, hating his presence, wishing horrible things would happen to me. After a few minutes of digging, he walked back to his car and took the piece of newspaper out of the trunk. He put it gently into the hole he had dug. Then he looked up at my window. I turned away.

On her monthly visits, Mrs. Moen kept asking me if I was happy, if I was content. I kept saying yes, I was happy, and yes, I was content. I was scared that if I told the truth, I would be sent back to training school.

I did what Uncle George wanted more and more often. Uncle George was changing. He talked about things I shouldn't have heard, things I didn't want to hear.

"Alice can't have sex; it hurts her too much. We tried about five years ago after her operation, and we haven't since."

I didn't understand what he was talking about. I wished he wouldn't tell me these things.

"You remind me of the first girl I had sex with. We were just kids, and we went out to the bush; it was good."

Why was he telling me this? I tried to shut my ears. His voice was making my head throb. I felt nothing but hate for him and myself for doing these horrible things to him. At these times, it was almost as though I left my body, or that my body became numb. The only thing I felt was the pressing pain. His words made me sick. Many times, I would go into the bathroom and vomit after these episodes. Uncle George didn't tell me I was going into his room anymore; he just said, "Well, it's about time for you know what."

I did what I was supposed to.

Our relationship outside the bedroom changed. I never talked to him anymore. We didn't tickle or fool around. He was no longer the father I'd never had. I never wanted to be around him at all. For a long time, he had been the only person I could still look in the eye, but now I couldn't even do that anymore.

I felt dirty all the time. I felt alienated from my peers. They weren't doing what I was doing. I wanted to tell someone about it, but there was no one to tell. I wanted to run away. But where would I go? I thought about the girls who had run away from training school. When they got caught and were returned, they told stories of having to do anything for a place to sleep. They slept with men, did drugs, anything to get off the streets for a night. I was too scared to run away.

I thought of telling Mom, but something inside of me knew that she would not, or could not, help me. In the meantime I kept missing her and writing to her.

November 1967

Dear Mom and John,

Hi how are you? I got your letter. Right now at school we are having our exams. I have not missed one day of school yet this year. You must be happy now that you have your own home. Say hi to John for me and how is he doing? Do you think that you will be able to get another record player? I seen Mike [Lyle's son] in the store one day and is he ever cute. I have never seen Kenny [Jeanne's son], but I want to so bad. Have you got everything unpacked in your house yet. I wish we could see it. Aunt Alice is coming to Windsor on Monday. Last time Aunt Alice was in Windsor she got some nice blankets like you have blue and pink. Well I guess that's it for now.

With Love

Barbara

oxoxoxoxoxoxo and many more

Christmas was rapidly approaching, and Grandma wrote to ask if we would be able to come to her house for the holidays. Excited, we asked Mrs. Moen for permission. She agreed, much to Aunt Alice's dismay.

Our entire family would be at Grandma's for Christmas, including Mom. We were counting the days. Aunt Alice was resentful.

"I don't know why you are so happy to see your mother," she said to me when we were alone doing the dishes one evening. "She is the one that put you in training school."

She never said these things if Uncle George or Mary was around. Usually, I could ignore her, but now, with things the way they were with Uncle George, I felt vulnerable to her digs. I no longer had an ally.

Uncle George was getting more and more demanding. I tried to avoid him. My change in attitude toward him was becoming apparent to everyone, even Aunt Alice.

"Barbara, why are you ignoring Uncle George? He has always been so good to you."

"I'm not!" I retorted venomously.

The more I detached myself from Uncle George the more insecure he became.

"You aren't going to tell your mother about this, are you Barbara? Remember what will happen, you'll go back to that school. Your mother doesn't want you anyway, but you know that already. Just remember who started this a long time ago."

"I know, I know," I said, impatient for him to stop.

Grandpa came to pick us up on Christmas Day. It was so uplifting to see my family. I hadn't seen them for so long. Jeanne and Ray had a girl and a boy now, and Lyle and Julie had one boy. I felt shy, unsure of myself around the family. Yet I also felt a sense of belonging.

Mom and John were the last to arrive. I kept asking Grandma when they were coming.

"Soon, Barbara, soon."

Finally, they walked in. I rushed to Mom. It had been at least a year since I had seen her. She hugged and kissed Mary and me. I was glued to her side for the rest of the day. She told me I was pretty and that she loved me and missed me. She promised that we would be together again soon.

During my stay at Grandma's, I had fantasies about living there again. Even if she did love Mary more, I didn't care; I could live with it. When I talked to Mary, I discovered she wanted to stay too. We decided to ask Grandma.

"Grandma, we miss being here a lot," Mary said rather hesitantly; she never spoke about her feelings easily. I wished she would be more forceful, but I didn't say anything.

"Well, Grandma misses you girls, too." She put her arms around us, pulling us close to her.

I couldn't stop myself. The tears rolled down my face, and I blurted out, "Grandma, can we please come and stay with you? Aunt Alice is so mean, she hates me. She always says horrible things about Mom. We hate it there so much."

Grandma pulled back from me, obviously shocked by my words. Mary too seemed surprised by my bluntness, but she continued when I stopped. "Grandma, can you please talk to Mrs. Moen?"

Grandma looked at Mary. I knew Mary could reach her, but I couldn't.

"Both you girls feel the same. I'm shocked. I thought everything was fine. But I don't feel there's anything I can do. You're wards of the court now. I can't just take you away from the Belanger's."

So, we went unhappily back to the Belangers'

When Mrs. Moen came that month, we broke down and told her how we felt. She said she would talk to Grandma and get back to us as soon as possible. Before leaving, Mrs. Moen talked it over with Aunt Alice, who seemed surprised to learn of our discontent. After Mrs. Moen left, she told us we were ungrateful, and that Grandma would never agree to take us in.

But she was wrong. Grandma did agree. Within two weeks, we were on our way to live with Grandma and Grandpa.

Uncle George was in his usual panic about me telling anyone. I assured him I wouldn't. But I knew in my heart, one day I would have to tell someone this ugly secret.

Chapter 8

Our new home was a one-and-a-half-story white frame house in Kingsville, Ontario, with a double-car garage and an old garden shed in the backyard. Grandma turned her sewing room into a bedroom for Mary and me. Grandma and Grandpa's bedroom was across the hall from ours on the main floor. Uncle Jack, still living at home at forty-one, had the entire upstairs—a huge room with sloped ceilings and lots of windows. The living room was bright and inviting, with an electric log set in the imitation fireplace, which Grandma turned on for special occasions. On the mantel above stood pictures of children, grandchildren, and great-grandchildren.

The basement was unfinished. On one side, Grandpa, a skilled craftsman, had set up a workshop, well stocked with tools and the materials to make a tool. Another part of the basement was partitioned off for the laundry. That left a large empty area in the center. After much coaxing, Mary and I convinced Grandma to let us make a sitting room for ourselves. We brought our record player and records down from our bedroom and used the lawn furniture that Grandpa was storing for the winter. We pretended it was our apartment and spent a lot of time there until we made friends and spent less and less time at home.

Grandma and Grandpa did everything for us without hesitation. During cold winter mornings, Grandpa dug the car out of the snow just to drive us to school, although the school was just a short distance and we insisted we could walk—he seemed to want to do this for us. And he was forever fixing our glasses when the arms came off, jewelry boxes that we had locked and then carelessly misplaced the key, clips on our necklaces or bracelets, and anything else we happened to break.

Every morning, Grandma poured cereal into bowls for us and filled our glasses with fresh-squeezed orange juice. Beside our place settings sat a vitamin C and a cod liver oil pill, as well as our lunches, always including dessert, neatly enclosed in a brown paper bag.

I found it amusing to watch Grandma and Grandpa together. Grandma would nag at Grandpa if he happened to forget something while out shopping.

"Oh Dad, you've forgotten the bread again. Didn't you read the note that the money was wrapped in?"

"Oh Jesus, I'll go back and get it. I don't know why we need bread anyway. Jack is the only one who eats it. He should go and get it."

"That's not true, and anyway, I sent you to the store, and you were supposed to get it."

"Alright Mother, you are right." And then, with a whimsical look: "What was it again I was supposed to get?

Sometimes they nattered away about Uncle Jack as if he were four years old—whether he should wear this coat or that or buy this or that car. Mary, if she happened to overhear this, would roll her eyes and walk away.

Although Grandma was ten years younger than Grandpa, her health was not as good as his. Since her heart attack, she had become progressively weaker. She needed bypass surgery to replace a clogged artery, but would not agree to have it done. She had never had an operation and was proud of the fact that she did not have a scar anywhere on her body. Her health was so weakened that she could no longer walk to a neighbor's house three doors away to get her hair done. I loved doing hair and was glad to do Grandma's hair in pin curls each Friday evening.

I felt relaxed and comfortable with Grandma and Grandpa. Grandma no longer compared me to Mary or made comments that made me feel inadequate.

I quit wearing my glasses except when I really needed them. I bought some new clothes that included shorter and tighter skirts, and I was letting my hair grow long. I began to feel normal, like I fit in.

As my life was changing - or I was changing - I no longer felt the need to compliment other girls to make them like me. Instead, I was the one receiving compliments. The girls seemed eager for me to like them. Best of all, I became fast friends with Joanne. She was cute and petite, and we got along great. She lived only a few doors away, so we were always at each other's house. Grandma liked Joanne and allowed her in the house. Grandma was choosy about who came into the house.

There was also a girl near our age named Patty who lived next door. She went to a different school, so we didn't see her very much. But one afternoon, a few weeks after school began, I saw Mary out in the driveway talking to her. Mary came into the house

"I was just talking to the girl who lives next door. She says there's a place in town everyone hangs out—called Bruno's. It's a restaurant, but she says there's a room with a jukebox and a dance floor. She said we should check it out. Do you want to go after supper? It's not very far, we could walk from here."

I shrugged. "Sure."

From the outside, Bruno's looked like an ordinary restaurant, but inside it was full of teenagers, and we could hear the strains of "Spooky" coming from a room off to one side. Everyone seemed to know each other; they were laughing, dancing, calling out to one another. Mary and I found an empty table and sipped our Cokes, looking around us, pretending we fit in. We felt awkward but at the same time glad to be there, glad to be included.

To my surprise, a boy with sandy hair and intense hazel eyes came and sat down beside me. He looked older and was quite good-looking.

"Do you want to dance?" he asked. I thought he must be asking Mary, but Mary was nudging me, and when I ventured a glance, he was looking at me with those intense eyes.

I nodded, the words sticking in my throat. The song, I could hear, was a slow one. I had never slow danced with a boy before. I was terrified I'd do something wrong.

Randy put his arms around me, and I could smell a mixture of deodorant and sweat emanating from his shirt. I felt uncomfortable being so close to a boy. I tried to pull away, but Randy's arm pulled me in closer. I concentrated on not stepping on his feet until the song was over.

He came back to the table and sat down beside me. The conversation was awkward. I didn't know what to say, and Randy seemed a naturally quiet person, although he did try to draw me out.

"I have never seen you around before—are you new here?"

I nodded.

"What grade are you in?"

"Nine."

There was a pause. I could tell he thought it was my turn to say something, but I couldn't think of anything.

"I quit school in grade ten," he said finally.

I looked at him with new interest. "Do you have a job?" I envied him not having to go to school.

Randy nodded. "I work in town—at Aztec Printing. It's a small printing shop," he added, seeing my blank look. "I run one of the machines. We print the Kingsville Gazette."

There seemed to be nothing else to say. I couldn't think of anything to ask him. Randy offered to buy Mary and me another Coke, and when he came back, we sipped our drinks and watched the other kids until it was time to go. Mrs. Moen, our social worker, had set our curfew at ten o'clock on weeknights.

"It's quarter to ten," I whispered to Mary. She nodded and I turned to Randy. "We have to go home now."

"Can I walk you home?"

"No, it's okay," I said. I was too shy to say yes.

"Can I at least get your phone number?"

I mumbled our phone number while he wrote it down on a napkin.

The next night, Randy called. He seemed to want just to talk. I didn't know how to talk to a boy on the phone. Again, I let Randy ask the questions. There were lots of awkward pauses.

"Who was that?" Mary asked when I got off the phone, smiling knowingly.

"Just Randy," I shrugged. I tried to look indifferent, though secretly I was flattered to have a boy call me.

"He's pretty cute," Mary said, looking at me closely for my reaction.

I shrugged again. I thought Randy was good-looking too, but I didn't feel any real attraction to him.

After that, Randy called every night.

During his usual evening phone call a couple of weeks later, Randy said, "Will you meet me at Bruno's in half an hour?"

"Sure, we were going to go anyway," I said indifferently, but inside my stomach went into a knot of fear. Why did he want to meet me? Was he going to tell me he didn't want to see me anymore?

Mary and I arrived at Bruno's at 7:30, and I looked for Randy, but he hadn't shown up yet. Around 9:30, Mary and I got ready to leave. I looked out the window. Randy was standing outside waiting. Nervously, I put my coat on. A blast of cold air greeted us outside. Randy looked agitated. I whispered to Mary to go on ahead.

"You saw me out here—why didn't you come out?"

I shrugged. I didn't know how to explain it. Randy offered to walk us home. As we began walking. I could feel Randy wanted to say something to me. His agitation made me feel distant.

Finally, Randy stopped walking.

"Here, I got this for you."

He pulled out a box from his pocket and opened it, lifting a ring from inside. He gave me an intense look. "Will you go steady with me?"

"Yes," I said, not thinking, unable to take my eyes off the ring. It was gold with a blue stone. "You bought this for me?"

"Well," he blushed, "actually, I bought it a couple of months ago—for another girl, but she hardly wore it. We didn't go steady very long."

He held it out, and I put it on the third finger of my left hand. It slid on in a perfect fit. I felt a rush of joy. I have a boyfriend now. Somebody cared about me. I couldn't wait to show Mary.

Randy and I became inseparable. We met for lunch together every day. We spent the evenings together after supper until my curfew. Mary usually came with us. She didn't have many friends and often stayed home in the evenings reading or doing homework. Since I was nervous about being alone with Randy at first, I urged her to come along.

I wasn't wild about Randy, but I was glad to have someone to hang out with. All the kids from Bruno's told me how good-looking he was. He was small in stature, standing about two inches taller than I at five feet seven, but very muscular from lifting weights. There was a dark spot in one of his eyes that looked like a freckle on his iris. At first, I couldn't help but stare at it. Strangely enough, almost right from the beginning of our relationship, I had no problem looking Randy in the eye. I began to feel safe with him, and no longer needed Mary to come along with me, although she still did.

Randy's foremost ambition was to buy a car; he was seventeen and had had his license for a year now. Soon after we started going steady, he bought a black MG sports car. I was excited to have a boyfriend with such a neat car. There were only two seats in it, which meant Mary had to curl up in the opening behind the seats. Once Mary found a boyfriend—a boy named Gary—Randy and I finally had a lot of time alone together.

The first time he tried to kiss me—on the front porch of Grandma's house—my arms hung limp at my sides.

"Put your arms around me," Randy said impatiently. I reached my arms hesitantly up around his neck as I'd seen women do in the movies. It felt awkward. What if Grandma came out and saw us? The January air was cold, and I wanted to get in the house where it was warm. But Randy was pulling me in close to him. I could feel the tenseness of his body. I pulled away. I hated the sound of his breathing.

"What's the matter, Barbara? Don't you care about me?"

I could see the hurt in his eyes.

"Yes, but—" I didn't know what to say. I didn't know why I pulled away. I just knew it felt uncomfortable. I felt uncomfortable touching anyone except maybe Mary and

Mom. I liked to be with Randy to talk, but I didn't want to be physically close. But it was important to him, so I forced myself.

As we became closer, I felt a stronger and stronger need to tell him about Uncle George. I needed to confess this secret so that he would know what kind of person I was before he fell too deeply in love with me. I felt I owed him that much.

One evening, after we had been dating a few months, Randy and I drove to the beach. We often went there on Friday nights. Randy parked the car and leaned over to kiss me.

I pushed him away. "Randy, I have to tell you something."

Randy looked at me sharply. My voice was different—I knew it didn't sound like me. I looked down at my hands fidgeting in my lap. They were clammy with sweat. I could feel the blood pounding in my ears.

"Randy, I need to tell you—" I spoke so low I could feel him straining to hear. I couldn't look at him.

"I used to live with my Uncle George and my Aunt Alice, and my Uncle George, he said I used to—" I choked on my words.

Randy grabbed my hands and held them tight so they would stop shaking.

Tears streamed down my face as I told him the story.

Randy squeezed my hands tighter.

I closed my eyes and concentrated on the painful pressure of his grip. The words came out almost in a whisper.

For the first time I had said it. It seemed different saying it out loud. I waited for Randy to say something, but he was silent. Finally, I raised my head and looked at him.

"Goddamn son of a bitch," he said. "I'll kill him."
He pounded the dashboard with his fist. "Shit."

I stared at him and let him pull me to him. He was angry at Uncle George, not me. But it had been my fault. Why wasn't he angry with me? My mind was spinning.

I made him take me home, overwhelmed by confusion.

Lying in bed, I felt relief. I had told someone, and he didn't hate me or blame me. I wondered if it really wasn't my fault. But if it wasn't, then whose fault was it?

I fell into a restless sleep.

Mom wrote to say she and John had parted and she was living in a small apartment above a restaurant in Windsor. Grandma and Grandpa were pleased. Grandma said Mom was better off without John and invited her to come and spend a few days with us. I was overjoyed.

Mom turned into a helpless little girl while she was around Grandma. They were always in conflict over one thing or another. Grandma disapproved of Mom wearing makeup and keeping her hair long.

"Mildred, why don't you cut that hair off? You're far too old to be looking like that."

Mom closed her mouth tight into a grimace.

Grandma took a deep breath and walked away in disgust.

After a few days of this aggravation, Mom became frustrated. One evening, she asked Uncle Jack if he wanted to go out for a few drinks. When Grandma discovered Mom and Uncle Jack had been out drinking, she was furious.

"You came here to see your children, and you are going out to hotels drinking."

Mom ignored her and went out the next night, and the following night again.

Mom and Uncle Jack stumbled in late one evening to be confronted by Grandma's serene face. "Mildred, if that is how you are going to act around your girls, out drinking every night, not to mention taking your brother with you, then you had better pack your things and leave."

"Ma, I have to have a life of my own. The girls are out with their boyfriends anyway."

"That is no excuse for what you are doing." Grandma's voice was cold.

> The next day, I went into my room to find Mom packing her suitcase. My heart sank. "Mom, do you have to go?"

"Yes dear, your Grandma doesn't understand me. I must have a life too. I'm not young anymore, and I'm entitled to enjoy myself."

I wished Grandma would treat Mom as well as she did Mary and me. I was angry she was leaving, but I understood why she had to go.

Mom kissed Mary and me goodbye, and Grandpa drove her home to Windsor

The Sunday after Mom left, Lyle and Julie came out for dinner. They came out once a month with their little son Mike, who was one and a half. They had expected to see Mom there and were surprised and disappointed to find her gone.

The first few times Julie and Lyle had come I had felt shy, but Lyle soon made me feel at ease, telling me jokes and making small talk. He had an easy, comfortable manner about him. He was also very handsome, and I felt a strong feeling for him, though I hardly knew him. He was very gentle and loving with his son.

"How's work going, Lyle?" Grandma asked.

"Pretty good, the factory is about the same as usual."

An ash from his cigarette fell on the carpet. Casually, he stepped on the ash and ground it into the carpet. No one else but me seemed to notice. When Lyle looked up and found me watching him, we began to laugh, leaving the others wondering what was so funny. This secret, unspoken rapport we shared made me feel good inside.

As a result of all my extracurricular activities—the main one being Randy—I failed grade nine. Grandma didn't make any comments about our grades. Our rules were set by Mrs. Moen, and Grandma seemed to accept the fact that she had no control. She was seventy now and, with her serious heart condition, could not afford to get upset. It was easier for her to let us do as we pleased. She never asked us where we went, although she did make it clear she didn't want us bringing Gary or Randy into the house.

The relationship between Grandma and me was becoming more caring and understanding. I felt a connection with her. When she cried, I could feel her pain. If she asked me to do something for her, I did it without resentment. I was so happy to be here. I felt it was my obligation to do the things she asked. Even though they didn't know it, Grandma and Grandpa had saved me from a torturous life with Uncle George.

I wouldn't talk to Randy about my feelings. I listened to him talk about marriage, but remained aloof and detached, which seemed to make him try harder.

The closeness Randy wanted was making me feel more and more uncomfortable. I spent more time with Joanne and eventually broke up with him. But that didn't stop him from calling me every night until I gave in and we reconciled. It felt so good to have someone telling me how much they loved me.

Every night when we were together, Randy told me he loved me. I could feel he wanted me to say it back. He never said anything, but I could tell by the look on his face that he was hurt. I tried to bring myself to say those words to him, but they wouldn't come. Despite these difficulties, our relationship continued in an on-off fashion. I broke up with Randy at the drop of a hat. If he forgot to call me or picked me up a few minutes late, or if I felt he hadn't paid enough attention to me, I became enraged.

"You are just using me; you don't care about me!" I screamed.

"I do Barbara! I'm sorry! I'm sorry!"

"I don't care. I never want to see you again!"

I threw the ring at him and stormed away.

After these episodes, I became even more convinced of his love for me. But when I was with him, he seemed to overwhelm me. I felt so smothered, so controlled. Randy talked of nothing except what it would be like when we got married, what our life would be like, and how many children we would have. I wished he would stop, and we could just enjoy the moment. A commitment was scary, and the idea of marriage was a nightmare for me.

I was confused by my feelings. I didn't understand why I kept breaking up with him, testing his love for me. I only knew when I went back with him, I felt surer of his love for me.

On Saturday mornings, Mary and I got up early to get our chores done so we could go out. One Saturday, Mary said she had somewhere important to go and couldn't do her chores. She left about ten o'clock that morning with Gary. Grandma was not her usual self. I asked her what was wrong.

"Oh, Grandma's having a bad day," she said. Her voice didn't sound like her own. "I'm finding it hard to get a good breath today. Do you mind helping clean the kitchen? I know it's Mary's job, but she went out somewhere with Gary."

"No, I don't mind." I feared the way Grandma looked. She was pale and breathing hard.

Mrs. Moen called while I was cleaning. "I won't be out to see you girls this month, Barbara. I'm being transferred. There will be a new social worker assigned to you soon."

"Oh, okay," I said. I was disappointed, I liked Mrs. Moen. But I didn't know how to tell her.

I finished my chores at about noon. Grandma was sitting on the sofa. She didn't look good at all.

"Can I get you anything?"

"No dear, you go out with your friends."

I went into the bedroom to change my clothes and get ready. Before I left, I went into the living room again.

"I can stay home if you want."

She turned to me with a distant look in her eyes. "I think my time is coming, Barbara."

Grandma always said things like this, but this time something was different. I reached for her hand.

"You are a good girl, Barbara. Now go on. Get going."

I hugged her and left to meet some friends for a Coke at Bruno's. Within a couple of hours, a lady I vaguely recognized as our neighbor came looking for me. I could tell by her face that something was wrong.

"Barbara," she said, "I've been looking for you. Your grandmother is not good, you need to come home. I'll take you." She put her arm around my shoulder.

I felt numb as I got into her car and sat silently. When we turned down McCallum Street, I saw a hearse pulling out of our driveway and burst into tears.

There was an unnatural quietness in the house. I walked in hesitantly. Jeanne was sitting with Grandpa at the kitchen table. The pain on his face was worse than I could ever have imagined. Uncle Jack was in the living room, babbling away about how he could not live without his mother. Mary appeared calm, almost numb.

"Gary and I are going to Windsor to get Mom," she said.

In an instant, they were gone. Jeanne sat down with me, and we cried.

A few hours later, Mary came back with Mom. Grandpa went to her and buried his face into Mom's shoulder like a young child.

After the funeral, Mary went to stay with Mom; she couldn't stay in the house. I was left alone with Grandpa and Uncle Jack. The emptiness in the house was eerie. Grandpa was sad all the time. He didn't even bother getting up early anymore. He didn't putter around the house; he just sat and stared into nothingness.

I wanted so badly to make everything right for Grandpa and Uncle Jack that I tried hard to be cheerful and ignore my pain. But I couldn't do this for long. Grandma had given me the best home I had ever had. I couldn't share my pain with anyone, not even Randy. I hadn't seen him since the funeral, and he gave up calling after a while, probably because he sensed my need to be on my own, rather than because he was discouraged. I had never given him much encouragement anyway. I withdrew into myself as I always had, drawing on my inner strength.

I began missing school again. Since I never did my homework, I bullied the other kids, demanding they give me theirs. I was even getting into knock-down, drag-out fights with other girls. This got me reported to the principal, and numerous times, I was given warnings and detentions. But I didn't care about anything. I continued doing as I pleased and ignored the rest of the world.

The guidance counselor from school called the minister from the United Church to talk to me. Mr. Moore was a tall man, with a broad, kindly face and thick, wiry eyebrows. He spoke to me with gentle concern in his almond-shaped eyes. But his words meant nothing.

At home, I cooked and cleaned for Grandpa and Uncle Jack and gave an appearance of being happy. When the school called Grandpa about my behavior, he was surprised. In his state of mind, he didn't understand what the school wanted him to do. When he asked me about it I told him to ignore them.

Ultimately, I got suspended from school and was eventually expelled. I stayed home and took care of Grandpa and Uncle Jack during the day. Since Mrs. Moen had been transferred, no one had been out to visit. I was hoping they had forgotten about us. I was perfectly content just to stay home and take care of Grandpa and Uncle Jack for the rest of my life.

One morning, I was awakened by the ringing of the phone. On the other end, a man's voice said he was replacing Mrs. Moen temporarily, that he would be out to talk to me in about an hour, and would I please wait there for him. When he came to the door, there was another man with him.

"Barbara, we have come to take you back to Lindsay."

At the word Lindsay, my heart started to pound. My one thought was to escape. I would not go back to Lindsay. I ran into my bedroom to get out of the back window.

They came after me, knocking on the door. "Barbara, come out here."

"I'm changing my clothes," I called out. I got halfway out the window and looked down, and there was one of the men standing under me.

"Please," I said, almost in tears, "I don't want to go back there, I hate it there. Please don't send me back there."

They dragged me into the car. Grandpa stood by, watching helplessly. He came to the car window and spoke to the one behind the steering wheel. "She is not a bad girl really."

He kissed me goodbye. I wondered who would take care of him now.

I wrote Mom from training school:

Dec 7, 1968

Box "4000"

Lindsay, Ontario

Dear Mom,

Hi, how are you fine I hope. Well I had promised the principal I would not skip school anymore and I wasn't going to but I guess I had too many chances. They phoned at nine o'clock and said they were coming over to talk to me so I waited and he said we are taking you to Lindsay I put up a pretty big fuss because I don't think I deserved this. But it is different now there is Junior, Intermediate, Senior and Gold Leaf. If you are good for 50 days in each you get promoted and returnees start at intermediate. So if I am good all I have to get is 100 days then I will be out. I could be out by March or April. Please come up here for Christmas day. I know I am asking a lot but it would mean the world to me. I am really lonely in here. It wasn't too bad before when Mary was in here too.

Will you send me a parcel as soon as possible with candy, lipstick (white) emery boards, noxema, hand lotion. Kleenex, a brush and comb and a pair of keeper earrings thanks a million.

Love to everyone

Barbara

Chapter 9

"A fifteen-year-old girl living alone with two men is not an acceptable environment." Mrs. Jarvis' appearance was intimidating, her too-black hair pulled back into a tight roll and her thick glasses making her eyes appear small and severe. She was the social worker who had been assigned to me since I had returned to training school. She came to see me once a month for an hour-long visit, during which we talked about my family, why I didn't go to school, what I wanted to do when I got out of training school, and where I could live. Although her manner did not display it, I got the feeling that she did care about me.

"Why couldn't I have gone to my mother's, like my sister did?"

"Because Mary is 16 and doesn't have to go to school anymore. Your mother's home is not appropriate for a schoolgirl. If you can think of a home where you would be happy, we'll be pleased to see if it meets our requirements. If not, we'll look for a suitable foster home for you."

With these words, I was dismissed.

How was I supposed to suggest a home? I couldn't go to Mom's or Grandpa's, and I would never go back to the Belangers'. I tried to think of anyone who had been nice to me. I had to get out of here. I hated it even more than I had the last time.

After much thought, I remembered Mr. Moore, the minister from the United Church in Kingsville who had come to talk to me at school. He had seemed genuinely interested in my welfare. Maybe I could live with him. I would still be close to my friends, and I could take care of Grandpa and Uncle Jack. I couldn't wait to tell Mrs. Jarvis about him on our next visit.

"Oh, you sure came up with that name fast," she said when I suggested the Moore's. "We'll check this out and let you know how it goes. Have you ever talked to them about living there?"

"No, I never thought about living with them before now."

"Okay, thanks Barbara, I'll let you know what their response is."

Mom was still living in her apartment over the restaurant. In her last letter, she mentioned she was seeing Lionel again. He had recently moved to Sarnia but came to Windsor on weekends to see Mom. He was trying to persuade Mom and Mary to move to Sarnia. Mom told him she didn't want to move and wrote me to say she would be staying where she was for now anyway.

During my two-month stay at training school, I wrote a lot of letters to Mom.

(These are the unedited letters that I wrote to mom. When she passed away, I was given them by my brother.

Dec 21, 1968

Box 4000

Lindsay Ontario

Dear Mom,

Hi how are you? Fine I hope. I received your letter on Monday. I was very disappointed in fact I was crying, I wanted to have a nice Christmas also. Oh well I hope you do If anyone has any gifts for me I can have them. They can be wrapped in gift wrap they are nicer like that.

You will probably receive this after Christmas. Do you know when you will be coming up. We wrote our exams this week I don't think I did too good on them but we have them every month here so I will try harder next month.

I will write Mary every week too. I hope she writes back.

It doesn't even seem like Christmas around here. Maybe you will be able to come up around the end of January or beginning of February. Mom will you talk to Miss Corley [our new social worker in Windsor] about me coming home to your house when I get out because I will be almost sixteen, or sixteen. I will go to school because if I get all of my schoolwork good in here then when I get out I will keep on going to see if I get my year.

I hope I get some gifts maybe it will be more like Christmas. In my parcel each month it doesn't matter how much candy I have.

I made you a big yellow doily I hope you like it. Right now, I am embroidering two pillowcases I have one done. I have gained four pounds in here. I don't need my boots I have a pair but if you already sent them it is alright.

Don't forget to send up my three pairs of earrings, - my blue ones, and my picture of myself, and my pictures out of my wallet. I want to show the staff the picture of Mary.

Most of the girls went home for Christmas but I came a week too late. I will get the next leave; I think it's in March.

Well I don't think I will hear from Dad cause I haven't written him. He doesn't care about me so I won't be bothered. I have made 16 good days so far. If you are good in school you can get a prefect of 5 days every second week. I am going to really try. We have to make 16 points out of 24 to earn a day, and I have made 22 and 23 and 24 every day.

Well this is getting long so I think I will close now and write Mary.

XOXOXOXOXOXO Love Barbara

P.S. I got 78% on my penmanship exam. Did Grandpa get my letter?

I received news that I would be leaving soon and going to live with the minister and his wife.

Dec 28, 1968

CAN I COME HOME NOW?

Box 4000

Lindsay Ontario

Dear Mom,

Hi. How are you? Well it is Saturday afternoon, and I wasn't doing anything so I thought I would write you.

I was so happy to talk to you on the phone on Christmas day. Christmas was nice here. I got a pair of silk panties (blue), a little China cat, a pair of panty hose and a necklace and earrings, but I gave the earrings away because they were not pierced.

Mrs. Jarvis never said anything certain about me leaving, just the second or the ninth of January, she wants to get me started before school starts in January. There is another girl in here getting out soon too and I am hanging around with her. There are a few girls in here who plan on making our last days rough, but they were taken care of by the staff.

Mary said that she wrote but I did not receive it yet. I hope I like it at the Minister's I think I will because all my friends are there. I hope I can come home to your house in June.

I will probably know for sure on Monday when I am going home.

I will not be able to go out every night there. I want to make all my own clothes when I get out, so if you get a hold of a pattern or any material keep it for me O.K.

I'll be so close to Grandpa's I could go over to do the ironing for him once a week. Has Jeanne helped? I felt so much better after I talked to you on the phone.

There were quite a few people with visitors on Christmas here. There was a Quartet here last night one of the guys in it liked me, was he ever cute, he said he was watching me all through the time they were singing, and he gave me his address. I forgot to ask Mary if she got her diamond.

Well, I am going to write to my girlfriend Jo-Anne, so I'll close now.

Love Barbara

See you soon

Jan 3, 1969

Lindsay Ontario

Dear Mom,

Hi. How are you? Fine I hope. I received your letter and the card. What's the matter with dad didn't he give us anything for Christmas? On Thursday the advisory board meets and then I will know for sure if I am leaving. If they say no I will be very disappointed. I hope I can come home to your house in June. Did you ask Mrs. Corley about it. Thanks for the dollar. Now I have some money to buy cigarettes on the way home. I wrote to the Minister & his wife. I am kind of scared to go there, but I hope it works. We are having a dance here tonight.

I made a pair of baby's soakers are they ever cute, now I am making the hat to go with it. The doily I made you is huge, it turned out bigger than I expected it to.

I got four letters on Monday night I was really happy. I got a planters wart burnt off the bottom of my foot. The only part that hurt was the needle to freeze it.

I can't wait until Thursday. I can go see Grandpa

It has only been a month since I came here but it seems like five I like that comb and brush you sent it is really different.

I want my big picture but don't send it.

I should have asked you to send up my makeup and earrings so I could wear it home if I go, but it won't come in time.

Well, I can't think of anything more to say right now so I'll close.

Love Barbara

XOXOXOXOXO and more

P.S. Say hi to John if you see him and tell him I won't make anymore mistakes.

Jan 11, 1969

Lindsay Ontario

Dear Mom,

Hi, how are you? Well, I am still here. You know what the holdup is, it is because the Minister and his wife are on an extended Christmas holiday. They are expected back the beginning of this week or next. Then it will be brought before the advisory board on the Thursday after that, then I can leave the Friday after. I am sick of waiting and I mean it.

The other night I was crying, and I felt sick and everything, and none of the girls in here except one likes me, and it is kind of rough.

The school told me something about you moving to Sarnia is Mary going too. Will you send me my earrings and makeup so I can wear it home. Send it as soon as possible so I can have it by Monday.

I have made 36 good days but that doesn't matter. I am going bowling this afternoon.

Right now I am going through the hardest part of my life I think, I am so nervous my hands and everything. Before I had Mary to share my problems with and I really miss her.

Nobody ever writes me.

I want to tell you one thing this is my personal feeling, so don't get mad please. I think you are crazy to go to Sarnia cause you are hurting a lot of people in my opinion.

Well I am going to start crying again if I don't end this letter.

All my love Barbara

XOXOXOXOXO and more

P.S. Will you send me some candy also. I can have a lot. But if it won't be here by Monday don't send it O.K. I am not going to write Mary this week. Would you send my big picture of myself I want to show it to someone.

Jan 25, 1969

Lindsay Ontario

Dear Mom,

Hi. How are you? Well remember on the phone I told you it would be this week or next, well it is next week. It will go through the advisory board next Thursday and I have to go to see Mrs. Jarvis Friday at 9:30 and she will tell me the answer and if it is okay then I can leave on Monday possibly.

Well I had one friend in here and she left today at 2:00 now I am alone and depressed. I just hope I can leave Monday. I was happy to receive your letter and Mary's, and my parcel. I just finished eating all the chocolate. I am not going to use my make-up cause then everyone will want to use it. I just want to use it to come home with.

Mom I really want to come home in June to be with you and Mary. I hope I can get along there till then, I want to come to your house for a weekend. I got the picture too.

I really do miss you so much Mom. I wrote Mary a five-page letter and now I have nothing left to say to you except I really miss you a lot, and I really love you Mom and no one can ever take your place.

Love Barbara

XOXOXOXOOXOXOXOX and more

P.S. Did you ask Mrs. Corley about me coming home in June?

(Mrs. Corley was the new probation officer assigned to Mary and me after Mrs. Moen's transfer.)

I did leave the following Monday, taking the train to Windsor. As I entered the station, I saw the minister and his wife in the distance, straining their necks to find me in the crowd. When he spotted me, Mr. Moore began waving his arms frantically. I made my way through the hordes of people, trying to keep the Moore's' in view. I had never seen the minister's wife before, but somehow she looked as I pictured her: tall and thin, her dark hair done up so perfectly I was sure she had just stepped out of a beauty parlor. She looked squeaky clean. Her clothes fit perfectly, as though they were made specifically for her. She was attractive in a plain sort of way.

The minister's dark hair was greased neatly back exactly in the way I remembered it when he had come to school. He introduced me to his wife.

"Barbara, this is Joan, and please call me Peter."

Joan reached her hand out towards me. Her hand was cool in my apprehensive grasp.

On the way home, we stopped to get something to eat at one of the restaurants along the highway. While Joan and Peter drank their coffee after the meal, all I could think of was how much I wanted a cigarette.

When we got home, Peter showed me the room they had fixed up for me. It was bright and cheerful, with a single bed, a chest of drawers, and a circular mirror on the wall over the dresser. At the end of the bed was a big trunk; it looked like a hope chest. I wondered for a long time what might be inside before I gave in and opened it. I had been thinking of some mysterious hidden treasure; instead, I found pillows and blankets.

The old brick house was attractively decorated in a Victorian style. Upstairs were three large bedrooms and a bathroom, and downstairs a small living room, a large dining room furnished with a huge wooden table and eight press-back chairs, and a small, somewhat plain kitchen, where we had our meals. The dining room was used only for company. The front porch was winterized. A bowl filled with candy and chocolate bars sat on one of the porch tables. I was told I could have an unlimited supply and took advantage of this pleasure until I got tired of candy.

The house stood beside the United Church. The Moore's had been there less than a year. They were in their early thirties and had no children. Peter was much more outgoing and friendly than Joan. I found her cold and serious and didn't particularly like or dislike her.

Joan and Peter were unlike anyone I had ever been around. They were calm, soft-spoken people who were openly affectionate and loving towards each other. I was not accustomed to this way of being and felt uncomfortable around them, particularly when they also tried to show affection to me.

Despite my resistance, they tried to be parents to me. They talked about how far I should go in school and how I should dress. "Barbara, those Levi's are boys' pants," Joan commented. "They don't look good on girls."

I shrugged. Everyone wore boys' Levi's, but what was the point in explaining?

"Why don't you wear nice dress pants or skirts? Jeans are worn by people who aren't quite—well, the right kind of people."

I had never been around such judgmental people, never heard these kinds of attitudes expressed before. It filled me with anger.

They insisted I go to Sunday school and church each week without fail, which I hated.

"None of my friends go to church, I don't see why I should have to go every week."

"It's important that you go to church, Barbara. Everyone should go to church—your friends too. People who don't go to church..."

I glared at Peter, resenting his implied judgment of my friends, resenting his trying to be a parent to me. I *had* parents.

The more uneasy I became, the more time I spent away from them, despite their efforts to be social. I made up excuses to get away: I had to do my homework, or I had to study, or I had to go here or there.

"Barbara, we're going to think you don't like it here if you don't start to spend more time with us."

"It's just a really busy time for me at school now. I've got to get caught up on a lot of stuff I missed."

Another thing that irritated me was that when I had a bath, I was not allowed to lock the bathroom door.

"We all trust each other around here," Peter asserted.

I tried to have my baths when no one was home. If I couldn't, I had the fastest bath in history, listening all the while for footsteps.

There were all kinds of rules set up for me, no matter how much I protested that they were being unreasonable, they would not give an inch. I was losing my friendship with Joanne. I couldn't even go for a Coke after school. I began to feel like I was living in a shrinking box.

After one month, I ran away to Mom's apartment in Windsor.

When Mom opened the door, I started to cry and hugged her tight. As she returned my hug, I felt loved. But when I told her what had happened, her reaction was not what I expected.

"You can't stay here; the authorities will find you." Her voice was cold.

I couldn't believe what she was saying.

Mary walked in just then and stood beside Mom, looking on with disbelief.

"Where will I go?"

Mom's face was expressionless.

Mary spoke up. "You can't just turn her away."

"I have to do this," Mom insisted. "I'll get in trouble if I hide her."

Mom and Mary argued back and forth until Mom finally said, "If you care so much about her, Mary, then maybe you should leave with her."

I stared at her, feeling numb.

"Come on Barbara." Mary grabbed my arm and pulled me through the door with her.

We went to the phone booth, and Mary called Gary to come and pick us up. The two of us spent the night in Gary's car, parked in his parents' driveway. His parents had no idea we were in the car.

The next morning, we were not sure of where to go or what to do. Eventually, we decided to go to Jeanne's, hoping she would help us.

"I had a feeling you two would show up here," Jeanne said, opening the door reluctantly.

We sat down and poured out our stories to her. When we finished, the look on Jeanne's face was sympathetic. Mary and I turned to each other and breathed a sigh of relief.

"Mrs. Corley called me and said if you two showed up here to call her. But don't worry, I'll explain to her what happened."

I felt so thankful to Jeanne for her kindness.

Mary and I gathered from what we could hear of one side of the conversation that Mrs. Corley would not be able to get out to see us for a while.

"Oh yes, I can keep them here until you can get out. Yes, Barbara *will* continue going to school."

As Jeanne hung up the receiver, she looked directly at me. "I suppose you heard."

We nodded and promised to stay with her until Mrs. Corley could get out to see us.

I continued going to school.

Chapter 10

A strong odour awakened me. I felt as if the insides of my nostrils were burning. I lifted my head, unsure where I was. The silence around me was deafening. Then a vision flashed through my mind. A vision of the car going off the road and banging into, and over, things.

I looked to my left, but I couldn't see Richard. I turned the other way to find Jan slumped over the dashboard.

"Jan, wake up." I shook her. "We must have been in an accident."

She lifted her head and looked around in confusion.

There was scarcely any windshield left, so it was easy to climb through. We slid down the front of the car. The hood was so mangled it pointed towards the ground.

I looked for Mary. I stumbled to the back of the car and peered through the back window. Gary, half on the seat and half on the floor, was trying to pull himself out through the side window. Mary was lying across the seat flat on her back, unmoving. Her stillness scared me.

"Mary! Mary!" I shouted. Gary had pulled himself out. I ran around to the side and reached my hand through the broken window to try to wake her. Suddenly, she started to moan. "Mary, are you okay? Mary, it's okay, you're alright."

The awful moaning sound continued through my words.

"Mary," Gary said. "Mary, can you hear us?"

She kept moaning. Gary and I looked at each other, scared. "Where's Rick?" Gary's voice was desperate.

We searched around the car. The driver's door was completely torn off. Richard was lying on the ground beside the car, a cloth or blanket covering his head. I pulled back the cloth. He didn't move. His face looked peculiar. Jan, Gary, and I stared at him. In the distance, the sound of sirens grew nearer and louder.

I headed to the back of the car to Mary again. I didn't get very far before I fell. My leg felt like rubber. I looked at my blood-soaked hands and screamed.

Jan rushed over and put her arms around me. "It's okay, it's okay."

Then she touched her face. It was covered in blood. I could not see where it was coming from.

"*Oh no, my face, my face, my father is going to kill me*!"

Two ambulances arrived, and a wide circle of people gathered around us.

A police officer bent over Richard. "It's too late for this one," he muttered to no one in particular.

"Get the girl out of the back seat first, she's pretty bad!" someone else shouted.

As they carried Mary past me on a stretcher, the horrible moaning became louder and louder. The back of her head was covered with blood. She was put into an ambulance. Gary got in the front seat of the same ambulance, and they sped off with screaming sirens.

I was scared for my sister.

By the time the attendants had brought stretchers for Jan and me, my leg felt as if it was not attached to me anymore. Our ambulance, too, raced to Leamington General Hospital.

I couldn't believe what had happened since the afternoon. When I got home after school, Mary had been anxiously waiting for me.

"Barbara, remember that favour you owe me?"

I looked at her blankly.

"Oh, never mind. Do you remember Gary's friend Richard?"

"Yeah, vaguely, why?"

"Well, he broke off with his girlfriend and wants to go out with you tonight, isn't that great?"

I wasn't sure if it was, or not—I could barely remember what he looked like.

"We're going for a drive to Point Pelee," Mary said.

"We have to see if Jeanne will let us go," I said. "Besides, I thought your friend Jan was coming over tonight?"

"She is," Mary replied impatiently. "Barbara, do you want to go or not?"

I thought about it for a moment and shrugged. "Sure, why not."

Jeanne said we could go if we were home by 10 o'clock.

Jan arrived after dinner. She was tall and thin and always dressed very stylishly, like a model. Tonight, she was wearing brown leather pants, and Mary and I oohed and aahed over them.

At 7:30 Gary came to the door for us. Gary and Mary got in the back of Rick's car while Jan and I slid into the front.

"Hi," Rick said, grinning at me.

As soon as I saw him, I remembered seeing him around with a girl named Pat. I was glad I'd come; he seemed like a nice person.

Gary introduced Jan and Rick to each other.

I could smell the alcohol on Richard's breath as he leaned his broad face in front of me to say hello to Jan.

On the way to Point Pelee, Richard pulled a bottle of beer out from under his seat.

"Anybody want a drink?"

He passed the bottle back to Gary.

"No thanks, you know I don't drink." Gary pushed the bottle away. The rest of us also refused.

Richard was driving fast and recklessly, and we were laughing and joking. We enjoyed the excitement, the quick turns, and being gently tossed around inside the car.

"Oh no, I'm going to be sick." Richard pulled the car onto the gravel on the side of the road, squealing the tires as they left the pavement. He jumped out of the car. We all laughed as he staggered away.

"That feels better," he said when he returned. He started the car again. "Is everybody ready?"

"Yeah, let's go! "Jan and I cheered.

Richard threw his empty bottle out the window. He stepped on the gas so hard that the car sped around in circles on the gravel.

"Hey, watch it, Rick, take it easy eh!" Gary called from the back seat.

"Mary, keep him busy back there, will you?" Richard joked.

The car swerved, almost went off the road, and swerved back again. I began to be frightened. Jan was giggling.

The car swerved again. I could hear the crunch and spray of gravel as the car left the paved road. Richard turned the wheel hard left, jerking us around inside. I put my hands on the dashboard to secure myself.

"Don't be scared," Richard said. "I've been through the park three times today, and at higher speeds than this."

"I bet!" Jan piped up.

Her words were exactly the challenge Richard was looking for. He stepped down so hard on the gas pedal that I felt myself being thrown hard against the back of the seat. Within minutes, I could feel the car banging and bumping over things, and my body being thrown around. Then everything went black.

The Leamington Newspaper of February 19, 1969, read:

YOUTH DIES IN PELEE CRASH

Point Pelee National Park — One Mersea youth was killed, and four others were injured, one critically, when a car hit a tree in the park shortly after 8 pm Tuesday.

DEAD IS RICHARD Shafer 17, R.R.# 5, LEAMINGTON

In hospital is Mary Rose Bennett 16, who is critically injured and suffering from massive lacerations to the head and possible back injuries. Also in the hospital is her sister Barbara age 15. Both sisters are from R.R. # 2, Kingsville.

Two other passengers in the car were Jan Devitt 17 of R.R. # 2, Kingsville, and Gary Beetham also of Kingsville.

Miss Devitt is suffering from lacerations to the face and arms and shock. Gary Beetham has possible back and leg injuries. Barbara Bennett is also suffering from back and leg injuries.

Police said the car was headed north on the Point Pelee Road when it failed to make the first curve on its way from the end of the Point to the gate. The car left the road, bounced over a shallow ditch, sheared off underbrush and small trees until it hit a tree about 2ft in diameter.

The roof of the car was completely peeled back by the impact and the seats in the interior of the car were jarred loose from their fastening.

Dr. James Taylor of Leamington, coroner, pronounced young Shafer dead and said cause of death was likely a fractured neck. The four passengers were taken to Leamington District Memorial Hospital for emergency treatment.

"God must have been watching out for you," the doctor said as he examined me. I had a broken kneecap, with fluid on the knee, and a few minor cuts.

"What about Mary?" I asked anxiously.

"Your sister's unconscious, and her leg is broken in two places," he replied evasively. "We're keeping close watch over her."

Jan had a large cut over her top lip and a very deep cut on her inner arm. Her leather pants had protected her legs from the broken glass. Gary had pulled muscles in his back but had no cuts and needed no stitches.

Jeanne, Ray, Mom, and Dad spent most of that night at the hospital, as did Gary and Jan's parents. I couldn't get anyone to tell me anything about Mary.

The next day, Aunt Alice and Uncle George came to see me. Aunt Alice tried to smile. "Well, Barbara, you're lucky," she said, tapping the temporary cast on my leg.

"Hello Barbara," said Uncle George.

Aunt Alice pulled up a chair.

"It's such a dreadful thing, your sister—."She caught herself, then rushed on as if she couldn't help herself. "If you had stayed at our place, this never would have happened."

I listened with indifference. Uncle George stood in the corner and said very little.

I wished they hadn't come. I could barely look at them.

Jeanne and Ray came most days to visit.

"I've got a lawyer starting proceedings for us to sue Richard's insurance company," Ray said during one visit. I was surprised. I didn't know anything about lawsuits or even that I would have a case. "I don't know if we'll get very much, but..." He spread his hands.

"When you get out, you can come and stay with us until you recuperate," Jeanne offered. "I asked the doctor, and he said they want to keep you a few more days."

"How's Mary?"

Ray and Jeanne exchanged a look. "She's coming along," Jeanne said vaguely.

"Will she be able to leave when I do?"

"No, no, I don't think so," Jeanne said. She looked at me. "Barbara, it's pretty serious. They weren't sure she would make it through that first night. But she's progressing—there may be the possibility of brain damage. The doctors aren't sure."

I felt numb. "I want to see her."

"The doctors think you should wait," Jeanne said. She was uncomfortable. The nurse came in just then to say visiting hours were over and Jeanne looked relieved.

Jan came over to sit on my bed after they left. "I wish I could get out of here. I don't know why they're keeping us so long. I'm fine," she grumbled. "Sally Griffith phoned me this morning. She was at Richard's funeral yesterday. She said it was really sad. Richard's family is taking his death hard."

I nodded. I still couldn't quite believe he was dead. I thought of Mary. What would I have done if she had died?

Gary, Jan, and I were discharged from the hospital after seven days.

I still had not been allowed to see Mary, but her birthday arrived two weeks after the accident, and I was finally able to see her. Grandpa, Uncle Jack, Jeanne, and I went to visit.

No one had prepared me. Her head was wrapped in bandages. Her face was swollen to almost twice its size, and her irises were completely black; there was no hint of colour. Her leg was in a splint. When she turned her head, I could see that the bandages and her pillow were drenched in blood. I couldn't hold back my tears.

She didn't seem to know who we were. We tried to talk to her, but she was incoherent and confused. She kept twisting and turning to try to pull her hands free from the straps that held them down.

The sight of this distressed me. "Can't we untie her?"

Jeanne went to find a nurse.

"Just watch that she doesn't grab at her bandages," the nurse said as she released Mary from the straps.

Mary wouldn't stop pulling at her wrappings, and within a few minutes, we had to ask the nurse to tie her up again. Even though she didn't seem to understand us or even know we were there, we kept talking to her. At one point, she lifted her head and looked toward Grandpa.

"Where's Grandma?" she asked. Her voice was barely audible. Before anyone could answer, she had gone back to sleep, or wherever it was that she went. Grandpa was the only person she acknowledged in any way. She looked at the rest of us as if we were strangers. After a short visit, we wished her a happy 17th birthday and left.

Walking in silence with Jeanne to the car, I wondered why I had been spared. Why had this happened to Mary and not me? I reflected on what the doctor had said, wondering if God was watching out for me. I had never given much thought to God.

During the drive home, I asked Jeanne about Mary. "Will she ever remember us?"

"According to Doctor Corrigan, she has brain damage and has had over a hundred stitches in her head."

"But is she going to get better?" I interrupted.

"Doctor Corrigan said it's too early to tell how extensive the damage is. She should improve a little each week as the swelling of her brain goes down."

I felt sadness wash over me. It was as if I had lost a part of myself. The sadness was mixed with anger. It wasn't fair. Why had I been spared and not Mary?

I loved being at Jeanne and Ray's. They had three kids, and I babysat them and played games with them. It seemed like such a normal family: Mom, Dad, kids, and a dog.

I wasn't enthusiastic to go back to school. This was my second year in grade nine and all my instincts told me I wouldn't pass this year either; I just wasn't interested. I had missed too much school, and too many things had happened.

I used any excuse to get out of school. Many times, I took the afternoon off to go see Mary in the hospital, though I found it difficult to spend a lot of time with her.

She did seem to be improving, but it was more physically than mentally.

One day, while I was visiting, we seemed finally to be making headway and having a coherent conversation when Mary suddenly sat straight up in bed. Her eyes were looking expectantly towards the door.

"Are you waiting for someone?"

"Yes, my little sister is coming."

I didn't know what to say. "I'm right here, Mary."

"No, no, I mean my little sister with the red hair and ponytails."

"Mary, I *am* your sister. It's me, Barbara."

But she kept shaking her head. Despite my insistence, she would not believe me.

I was very disturbed by this visit and did not go back again for a week.

Mrs. Corley was finally coming to see me, which meant I got a legitimate afternoon off from school.

Mrs. Corley was young, in her early twenties, I guessed, and very attractive. I felt at ease with her.

"How's your leg, Barbara?"

"Oh, not too bad."

She asked about Mary. She was going to see her after she left me.

"Well Barbara, how about telling me what happened at Peter and Joan Moore's?"

"I hated it there. They treated me like a baby. I don't want to go back there ever. I don't belong with them." My voice was strong, filled with certainty. I didn't want to live with any other families. I just wanted to take care of myself; I didn't trust other people. I knew what was best for me.

"Well, Barbara, you've got me stumped. I can't see any benefit to sending you back to training school because while you're in there, you're as good as gold. We can't very well rehabilitate someone who doesn't appear to need it. You outsmarted us; you came up with the minister and his wife just to get yourself out of training school. If we send you back, you will probably trick us again. How about you tell me what you want to do with your life, Barbara? And I want you to be truthful."

I was embarrassed to discover my motives were so transparent. However, I knew exactly what I wanted and told Mrs. Corley without hesitation.

"I would like to quit school next month when I'm sixteen, get a job, and move into a boarding home."

Mrs. Corley seemed briefly stunned by what I had said. "That has possibilities," she said after a moment's silence. "I'll tell you what, when I get back to my office, I'll ask around. As soon as I find any information, I'll let you know, okay?"

I was surprised by her immediate acceptance of my proposal. But I doubted she would find what I wanted.

I was becoming frustrated with having to spend useless time in school. I didn't care about anything anymore. I never did my homework, so I tried to copy it from the other kids. Soon they began to resent me and refused to give me their work. I became physically abusive, pushing and shoving them until they gave in. My anger was getting out of control. Usually, I was late for class and often convinced others to skip school with me. I never studied for tests. When a test paper was handed to me, I looked at it for a moment, then walked up to the teacher's desk, put the blank test on it, and walked out.

During class, I was disruptive, writing notes to others or making fun of the teacher when her back was turned. I was constantly sent out of class for disrupting the other students.

Eventually, the principal called Jeanne in. Jeanne tried to talk to me, but it was no use. I didn't care, and I wasn't scared of threats anymore. The only thing I seemed to be able to feel was anger. It became harder and harder for me to feel anything other than a boiling rage within.

Mrs. Corley called. "I think I've found just the place for you, Barbara. It's a halfway house for girls 16 to 25, called "The Inn."

I listened in surprise. I was not accustomed to things working in my favour. Glad as I was to hear this news, I felt a sinking feeling inside and reluctantly let go of my secret hope of ever being home with Mom again.

"You can quit school and get a job," Mrs. Corley was saying. "The only problem is, The Inn hasn't opened yet." She hesitated. "It's not due to open until the 25th of April."

"But I'm quitting school on April sixth, the day I turn 16," I declared with determination. I was scared she would say that I had to stay in school until April 25th.

She did not.

At school, I spent more time in the office than in the classroom. I never felt fit in with the other kids, I had lived a different life. No one understood me or knew how I felt deep inside.

My 16th birthday finally arrived, and I went into the office to quit school. When I came home Jeanne had prepared a small birthday party for me. She and Ray bought me a pair of bell-bottom pants. I was so proud of them. I was the first girl in town with bell-bottoms.

The next few weeks passed quickly. I went to the hospital to say goodbye to Mary the evening before I was to leave for The Inn in Windsor. She had improved a great deal. She had most of her memory back and knew who I was. Her leg was in a cast and the bandages were off her head. The hair was beginning to grow back where it had been shaved off.

Afterward, I went downtown to say goodbye to my friends. I couldn't wait to leave the next day and to be in charge of my own life

Chapter 11

The Inn was rooted on the corner of Wyandotte and Windermere Streets in Windsor. It reminded me of a castle with its towering roof reaching to the sky. A large veranda with square wooden columns wrapped around two sides of the house with steps leading up to both front and side entrances. Mrs. Corley parked the car closest to the Windermere Street entrance. I felt apprehensive beside her as she rang the doorbell.

A pleasant-looking woman smartly dressed in a tailored skirt and jacket opened the door. She looked to be in her mid-thirties, with short dark hair, bangs straight across her forehead and a generous smile.

"Oh hi, come on in. You must be Barbara." She reached her hands towards me, taking mine in both of hers. Her hands were warm and welcoming. "I'm Irene."

She led Mrs. Corley and me into the foyer and then through to the living room, which was separated from the foyer by four carved columns extending from floor to ceiling. The living room was like something out of a movie. A ceiling lamp hung down on a cord from the center of the room. The wallpaper was an old-fashioned faded pattern that looked like it had at one time matched the ruby material of the drapes. The furnishings, also old fashioned, were a mismatched assortment of chairs, end tables and a sofa covered in the same red velvet material as the drapes. I had never been in such a room.

"I realize the living room is a little staid," laughed Irene apologetically, "but with our limited resources at the moment it's the best we can do. How about a tour of the rest of the house, Barbara?"

"Okay."

As I followed her back into the hallway, I caught a glimpse of myself in the mirror that hung on the wall over the sofa. My straight auburn hair was just past my shoulders. I had let my bangs grow out and they had finally begun to blend in with my longer hair. Everyone said I had turned out pretty, but I didn't feel pretty.

Mrs. Corley and I followed Irene through a narrow hallway with a door on either side. One led to the unfinished basement, where the washer and dryer were kept, the other into a two-piece bathroom. Irene opened a door at the end of the hallway.

"This is our dining room. I know it looks immense but we're hoping it won't take too long to surround this table with many young women like you Barbara."

I felt intimidated by its size but warmed by its coziness, an effect created somehow by the tall windows and heavy drapes, and the dark wood floor.

"This is supposed to be my office, but for a while, it will also be my home." Irene said, showing us into a small room with a desk and a sofa. The desk was piled high with unopened envelopes and papers. "Until I can find a housemother I'll be sleeping here on this pull-out sofa."

The next door we went through brought us back to where we had started.

"Well, that's the downstairs, what do you think so far?" She smiled at me.

"It's great, it's so big." It was all I could say.

We walked over to the beautiful wooden staircase.

"Are you ready to go upstairs?"

"I'm going to pass this time," Mrs. Corley said, " I've already seen the upstairs. I'll go out to the car to get Barbara's suitcases." She pulled her spring jacket over her shoulders as she disappeared out the door.

The stairs creaked as we went up. Right at the top, Irene showed me an undersized room that had a folding door, the kind you would see on a closet. I wondered if this room had been a closet at one time. It now contained a dresser and pull-out sofa.

We turned to our left and walked through two large oak doors into a beautiful room with a bay window. In the center of the room, three sofas covered with dark brown fitted covers had been arranged in an open square, each facing out into the room. Two dressers with attached mirrors each stood in a corner, with a large wardrobe between them.

The next room was almost the same. It too had a wardrobe, a triple dresser with an attached mirror, and two sofas in the middle, these covered in orange fitted covers.

"I think we'll put you in this room," Irene said as she slid the doors back into the walls, so they disappeared.

On our way downstairs, I thought what a warm feeling I got from this old home. I also liked Irene; she seemed very confident and straightforward. You knew where you stood with people like that.

That evening Irene made dinner for the two of us, and we ate at the wooden kitchen table. I felt awkward in the unfamiliar surroundings. I didn't know what to talk about, so I let Irene do the talking.

"We want girls to feel independent here, but there will be certain house rules."

I nodded as she explained there would be a curfew of ten o'clock on weeknights and midnight on the weekends. It was the same as Mrs. Moen had set for Mary and me.

"Each girl will be responsible for keeping her room clean and doing her laundry. And on Saturday, everyone will clean the house from top to bottom."

"Does that mean I have to clean it all until the other girls come in?"

Irene smiled at my panic. "Oh no, I'll help. Besides, I don't think it will be too long before you have a lot of company."

The next morning, she called me into her office.

"So, Barbara, what do you plan on doing with yourself?"

"I want to get a job."

"With the little education you have, you won't get much of a job. Are you sure you won't consider going back to school?"

"No, I hate school. I never do well in school." I was adamant.

She tried to persuade me. "We can give you some aptitude tests to see what you're good at, and we can go from there."

"No, I just want to work."

Irene sighed. "I'm expecting another girl tomorrow, Collette, who has also quit school. You can go down together to register with the employment center later this week."

Collette breezed into the house as if she owned it. She had shockingly bright orange hair, obviously dyed, an amazing amount of make-up, and eyebrows that had been drawn in with an eyebrow pencil, her own shaved off.

"This will be your room, and this will be your bed," said Irene. "Maybe Barbara will help you put your things into that dresser." She pointed to the dresser closest to the bed she had chosen for Collette.

After Irene left the room, Collette turned to me. "How can you stand that bitch?" She proceeded to put her clothes in the opposite dresser to the one Irene had chosen. All the while she chattered away. "I just can't take living with my old lady. She's just been so weird—ever since I got out of training school."

"You were in training school?"

Collette misinterpreted my surprised tone. "Yeah, so what?"

"No—no, it's not that—I was there too."

"No. Really? When were you there? Which one were you in?"

It turned out Collette had been there the same time as I had, the second time, only she had stayed in Galt. It also turned out she was from the Drouillard Road area. We were surprised we had never run into each other before.

"Why did you go to training school?" I was genuinely curious.

"I was a prostitute with my mom," she said nonchalantly. "We lived in Montreal."

I was stunned. I wasn't sure whether to believe her. I could tell she was very dramatic; maybe this was just a way of getting noticed.

I told her almost nothing about myself. I would only tell people certain things, once I had gotten to know them, and only things that I was sure they wouldn't use against me or try to hurt me with. I wondered how Collette could tell me so much and be so open. I wondered why she wasn't scared like I was. She didn't seem to notice my silence, though. She just seemed to need to talk to me.

On Friday, Collette and I registered for work. By next Monday, we were working in an apple packing plant, making $1.20 an hour, and working forty hours a week. After paying Irene $10.50 a week for room and board, we had plenty of money left for clothes and cigarettes.

Despite our differences, we hung out together. Collette made me feel needed—a feeling I enjoyed. When we argued, she bought me things, trying to buy back my friendship. I was flattered. Aside from Mary and Joanne, who I never heard from anymore, no one had ever really wanted to be my friend before.

The Inn's ten beds filled up quickly. Some girls stayed for months, some only for days. Most had family problems and couldn't live at home. Some had come from training school; others had been in jail.

Mrs. Calvert arrived as our new housemother a few weeks after I arrived. I was immediately drawn to her, though I was sure she wasn't aware of my feelings. I was an expert at hiding them. She was a tiny woman in her fifties; her hair was greying, but she always kept it in a neat, attractive style, like the rest of herself. She wore makeup and always seemed to be rubbing lotion onto her hands. Her glasses dangled from a cord around her neck. She was divorced, and her two children were grown and living on their own.

Most of the time, she was very soft-spoken, but she could be firm if a girl was late coming in or neglectful in doing her chores. I never got into trouble with her, and although I didn't talk that much with her, I felt close to her. Occasionally, she put an arm around me or a hand on my arm when she spoke to me. I wasn't able to reciprocate her touch, but I found it comforting.

We had volunteer cooks come in on weeknights, though on weekends we had to cook for ourselves—weekends could be a hungry time. Most of the volunteers were housewives, and one night a week, a "brother" from the church came to cook. He told jokes and teased some of the girls—mostly Charlene, a girl from Montreal. She was easygoing and would tease right back. I envied her ease; I felt uncomfortable around men, especially middle-aged men.

One Saturday, I snuck out of the house to go shopping before Collette could join me. I had been with her every day all week since we worked together, and I needed a break. It was a warm spring day, and I felt good as I walked around town, wandering in and out of the stores.

When I came home, I paused outside The Inn and looked up at the big house. It came over me with a rush that I belonged somewhere. I had freedom and could make choices for myself. I was able to control my anger better. I still fought the feeling that someone might come and take me away suddenly or say I had to leave. Not that I felt I was in any immediate danger, but I still felt I had to protect myself, just in case—keeping my distance from people and not trusting anyone but myself. I liked the feeling of not being smothered, the way I had been with the minister and his wife. I looked up at my bedroom window and breathed in deeply.

Collette came to the door. "What are you standing there looking like an idiot for, Bennett? And where have you been? Come 'ere, I want to show you what I just bought at Steinberg's. I bought you something too. Come in."

She chattered away as she ran up the stairs ahead of me. I was surprised but glad we hadn't met downtown. I stopped in my room and found Irene talking to a stockily built girl with a dark complexion who was unpacking her clothes. This must be the girl Irene had told us was coming who was pregnant.

"There you are, Barbara," said Irene. "This is Lynn. She's going to share this room with you."

Lynn and I looked at each other. She didn't look pregnant, but it was probably too early to tell, and she was a big girl anyway. I thought if she lost weight and put on makeup, she would be quite attractive.

I always felt embarrassed meeting the new girls. I never knew what to talk about. Usually, I didn't try, just kept to myself. I'd never shared a room with anyone but Mary before; I wasn't sure how I felt about having Lynn there. Something about her scared me at first. Maybe because she was big and tough-looking. But that feeling soon went away.

At night, when the lights were out, we talked.

"How long do you think you'll stay here, Lynn?"

"I guess until I'm ready to have my baby, then I'll have to go somewhere else."

"Are you keeping your baby?"

"I'd like to, but I'm not sure if I can."

"What about your boyfriend?"

"I don't have one."

I was silent. I didn't want to ask any more questions.

Lynn's voice came out of the dark. "I was raped."

"Oh," I said, inadequately.

There seemed to be nothing to say after this, and soon I heard the even rhythm of her breathing. But I couldn't sleep; I tossed and turned, thinking about what she had told me, wondering how I would feel in her place. I thought of telling her about Uncle George but couldn't bring myself to talk about it again. Nevertheless, I felt a kind of closeness to Lynn. I was the only one at The Inn she shared her story with.

After Lynn arrived I hung out more with her and less and less with Collette. Collette wrote me letters and bought me things to try to get me to be her friend again. She never bothered with any of the other girls. I felt sorry for her, I felt she needed me. I wasn't sure why either Lynn or Collette wanted to hang out with me, I didn't say very much, but I didn't dislike their company.

Although Irene was a difficult person to please and tended to be critical, I knew she cared for us. For the most part, I got along well with her and respected her, but many of the girls found her harsh and difficult. She expected things to be done right. Especially the way her office was cleaned on Saturday mornings. I didn't like cleaning so often I tried to escape.

"Where are you going, Barbara?" Irene came in the front door as I was trying to go out.

I shrugged. "Just out for a walk."

"Have you done your chores yet?"

Something in her voice reminded me of Aunt Alice. I could feel anger rising inside. I hated it when people told me what to do. I tapped my foot anxiously and crossed my arms in front of me. "I just need to go out, I'll do them later."

"No, you'll do them now, the same as the other girls." Irene's voice was threatening. I felt she was trying to control me. How dare she—I knew what was best for me.

"Fine, but I won't do them right." I turned and stomped back into the house and banged noisily up each stair.

"Barbara, get back down here!"

"No! Leave me alone!"

"Barbara I mean it, come down here."

By now there was a rage boiling inside me, I wanted to lash out. "No, leave me alone! I hate you! I hate you!"

I raced into my room and flung myself down on my bed, burying my head in the pillow. A minute later I heard Irene come into the room.

"Barbara, what is wrong? Calm down." She put her arm across my back.

I cringed. I felt cornered and threatened. I pulled away.

"There's nothing to be afraid of Barbara," I could hear her saying. "You don't need to be afraid. No one's going to hurt you."

I wasn't sure why she was talking about being afraid. To me, it felt only like I was angry. I finally let her touch me, and it didn't hurt—in fact, it felt good, I felt momentarily safe.

When my breathing returned to normal, Irene squeezed my shoulders and sat back, and looked at me with a concerned look in her eyes.

"Has someone beat you or hurt you at some time, Barbara?" she asked gently.

"No, not really," I said hesitantly.

"Has someone done something to you that you didn't want them to?"

"Why?"

"I'm just wondering why you feel so threatened. Something must have happened to you."

I shook my head.

The next morning I woke up with a cold sore. I waited for Irene to accuse me of chewing bubble gum as Aunt Alice had.

"Oh Barbara," Irene said at breakfast. "You've got a cold sore."

"I wasn't chewing gum. I don't know where I got this from."

Irene laughed. "They're not from chewing gum, they're from stress. It probably came from that outburst yesterday."

"Oh." I felt relieved.

One Sunday afternoon I was in the kitchen doing dishes when Irene called to me.

"Barbara, you have a visitor." I dried my hands and walked out to the foyer. I couldn't believe it; Uncle George was standing there. He was dressed up in a suit and tie, holding his hat nervously in his hand. I felt my stomach tighten.

"Mr. Belanger has come to see you."

My heart was pounding. Why was he here? What did he want?

"I'll leave you here to visit." Irene rushed off to her office.

We sat in the living room. Girls were milling about behind us.

"Alice is in the hospital, her legs again. I was just visiting her."

I didn't know what to say. I didn't care.

Uncle George cleared his throat. "I was at your mom's, and she gave me your address."

"Oh." I felt uncomfortable, uneasy.

Uncle George fumbled nervously with his hat, passing it from one hand to the other. I could tell he sensed something different about me. "Do you want to come for a drive?"

"No, I can't right now, I've got to finish the dishes." I thought of the rides we used to go on when he would tell me I was doing those horrible things to him.

"We've got two litters of pups now."

I wished he would leave, I was scared he was going to talk about before. I didn't want to talk to him about it. I didn't want to be alone with him. I didn't care about him, or his life anymore. I could feel my throat tightening up as a vision flashed through my mind of Uncle George lying on top of me. I was trapped, I couldn't move. I could hear his breathing and wanted to scream at him to get away from me.

"Well, I just wanted to see how you were doing."

He got up and moved towards the door. I followed, not saying anything.

"Here," he said, handing me a $20 bill. I looked at it, wishing I dared to give it back to him.

"Bye, Barbara."

"Bye." I felt numb.

As I walked back to the kitchen, Irene called after me.

"Barbara."

"Yeah."

"Who was that?" By the look on her face, I could see she was suspicious or uncomfortable with Uncle George.

I carefully made my voice casual. "Oh, I used to live with him and his wife."

Collette and I had to be at work by seven o'clock each morning. We had been working for about five weeks now. It was a tedious job, putting apples onto trays and then covering them with plastic and inserting them into the shrink machine, to make the plastic tight. But it felt good to be earning money, being independent, in control, and paying my way.

There was one man—Albert—a black man in his thirties—who made me nervous. I always tried to avoid him. Something in his eyes scared me. He liked to tell jokes, mostly dirty jokes.

Today, he started as usual. "Hey, did you hear the one about the farmer's daughter...." He was looking at me.

The others within hearing snickered when he came to the punch line. His eyes were still on me. I knew he was waiting for me to laugh. I couldn't. His eyes scared me.

"You don't think that's funny? You too good for my jokes, little girl?" He was getting angrier.

I looked away, trying to ignore him.

"Hey—look at me when I'm talking to you, girl."

I fumbled with the apples, thinking I should have laughed as everyone else did.

The next thing I knew was his hands were around my throat. He squeezed tighter and tighter until I gasped for air. I heard shouting and felt someone trying to wrestle him off me. He was knocked to the ground, and his hands came away from my throat.

I pulled free and tore out of the factory. I didn't stop running until I reached The Inn.

Irene found me sitting in the front entrance, shaking all over and trying to get my breath. "Barbara, what's wrong? What are you doing home?"

When I had calmed down enough, I told her what had happened.

"You should press charges," she said, her face filled with anger. "He can't get away with that."

I looked at her, shaking my head.

For the next few days, she tried to convince me, but I was too afraid. Collette continued working there for a few more weeks. She said Albert had been fired the next day.

One bright sunny day, about a month after the incident with Albert, Collette and I were walking back from the ice cream parlor. A black car drove by, and the driver honked at us. We looked quickly at the car and then away—it was no one we knew. Within minutes, the car was back. It pulled into the driveway in front of us, blocking our way. We couldn't see the driver, who was on the other side.

A voice came from within the car. "Hi girls, how are you?"

"Fine," Collette answered.

I stood by, frustrated at the nerve of this guy to just cut us off.

"Come here, I won't bite."

We bent down and looked through the open passenger window. The first thing I noticed was his blue eyes. They seemed to jump out, demanding to be noticed. His thick curly black hair seemed to have a mind of its own. On his chin were crumbs of food. Aside from the obvious disarray of his appearance, he was strikingly good-looking. Something about him appealed to me in an annoying kind of way.

"I'm on a break from work right now, so do you think you could give me your phone number quickly?" He was looking at me.

Collette began reciting our phone number.

"No, no," he interrupted, "I want her phone number."

"We live together, so her phone number is my phone number." Collette finished saying the number.

The driver wrote it on the inside of his cigarette package.

"What's your name?" He was looking at me again.

"Barbara," I said, uncomfortable about giving him both my name and my phone number.

"Bye, Barbara, I'll call you." His eyes looked directly into mine before he backed up and sped away.

Collette and I looked at each other, and she laughed.

"So, what do you think?" she asked.

I shrugged. "Crazy guy."

One Friday evening. Collette, Lynn, Irene, and I were sitting in the living room. Collette and I had planned to go out, as we usually did, but with everyone else out—even the volunteers and housemother—and just the four of us talking, there seemed to be no rush.

The stereo was playing, I was with the people at The Inn I was the most comfortable with, and I felt relaxed.

"Lynn, have you decided what to do about your baby yet?' Irene asked.

"I don't know, it's such a hard decision."

Irene looked at Collette and me. "What would you girls do?

"I'd keep it," Collette said. "You never know who will adopt it."

"Yeah, but they're supposed to make sure the people are good people," Lynn said. "That's what I heard anyway."

I thought about the Belanger's, how everyone thought they were good people. "I don't know about that," I heard myself say sarcastically.

"What do you mean, Barbara?" Irene asked.

"Well, I ... oh, it's nothing."

"Come on Barbara, what do you know? Tell me for the sake of my baby." Lynn implored.

I was trapped now. "Well, okay. I knew this girl who lived in a—well, it was like a foster home, and the man tried to get her to do things with him."

All eyes were on me now. I felt like running out of the room, but knew if I did that, they'd figure out it was me.

"What kind of things?" Irene asked, her dark eyes searching my own.

"Well, he used to say that she was—you know, doing it with him in her sleep and that if she wanted to stop she would have to do it with him while she was awake."

I could feel my speech quicken as my heart pounded in my chest. I was sure they could tell it was me I was talking about.

"She didn't do it, I hope." Collette piped up. I could feel myself flush as I heard Lynn's and her comments - "What a creep. What a liar."

"Oh no, she didn't do it," I lied.

Irene's response disconcerted me. "No one can have sex in their sleep," she said. "It would wake them up immediately." She looked at me and added gently, "I think this man was abusing your friend, Barbara."

Lying in bed that night, thinking about the reactions of Irene and the other girls, I felt ashamed. Why was I so stupid? Why had I believed Uncle George? These girls wouldn't have.

Irene must have known something was wrong; the next day she called me into her office.

"Barbara, I want to talk to you about this friend of yours."

I looked down at my fidgeting hands.

"You know, even if she had done what that man wanted her to, it still wouldn't have been her fault."

"Well, she didn't." I tried to hold my tears, but I couldn't. I began to cry uncontrollably.

Irene brought me a Kleenex and held my hands.

"This is you that you're talking about, this has happened to you, hasn't it?"

I nodded, trying to control my sobs.

"Was it that man who came to see you, that Uncle George or whatever?"

"Yes." I cried harder; it was finally out. I had told an adult.

I looked up at her. "Please don't tell anyone, Irene—no one knows." Irene sat with me until I stopped crying. For the next while, I felt such pain deep inside. Even though I had become suspicious of Uncle George, it was still upsetting to hear Irene confirming my thoughts. I wanted to hang on to the illusion that Uncle George was the one person, besides Mom, who loved me. Wrong again.

Chapter 12

Days later, there was a phone call for me.

"Hi, this is Roger. I drive the black car. What do you say we go out on Friday night?"

I was surprised by his aggressiveness. He was so forthright; how could I say no? But I was too afraid to go out by myself, what if he was a weirdo?

"Okay," I said, "but only if we can double date with Collette."

"The girl you were with the other day? Sure, sure. Do you want me to bring a date for her?"

"Yeah, if you could."

"I'll pick you guys up at seven."

Collette and I were still upstairs getting ready when we heard the doorbell.

"My date had better be good-looking, Bennett, or you'll be in trouble," Collette whispered to me before we headed down the stairs.

Irene, who was waiting at the bottom of the stairs, followed us into the living room, where we found the boys sitting on the sofa.

"Hi," I said, my voice barely above a whisper.

Roger rose to his feet. "Hi. This is Bill. Bill, this is Barbara and Collette."

We all said our hellos as Irene stood surveying our dates. "Now remember, I want you girls home by midnight."

Out on the street, Roger opened the car door for us. I couldn't help but notice how clean and shiny the car was. Collette and Bill got in the backseat, and I got in the front with Roger. I was surprised at how different he looked from before. His hair was neatly combed and looked almost wet—he must have put some hair cream on it. He was clean-shaven and wore light green cotton pants and a white cotton shirt. I hadn't noticed how skinny he was until he sat down beside me in the car—his legs made mine look heavy.

"Where would you girls like to go?"

"Some place fun," Collette called from the back. I felt embarrassed by her boldness.

"What about you, Barbara?" Roger asked in a very low voice.

"I don't care," I said, shrugging my shoulders.

"How about going to Detroit, just to drive around?"

"Great! Alright!" Collette and Bill called from the back seat. I was surprised they were already sitting close together.

"How about you, Barbara, would you like to go?" Roger asked again in a soft voice. He seemed to have a different tone of voice for me, and even his face got a soft look on it.

"I guess so," I said shyly.

I felt more shy than usual around Roger. Maybe because he was so outgoing and seemed so sure of himself.

On the drive through the tunnel to the U.S., it was very dark in the car, and I felt apprehensive. But Roger talked nonstop, which seemed to distract me from my fear. "Hey Bill, remember last Friday night going through here at sixty miles an hour?"

"Oh yeah, let's try it again."

"You girls game?" Roger was looking at me.

"Not really," I said.

I felt the car immediately slow down. "You don't like to go fast in a car?" Roger asked.

"No, I'm scared—I was in a car accident a while ago."

"Did you get hurt?" His face showed concern.

"Well, not really, but my sister did, and the guy who was driving got killed."

"Wow, where was this?"

"Point Pelee."

"Oh yeah, I remember reading about that ... hey, Bill, remember that accident during the winter at the Point, that was her." Roger pointed to me.

All this attention was making me feel self-conscious.

When we finally arrived in Detroit, we began driving through the suburbs. Roger seemed to know where he was going. He continued doing all the talking, mostly telling jokes or saying things to make everyone laugh. It would have been hard not to like him.

"Are you going where I think you're going?" Bill called from the back seat.

Roger just smiled.

I turned to the back, and Collette and I looked at each other with confusion. I began to feel scared. What if he dropped us off and left us here? Worse yet, what if he took us to a bar or someplace weird? I could feel myself starting to sweat. I felt trapped and threatened.

"There it is, there's the house," Roger said. He slowed down in front of a white frame house. "I used to go with a girl who lived there."

I sighed with relief, hoping now we would go back to Windsor. I needed to be somewhere familiar.

"So what?" Collette called from the back.

I laughed nervously at her boldness, yet I too was wondering why we were here.

"Well, she's not my girlfriend anymore, I just thought ..." I could tell Roger was embarrassed and had realized that coming here had been a stupid thing to do.

We headed back to Windsor and spent the next few hours driving around. All the while Roger was pointing out schools he had gone to and places he had worked. He didn't get along with his father, although he did say his father had bought him the car he was driving. I wondered why his father would buy him a car if they didn't get along. He had two younger brothers and an older sister who lived away from home. His father worked at Ford Motor Company, as my father had. His mother worked at General Motors. Roger had had two previous jobs and was now working in a factory.

We stopped at the Red Barn for a hamburger before going home. Sitting in the car eating our hamburgers, Roger asked, "Are you always this quiet or am I just talking too much?"

His question was so blunt I felt myself blush. I shrugged nonchalantly. "I don't know."

We were silent on the way home. I felt a little overwhelmed by all he had told me. As with Collette, I couldn't understand how he was so willing to reveal everything about himself. Maybe with Roger, it didn't matter; he seemed to have had a normal life. But I couldn't tell him about my background. If he knew the real me—if he found out, I'd been to training school, or if he knew what had happened with Uncle George and John—how could he still like me? I couldn't lie, I was a terrible liar. It was easier not to say anything.

Roger stopped the car in front of The Inn. I was opening the door to get out when he pulled me to him. I didn't resist. I kissed him, but I quickly pulled away when it was over.

Bill and Collette didn't even realize we were home. Roger practically had to pry them apart to get Collette to leave. That night, I lay in bed thinking about Roger and how confident he seemed. I envied his personality. I wondered if he liked me.

My question was answered the next day when he called and wanted to see me again.

My reserved, aloof manner seemed to pose a great challenge to Roger. I was so opposite to him. He seemed as intrigued by my quietness as I was by his ability to say whatever he wanted to people. He began to call every day and came to visit every evening. He seemed enthralled. I was flattered but suspicious. I wondered what he could see in me. I wasn't sure how I felt about him, except I was attracted to him and enjoyed being with him. This was something new, this feeling of physical attraction. I'd never felt this way with Randy. With Randy, I'd never really thought about whether I wanted to be with him; I'd just gone along with it. It felt good with Roger; I felt dating him was a choice I had made.

Toni, another resident at The Inn, was the first person I knew who did drugs. Drugs and alcohol were strictly forbidden at The Inn. Toni had sworn me to secrecy, not to tell that she smoked up at her boyfriend's. I was surprised, yet curious. As she was speaking, I was distracted by a familiar figure walking towards us up the street with two others.

"Toni, I think I see my mother over there." I could feel Toni looking at me, wondering at the nervous excitement in my voice. I hadn't seen Mom since the car accident in February; this was July.

As they came closer, I could see that the two others with her were Lyle and Julie.

My heart pounded, and my face broke into a wide smile as I got up to meet them.

"Mom."

Mom held me at arm's length, looking at me for a moment before we hugged. I could see she was aging. The way she was dressed embarrassed me: she wore very short, tight shorts that accentuated her thin legs and swelling abdomen, and a tank top that displayed her fleshy back. Somehow, her dressing this way made her look older, as if she were trying to be a teenager.

Julie, Lyle, and I said awkward hellos. I remembered Toni, behind me on the porch, "Oh, this is Toni." I introduced her around. There was an awkward moment.

"I'll see you later, Barb," Toni said, disappearing into the house.

"We came to see your new home," Lyle said, his eyes sparkling at me. He plunged his hands into his pockets. "We just live down the street. Julie and I have an apartment."

I felt shy with Lyle; at the same time, I remembered how we used to chase each other around. "Oh, I didn't know."

"Yeah, Ma was just visiting, so we thought we'd bring her to see this here place."

Mom stood silent, looking from Lyle to me as we spoke. I didn't know what to say to her; it was easier to talk to Lyle.

"Where's the baby?"

"Oh, Julie's sister is watching him. He's not such a baby anymore—he's almost two now."

"Come on in, I'll show you around." I felt proud to show them my new home. I felt somehow separate from them in a way I had never felt before. I didn't need them anymore. I was surviving on my own and learning to belong. Learning to be part of a world away from them.

As I introduced Mom to Irene and some of the other girls, I became even more embarrassed by the way she was dressed. She was still attractive with long red hair, but I wished she looked more like mothers were supposed to look—with longer, looser shorts and a blouse instead of a tank top. I was grateful to Irene; if she was surprised at Mom's appearance, she gave no sign.

After a tour, we sat back out on the porch. Mom seemed tense; she hardly spoke. Lyle talked casually about work. I wondered why Mom was uncomfortable. I could tell she was anxious to leave. I could feel my chest tightening in resentment. Why didn't she like my home? Why wasn't she as happy and at ease as I was here? I felt there was a new distance between us. I didn't need her; I had everything I needed here. I still felt great love for her as I always had, but now I didn't feel as desperate for it.

"Here honey," Mom said as they were rising to go. "Here's my phone number. I'd like it if you dropped over to see John and me sometime." Mom must have forgotten to mention that she and John had reconciled.

"I will." A warm feeling spread through me. I was glad she had made the gesture.

That evening at the dinner table, Toni asked about Mom. "Where does your mother live?"

"Just over on Albert Street."

"She is so pretty, she looks so young," Lynn interrupted.

I felt awkward and surprised at their reaction, but also proud that they thought she was pretty.

"Why don't you live with her? —She seems so nice," Toni asked.

"I don't know." I wasn't sure how to answer their questions.

"Would you like to live with her?" Collette asked.

"I guess." But I found myself hesitating, and this disturbed me. For the first time in my life, I was doubting that I wanted to be with Mom.

I phoned her the next week, nervous about how she would respond to my coming over, fear of rejection overcoming me.

"Tomorrow night? That's just fine, honey. I'll be here."

I breathed a sigh of relief when I hung up.

Roger was working the afternoon shift, and I didn't want to bring him over to meet Mom yet. I felt I had to prepare him first, warn him that my mother didn't look like other mothers. And then there was John, too, with his strange, quiet way of relating to people, the way he snickered whenever he was asked a question. I wasn't ready for Roger to meet them yet.

It was about a twenty-minute walk to Mom's. She lived two streets over from Drouillard. As I walked down the familiar streets, I remembered Mary and me hanging around together. I missed Mary. As I turned in the laneway leading to the front door, I could see the blinds were pulled as tightly down as ever, and the windows were all closed despite the mid-summer heat. I decided to follow the broken sidewalk around to the back door.

I was surprised to see the back door wide open. I walked up the two steps to the back porch. I could hear country music playing.

I called out softly. "Mom, are you home?"

"I'm here." Mom motioned from the kitchen for me to come in. She had on a light blue nightgown—she always wore nightgowns around the house. Some were embarrassingly sheer.

"Hi," I said awkwardly. I didn't know whether to hug her or not. I could see she was also at a loss, but she hesitantly touched my hands. "I'm happy you're here."

I reached my arms around her. I felt overcome with emotion. I loved her so much.

"Can I get you something, a coffee?"

"Okay." I had recently begun drinking coffee. As Mom was preparing the coffee, I sat down on one of the familiar grey and yellow kitchen chairs. I remembered the scared little girl banging back and forth on these chairs, listening to Mom and John arguing. The square table had four yellow placemats placed neatly around it. I wondered if Mom still kept her unpaid bills underneath them. Her make-up and nail polish stood neatly beside a round mirror at the place across from me, where she had been sitting before I came in.

"Where's John?"

"Oh, he's over at his mother's. He'll be home soon. He wants to see you." My stomach tightened at her words. She sat back down at the table across from me, with two mugs of coffee.

"So, what have you been up to?" I asked. Mom seemed much more comfortable here than she had been at The Inn.

"Well, I'm still babysitting, and I do a lot of sewing." She looked over at her sewing machine, which was sitting on the back porch.

While she talked to me, she kept looking in the mirror at herself.

"So do you like that place where you live?"

"Oh yeah, it's great. I've got a boyfriend now."

"Oh, what happened to that nice boy from Kingsville?"

"Oh, Randy and I broke up, but you'll like Roger. Maybe I'll bring him over one day."

"I'd like to meet him. So, are you going to school?"

"No, I quit, I hated school. I was working but ... I'm looking for another job now. Irene, the lady who runs The Inn, said she might have a lead for a job."

"Where was your other job?"

"Oh, just at an apple factory."

"You quit that job?"

"Yeah, it wasn't working out." I didn't want to tell her the details.

After a pause, Mom looked at me in an almost adoring way. "Gee, your hair is so pretty, Barbara. I wish I had your hair."

"Oh Mom, you have beautiful hair." I was embarrassed by her compliments.

"Your dad is living near here, now, did you know?"

I was surprised to hear her mention him.

"He'd probably like to see you. Maybe Jeanne could get you his phone number."

I heard a car pulling up the driveway. Mom looked at me, raising her eyebrows. "That must be John."

John looked the same, except he had more grey hair. I smiled at him yet felt uncomfortable under his gaze.

He looked me up and down in a most piercing way. "Hi Barbara, you're sure looking pretty these days—isn't she, Millie?"

I felt my face go red.

Mom smiled at me.

I began to visit weekly. I also got Dad's phone number from Jeanne and began to visit him too. Sometimes when I dropped in at Mom's, only John was home.

"Where's Mom?" I asked, seeing John at the kitchen table.

"Oh, out somewhere."

He kicked a chair out for me.

It felt like old times—we talked easily as we always had.

I put out of my mind the things that had happened between us.

With Dad, words did not flow so easily. Still, I found comfort in just sitting in the same room with my father and watching the Sunday afternoon movie. There was something about being able to look at the person next to me and see a resemblance to myself.

Dad was living with Verna, a woman he had met two years earlier. Verna was the only woman I had ever seen Dad with. She was an eerie person; something about her didn't seem right. She had a face like a bullfrog, and she was always puffing away on a cigarette. I wondered what Dad saw in her.

That summer Irene helped me find another job through one of her numerous contacts—this one at Goodwill Industries. I started out sorting clothes, which arrived in big green garbage bags.

Soon I got promoted to the tabulator. My job was to go through the boxes of clothes that had already been sorted and priced. I added up all the price tags of each of the boxes and entered the box number and the amount into a special book. It wasn't a great job, but it was better than packing apples.

I found it unsettling at first to work with mentally and physically disabled people. I couldn't help but stare. During the evening, when Roger and I were out driving, I talked about the people at work. Roger seemed genuinely interested and asked details about their afflictions.

At work, I sat by myself on my breaks, unsure how to interact with such people. But after a while, a woman named Sharon, who was physically handicapped, began to join me for a smoke. She wasn't much older than me. I was surprised to hear her talking about boys, clothes, and music, just like the girls at The Inn.

Still, I wasn't thrilled with my job at Goodwill and began making an effort myself to get another one. I watched for signs in restaurants and store windows and read the want ads.

Three months after I'd started at Goodwill, I read an ad in the newspaper for a job at a new Burger King restaurant that had just opened. I went down, filled out an application, and was hired right then and there.

I felt proud to have gotten this job completely on my own. I would be making $1.35 an hour, 10 cents an hour more than at Goodwill.

Jeanne called that Sunday to let me know Mary was finally getting out of the hospital.

"She's going to be staying with Ray and me for a while. Do you want to come and visit next Sunday?"

"Sure." I was relieved to hear Mary was getting out of the hospital. I had so much to tell her, mostly about Roger. It would be great to talk to her again and do things together. Somehow, I assumed if she was out of the hospital, she would be as she was before the accident.

Mary was in good spirits, but within minutes of talking to her, I could see she was different. She couldn't remember many things I talked about from our past. Sometimes in the middle of a sentence, she forgot what she had started to say. When I mentioned her head injury, she made an impatient gesture. "Oh, it's fine now, it's all healed."

Gary sat close by her side, very concerned and attentive. "We're going to be married as soon as Mary can," he said to me.

Mary took his hand and smiled. I had never seen her smile like that before. She seemed like a different person.

I stayed for dinner, then Gary and Mary drove me home.

"Come on in and see The Inn. You'll love it, Mary, you should see my room."

They came in with me, and I gave them a tour. I couldn't get Mary to respond to my enthusiasm. I wanted somehow to tell her my feeling of belonging here, but I didn't know how to say it. She and Gary sat on my sofa bed and admired the room. She didn't ask about my friends or if I was seeing any boys. There was a strangeness between us. The closeness we had shared seemed to be gone. After they left, I lay on my bed, giving in to a pang of sadness and pain that seemed to fill my whole inside.

Waiting for the bus on the first day of my new job, my stomach was doing flip-flops. This would be the first real job I had gotten on my own—what if I couldn't handle it?

The bus was coming. I panicked. I began walking down the street, I couldn't go. I knew I wouldn't be able to do the job. When I looked at my watch, it was 8:15. I was already fifteen minutes late. What was I going to do? I found myself walking back to the Inn.

Mrs. Calvert, our housemother, looked at me in surprise when I came in the door.

"Why, Barbara, what are you doing here?"

I felt rather sheepish. "I missed the bus."

"Come on, get in the car, I'll drive you."

"But I'm late, they probably don't want me now."

"I'll go with you and explain what happened, okay?"

"Okay." I agreed, embarrassed by my weakness.

Mrs. Calvert explained to my new boss how I had missed the bus. He was very understanding. I wondered what I had been afraid of.

I was a quick worker. I could make a Whopper in seven seconds. My boss was amazed; he brought people around to watch how quickly I worked. But I learned that making a Whopper in seven seconds was no advantage to me. I watched the other girls around me get taught other jobs or get promoted, but never myself. I felt doomed to make Whoppers for the rest of my life.

One Saturday, when I had a rare afternoon off work, three months after Roger and I began dating, he picked me up, and we went to the Red Barn for a hamburger. After driving around for a while, we ended up in the park, sitting in his car listening to the radio.

Suddenly, Roger sat up straight. "Do you like this ashtray?" He was looking me directly in the eye.

I didn't know what to say.

"Because if you don't, I'm throwing it out of this car. I don't want anything around me that you don't like."

Roger threw out everything that could be unscrewed or ripped off. I was stunned but flattered. Beside the car was a pile of knobs and other paraphernalia. I had never seen anyone do anything quite like this before. It had to be love.

Although I felt sure Roger loved me, I wasn't sure how I felt about him, except that I enjoyed being with him, and I even liked being in his arms in the car. He made me feel important and seemed unconcerned about the little bit I had told him about my fragmented family.

I did find him overwhelming at times. His hyperactive personality was wearing. When he brought me home after a date, I welcomed the silence of my room. I never told anyone my feelings. I felt I should be thankful someone loved me so completely. But when I tried to say I loved him back, I felt as if someone had put me in a straitjacket and gagged me. The words would not come.

One Friday evening, Roger was unusually quiet and withdrawn. I had never seen him like this. He barely spoke to me and even left early. At the door, he kissed me absently. "I'll call you tomorrow."

The next day, he didn't call. I stayed in all evening waiting.

"You and Roger want to come to the show with Bill and me?" Collette asked a few days later.

"Sure—except I haven't heard from Roger—he didn't phone last night or tonight."

Collette seemed unconcerned. "He'll call."

I still hadn't heard from him by the next Friday evening. I didn't go out with Collette, but stayed in my room, trying to think of what I had done wrong to Roger.

After over a week of silence from Roger, Collette said, "Well, have you tried to phone him?"

I stared at her, and a panicky feeling came into my stomach. I tried to look indifferent. "If he wants to call me, he can call me," I shrugged.

"Barbara, don't be such an idiot. It's driving you crazy. You might as well find out. Phone him."

She railed at me for three more days until I finally caved in. What did I have to lose? I called his parents' house.

"Are you the little girl from Wyandotte Street?" his father asked.

"Yes."

"Roger has gone to the West Coast. Didn't he tell you?"

"No." I tried to hold back the tears.

"You've got to watch Roger, he's a funny boy. He did this two years ago. Don't worry, he'll be back."

I hung up the phone and burst into tears. How could he do this to me? I hated myself for believing that Roger cared about me.

Collette had not found another job since leaving the apple factory.

"I've decided to move back home with Mom," she said one Sunday afternoon. "I've been talking to her a lot lately. I think things will be better now. She doesn't seem as freaked out anymore.

"I don't live too far, though, it's not as if we won't be able to still do stuff together."

I was glad. I still wasn't attached to her; I could easily say goodbye, but I liked doing things with her; she made me feel as if I mattered to her.

Collette moved home the next day, but we continued to see each other. She called me daily to see if Roger had come back.

After a month of agony, Roger came back. He offered no explanations and made no excuses. He tried his best to convince me he truly loved me and would never leave me again. I let him think I believed him, but in my heart, I decided I would never let myself be fooled again.

Roger found a job and moved out of his parents' house into an apartment right across the alley from The Inn. We began to spend a lot of time together alone in his apartment. Irene was concerned that we were spending too much time together, but I convinced her everything was fine and there was nothing to worry about. I did feel physically attracted to Roger, but I could always stop myself. I never lost control; I always knew what I was doing. When we came close, I stopped him. If we went too far or did certain things, I was reminded of Uncle George and immediately turned off.

Roger got very frustrated. "What is wrong with you, Barbara? You know I love you. If you get pregnant, we'll get married. I need you. Please."

"I can't, I just can't. I'm sorry." I began to cry. I wished I could do it with him and not feel so turned off. But it was hard to fight the feeling that all he wanted me for was sex, just like the other men in my life. I could not bear being used one more time. If I were going to have sex, it would be when I wanted to, it would be my decision.

Since Roger had come back, I had become extremely suspicious and didn't trust him at all. Each time he was away from me, I quizzed him on where he had been and with whom. I always wondered if he was going to come back or just leave the next night. We were constantly arguing.

Finally, I couldn't stand it any longer. The day after a particularly nasty fight, I called Roger. "We have to break up."

"What are you talking about?" He tried to sound scornful, but I could hear the fear in his voice.

"I want to break up. All we do is fight. I can't take it anymore."

"Barbara, you can't break up with me." Now he was beginning to sound desperate. "Please Barbara, we'll work it out."

"I'm sorry," I said and hung up the phone. I felt calm inside and relieved.

Chapter 13

For my seventeenth birthday, I received the best gift I could have ever received. Mrs. Corley and Irene agreed that I was mature enough to be released from my parole and to be legally on my own. My case was brought before the Review Board and approved.

My first decision as a free person was to move into my apartment. I felt confident and strong as I went searching for a home of my own.

I soon discovered that $36.00 a week was not enough to support myself in an apartment.

Discouraged, I went to Irene.

"You need a roommate," she said. "I think I know exactly the right person, too. A friend of mine has a daughter who's looking for someone to share an apartment with. I'll give her a call if you like."

At this idea, I became more optimistic.

Debbie came over the next day. I felt a little intimidated by her. She was tall and blonde and looked like Faye Dunaway in Bonnie and Clyde. She was adopted and came from a rich family. She was moving out because she did not want to listen to her parents anymore. She worked at Reitman's and seemed very confident and sure of herself. She had beautiful clothes, which she let me wear occasionally.

We found a bachelor apartment a short walk from The Inn—a three-story walk-up. It was to be available in a couple of weeks. Debbie and I spent the intervening time collecting furniture, kitchen items, and other odds and ends from Irene, Mom, and Debbie's family.

I looked around with satisfaction at the apartment after we moved in. It was a pretty tight squeeze—two girls in a bachelor—we slept together on a pull-out sofa—but it was my place. My first real home of my own.

As it turned out, my apartment was the furthest thing from a home I had ever known. Since Debbie and I were the only ones of our friends with our place, it soon became a hangout for kids wanting to get out of their parents' homes. Many were people I didn't even know—they were friends of Debbie or friends of friends. Most nights, they stayed until the early morning hours, and I soon became exhausted from lack of sleep. But I was flattered by all the friends I had suddenly acquired. I had never been so popular.

Occasionally, I went out to visit Jeanne and Ray, who were living in Kingsville. Ray came into town to get me. Mary was still staying with them while she recuperated. One Sunday in July, when Jeanne called to invite me for dinner, she said Mary had something to ask me. I had a feeling it was going to be about her getting married, although a date hadn't been set that I knew of yet.

When I arrived, the kids all ran to me. I loved Jeanne's kids—she had three: one girl and two boys. Mary and Gary were sitting together on the sofa. Mary was glowing. Before even saying hello, she held her hand out for me to see her diamond.

"Oh, is it ever nice." I hugged her.

"We're getting married in October. Dad's giving me the money for my dress and part of the wedding. Jeanne talked to him about it.

"Wow, that's only a few months away." Mary hadn't been out of the hospital that long, and I was wondering if she was going to be able to manage.

"I'd like you to be my maid of honour."

"Wow, I don't know what to say." I was happy for her. Gary had seemed anxious to marry her. He didn't say much but sat close to Mary's side and seemed very attentive toward her, while she chattered on about the wedding. The ceremony was to be at the United Church in Kingsville, and the reception at Gary's parents' home. We talked about the bridesmaid dresses. Jan, Mary's friend (who was in the accident with us) was to be the bridesmaid, and other plans all through dinner until it was time for Ray to drive me home.

One week later, Roger came into Burger King while I was working. Since he had started working at Chrysler's, which was right across the street, he often came in for lunch. Lyle also worked at Chrysler, and I knew they had met.

"So I hear your sister is getting married." I had come out into the dining room to clean tables. I sometimes used that as an excuse to come out of the kitchen area to visit with Roger.

"How do you know that?"

"Your brother."

"So, am I invited to the wedding?"

"I don't know, probably not."

"Well, you'd better see if you can get me an invitation, eh?"

I laughed; he was still the same. I wondered where he got the nerve to be so bold. I was intrigued and invited him to the wedding.

The night before the ceremony, Mary and I stayed over at Grandpa's since it was closer than my place or Jeanne's. I hadn't been back to the house for quite a while. The house still had that dark, oppressive feel without Grandma, and Grandpa seemed the same as he was when I'd left. But now, with the house quiet and Mary giggling nervously in the cot beside me, it was easy to believe Grandma was sleeping in the next room with Grandpa, and that I was fourteen years old again. I missed Grandma now, though ordinarily I rarely thought about her. I wondered how she would feel about Mary getting married.

"Mary, you'd better get to sleep, or you're going to be too tired to get married tomorrow, “I said in a hushed voice.

"I can't sleep, I'm so excited. I'm getting married, I could scream!" Mary squeezed these words out between giggles. She seemed to be getting back to her old self again.

The streetlight shining in through the window had created a perfectly shaped square on the rose-coloured wall. I stared at it with sleepless eyes and thought about Roger coming tomorrow.

It was a small ceremony. Just Gary's family and ours and a few friends. It was wonderful to see everyone—all the family came, even Lyle and Julie were there. Dad walked Mary down the aisle. She grinned nervously through the entire ceremony. She and Gary repeated their vows so softly I'm sure only Jan, I and Gary's best man, Butch could hear.

The minute the service was finished, Dad rushed away. I turned to Jeanne. "Dad couldn't stay?"

She shook her head. "He almost didn't come. I had to talk him into it—because of John I think."

I nodded.

I was sorry to see him go, but looking around at everyone at the reception—everyone so happy and joyous—I couldn't imagine him there. Somehow, he didn't fit this picture.

Lyle came up to me as I was pouring myself a Coke from the beverage table. "How are you doing, Barb?"

"Okay," I said. I felt shy. I hadn't talked to him since he'd visited me at The Inn.

"So I hear you know Roger?" I said nonchalantly.

"Yeah." I could see Lyle's face brighten. "What a funny guy. Where is he anyway?"

"Did I hear my name?" Roger came up beside me. He and Lyle began talking about work. Bored, I looked around the room. It was noisy and smoky, but I didn't find it irritating; it was a joyous kind of hubbub, with music playing and people talking and laughing and dancing. Mary and Gary were on the dance floor. I could see that Mary was tired; she tired easily since the accident, and her leg looked swollen. Mom and John were sitting in the corner quietly drinking, not talking to anyone.

"I'm going over to see Mom."

Roger and Lyle continued talking, only nodding slightly to acknowledge my statement.

"Hi, are you guys having fun?"

John snickered, and Mom motioned for me to sit down in the empty chair beside her.

"Where's Jeanne?"

"Oh, Ray and her are dancing over there," Mom said.

I looked through the heavy smoke to the dance floor. Sure enough, Jeanne and Ray were laughing and dancing up a storm, with Mary and Gary beside them.

"I never thought your sister would come through that accident and be able to marry so quickly," Mom said, offering me one of her Rothman's cigarettes.

"Yeah, she's doing well, and Gary seems to love her." I was almost shouting over the loud music, which seemed to be getting louder. I could see Gary's parents anxiously walking around the room, making sure everyone was taken care of.

Mom whispered into my ear. "Roger looks really good; you'd better hang on to him."

I smiled awkwardly.

After the reception, Mary and Gary drove off noisily in Gary's car—someone had strung a pile of tin cans to the rear. I waved goodbye, not sure when I'd see them again.

At the end of the evening, Roger and I kissed goodbye, and I promised to keep in touch. I could tell he was more eager to keep in touch than I was.

It was 1970, and it seemed everyone was doing drugs. Debbie and I started smoking grass, which we got free from the kids who used our apartment. I began smoking up daily.

I felt great, I didn't have a problem in the world. I looked forward to getting high when I got home from work. My days consisted of going to work, coming home, getting stoned, and eventually falling asleep. Day after day, I repeated this ritual.

Early one morning, I got an unexpected visit from Lyle. The last time I'd seen him had been at Mary's wedding months earlier.

"Barb, I'm afraid it's Grandpa. He died in his sleep in the night."

An image of Grandpa flashed through my mind. Tears filled my eyes.

"The funeral is tomorrow," Lyle went on. "Julie and I will come and pick you up around ten o'clock. The funeral's out in Kingsville

Mom fell apart at the funeral. She collapsed over Grandpa's body and had to be pulled away by Ray and Lyle.

That evening, when I walked into my apartment, people were sitting everywhere in a stupefied state. The smell of grass was heavy in the air. I was overcome by repulsion. I wanted to kick them all out. I went into the small kitchen area. A guy I'd never seen before handed me a joint. "Hey, baby, where have you been? You look uptight."

I took a hit and, after a while, didn't notice the oppressiveness of my environment anymore.

Two months of being stoned daily was taking its toll on me. I was becoming disorientated, even when I wasn't stoned. One day, a new person at work asked me my name. I panicked; I couldn't remember it. My mind was blank. I had to stop the drugs. If I didn't stop myself, I would never stop. I knew I was the only one in charge of my life.

Maybe if I just cut down a little bit at a time, I thought on my way home after work. The idea of not having a joint when I got home wasn't very appealing.

When the alarm went off the next morning, I jammed down the off button in irritation and pulled the pillow over my head. Another day of making Whoppers. I was sick of making Whoppers.

"Barb—" Debbie was shaking me. "You're going to be late. Get up, it's 8:30."

"Leave me alone," I grumbled.

Debbie ignored me and went about getting ready for her job. She didn't have to stand under a hot light making hamburgers all day, the way I did, with her hair and skin feeling perpetually greasy. She just got dressed up and stood in an air-conditioned store, showing people bright, fresh summer clothes. If she missed work, she could always go back home and ask her parents for some money. I had to be here; I had nowhere else to go and no one to turn to.

"Bye, have fun making your burgers and fries," Debbie called sarcastically as she left for work.

I could feel it coming back, the old anger and moodiness. I didn't want to talk to anyone. I didn't want to make Whoppers anymore. I didn't want to live with Debbie anymore. We were getting on each other's nerves. I hated going home to my apartment. I hated people always being there.

When I finally dragged myself out of bed and looked in the mirror, I could see crusty dark stuff on my lips. I pulled in closer to the mirror and opened my lips. My teeth were covered in dried blood. What was this? What was wrong? I grabbed a glass and took a gulp of water, and swirled it around my mouth. When I spit out the water it was red, almost pure blood. I was scared. I brushed my teeth, and the bleeding got worse. Eventually, it did stop, and I was able to go to work, but it continued periodically throughout the day. Each time I smiled, someone would say, "Oh, your mouth is bleeding." I was extremely embarrassed.

That evening I called Mom.

"Oh Barbara, that sounds like what I had, pyorrhoea." She said this all very casually, but her words frightened me—I knew she had had to get all her teeth out when she was quite young.

"So what should I do?"

"Take some hot water and put a spoonful of table salt in it, and mix it up well. Rinse your mouth three or four times a day, and you'd better get to the dentist."

I made an appointment with Mom's dentist, not sure how I was going to pay for it. The dentist confirmed my fears: I had serious gum disease and needed about $500 worth of dental work. I kept rinsing with salt water, and peroxide too, as the dentist had suggested. I had no idea what I was going to do about the dental work.

I began to spend more time at Mom and John's. I tried to talk to Mom about what was happening with me—my job, my roommate, my teeth, the drugs. I could tell by the way she quickly changed the subject that she didn't want to hear what I was saying. John listened to me while snickering and looking at me in the way he used to. My stomach tightened as I turned away

I started missing work and couldn't pay my share of the rent. Reluctantly, at the last minute, I went to Debbie.

"What d'you mean you haven't got the rent? You think I'm going to cover for you?"

She did though, and nagged me the rest of the month for the money.

"And are you going to be able to pay <u>this</u> month?" she demanded when I finally gave her the last of what I owed her.

I shrugged.

"I can't cover for you every month, Barb. What do you think I am? I've had it with this dump anyway. There are always ten million people in here, and there's never any food. I might as well go back home...." She banged around, making an angry attempt to put things away, gave up, and stormed out of the apartment.

A while later, she was back, with her father and two huge suitcases.

I was alarmed. "What are you doing?"

"I'm going home."

"You can't do that—how am I going to pay the rent?" Panic rose inside me.

"That's your problem. Maybe if you went to work, you'd make some money."

It was my turn to storm out of the apartment. When I came back, I could see Debbie's stuff was gone.

In a panic, I tried to go to work each day. The end of the month was approaching fast, and that was the second month I missed. Even if I worked ten hours a day till then, I wouldn't be able to pay the whole amount. When my notice of eviction came at the end of the month, I felt almost despair inside. I was a failure. I stared at the notice. I had thirty days to get out of the apartment. I had no idea where I would go. I couldn't go to Irene. I didn't want her to know how I had messed up.

I went to Mom and John's and poured out the whole miserable story.

> "Why don't you come and stay here?" John said, not looking up from rolling his cigarette. "We can put you on the couch."

I didn't know what to say. I looked at Mom, waiting for a reaction from her. Finally, she looked up from doing her nails.

"That would be nice dear. Why don't you do that?"

I hugged her.

"Watch you don't mess my hair, dear."

I quickly pulled away.

I didn't hug John; we didn't do that sort of thing. "Thank you," I said awkwardly. "I appreciate it."

John just waved his cigarette at me, brushing away my thanks.

When I returned to my apartment, I found two guys I had never seen before sitting at my kitchen table, injecting needles into their arms. The sight was sickening. I grabbed some of my clothes and ran out the door. They were hardly even aware of my presence; they were so high.

John came back to the apartment with me the next day to get the rest of my belongings. The guys were gone, but their syringes and blackened spoons were lying on the table. I got rid of them quickly for fear I would get charged with possession of whatever kind of drugs they had been using.

I kept my belongings in the basement at Mom and John's. The house had two bedrooms upstairs, but John was renting them out to make a little extra money. I slept on the sofa in the living room. Mom gave me lots of warm bedding, and the sofa was quite comfortable.

It didn't take long for John to start his old escapades again. During the evenings, if Mom was asleep or out, he would sit somewhere within my view and masturbate. If I moved away, he followed till he was within my viewing range. He never said anything; he just had a sort of grin on his face as he followed me. When I asked him to quit, his response was always the same: "What's the matter with you, are you cold or something?"

I thought of telling Mom, but knew it would just upset her. She and John weren't getting along very well, anyway. So I just tried to avoid him as much as I could.

I was still working at Burger King, but was becoming increasingly dissatisfied. I had to force myself to go to work. Many days, I couldn't bring myself to go. The thought of making Whoppers for eight hours was too much to envision.

I was one of the few girls still working there since it had opened a year earlier. Others had gone on to better jobs, gone back to school or gotten married.

My discontent was becoming hard to suppress. I thought of Irene. I hadn't seen her for so long. It was time to tell her about the mess I had made of my newfound independence. I went to The Inn.

Irene listened without commenting until I was finished.

"Barbara, now is the perfect opportunity for you to go back to school and finish your education."

"Not that again," I said.

"The only jobs you're going to get without an education are like working at Burger King."

I sighed.

"Promise me you'll think about it," Irene said before I left.

"Yeah, I will," I said. I wasn't as opposed to the idea as I had been a year earlier, but I still wasn't enthused.

"By the way, Barbara, are you feeling alright? You look kind of run down."

"Oh I'm fine, great, I've just found out I have a few cavities and they're bothering me."

The gum disease wasn't clearing up, and my teeth were rapidly deteriorating. I had an almost constant cold sore on my bottom lip. I felt ugly, dirty, and physically ill a lot of the time.

"Barbara," Mom said, "you'd better do something about your teeth, or you'll end up losing them just like I did."

I was impressed with the concern she was showing.

"I haven't got the money, and I don't know when I'll get it."

"Look dear, I want you to make another appointment, don't worry about the bill, I'll talk to Doctor. Perry."

"Mom, I know you don't have that kind of money."

"Never mind, just do what I say."

She was very firm, and I was in such pain that I accepted her offer. I went to the dentist and had the work done, and I never paid anything. Mom took care of it all, and never mentioned a word to me about it.

One Friday night, I went shopping with Mom and John. As we walked towards the entrance, a familiar figure wearing a motorcycle helmet caught my eye. I felt my heart do a thud.

"Hi," I said.

Roger lifted his helmet off his head and smiled.

"How are you doing?"

"Pretty good." I tried not to appear too happy to see him. It had been quite a while since we had gone to Mary's wedding together, and I hadn't seen him in Burger King for a while.

I was acutely aware that the attraction was still there. I could feel something stirring inside. I couldn't help but notice how long Roger's hair had grown and how even more striking it made his eyes.

We talked for a long time. It was obvious there were still feelings very alive within each of us.

"What are you doing tomorrow night?" Roger asked.

"Nothing."

"Would you like to go to a show or something?"

"Sure, that'd be great." I was relieved I would be seeing him again. I gave him Mom's address and anxiously awaited our date.

After the movie, we went to The Big Boy and ordered Cokes.

"I'm only down for the weekend," said Roger.

"What d'you mean?"

"I live in Toronto now. I'm staying with Ron—he moved with me. We're staying with his aunt and uncle in Mississauga."

I felt a stab of disappointment that he was living so far away.

"They are great, just like parents, only not so controlling."

"Do they live in a house?"

"No, an apartment. I'm working in a factory with Ron." As Roger shifted in his seat, I could tell he was getting sick of all this serious talk, and soon he started with his never-ending one-liner jokes. I had almost forgotten how much fun he was. It had been so long since I'd laughed this much.

The following week, he called me from Toronto.

“Barbara, I haven't stopped thinking about you since I got back here. I've never stopped thinking about you. I love you, Barbara."

Hearing those words from him again, a warm feeling spread through me. Though I still couldn't bring myself to say them back.

"I'm going to be in town on Friday. There's something I want to talk to you about."

"What is it?" He sounded serious. I felt a pleasurable panicky feeling inside.

"Not on the phone. We'll talk when I get to Windsor. Save Friday evening for me."

I waited anxiously for Friday to arrive. I had a feeling he was going to ask me to go back with him. The idea appealed to me. A way to start over. We could begin dating regularly again. Roger picked me up at seven.

"Your Mom's car?" I asked as I got in the grey Ford Falcon.

"Yeah, she loaned it to me for the weekend. Want to go for a burger?"

We went to a drive-in restaurant for a hamburger and fries.

I waited for Roger to bring up what he wanted to talk to me about, but he was silent. It was rare that he was so silent.

"What did you want to talk to me about?" I said between bites.

He shook his head. "After we eat."

"Ah, come on," I coaxed.

He shook his head again, his mouth full.

I couldn't budge him.

When we left the restaurant, we drove down to the Detroit River to a spot we'd been to many times, dubbed "Lover's Lane." Roger turned off the engine and pulled me close to him.

"I have been crazy without you, Barbara."

I turned and looked at him. I'd never seen him so straight-faced before.

"I don't want to lose you again; I want us to get married."

A nervous giggle burst out of me. I couldn't believe he was serious until I looked into his eyes. He was not kidding. I was tongue-tied.

Finally, Roger broke the silence. "Well, are we going to get married?"

"Don't you think we should just go out for a while and see how we get along?" I said hesitantly.

"When will we see each other, with me in Toronto and you here in Windsor? You'll just find somebody else and forget about me."

I laughed again nervously. Somehow, this was not as serious to me as it seemed to be to Roger. Angrily, he pulled away from me.

"How about living together? I could move up to Toronto with you?" I thought this was the perfect solution. After all, it was 1970, and a lot of people lived together.

"NO! We get married, or we never see each other again."

Roger crossed his arms on his chest, much like a child who can't have his way. I sat silently beside him. I didn't want to lose him, yet I was afraid to get married. I wasn't sure why I was scared but I was.

A moment later, Roger turned to me. "You love me, don't you Barbara?"

I nodded.

"Then we have to get married. I can't take seeing you and not being able to have you."

I could see the despair in his eyes.

He had given me an ultimatum. I had to decide quickly. I did care for him. I didn't want to be without him. Seeing him again made me realize how much I'd missed him the last year. It had to be love. If it was love, why not get married? In the back of my mind was the thought that if it didn't work, I could always leave, and we could get a divorce.

"Okay, "I blurted out.

Roger hugged me tightly. Suddenly, he was relaxed and happy.

I was numb, not sure what I was doing.

"Barbara," he murmured in my hair. "I have to have you. Let's go to a motel."

I nodded against his shirt. I knew he loved me. It would be alright.

The next morning as Roger drove me home, I felt close to him. I didn't feel like when Uncle George did those horrible things to me. Although the visions were not far from my mind.

When Roger dropped me off, I burst through the back door and into the kitchen. Mom was sitting at the table having her morning coffee.

"Mom, I'm getting married. Roger asked me to marry him. We're going to move to Toronto." Saying the words out loud felt somehow different than when Roger and I talked about it. I waited for Mom to say something to somehow make this feel more real, bring me back to earth, and snap me out of this state of whatever I was in. She didn't.

"That's wonderful dear. Now all my children will be married." She hugged me and began talking about the wedding. "Have you set a date yet? You'll have to invite the family. Lyle and Julie will come. It will be wonderful to see everyone. We'll have to get you a nice dress." Her eyes clouded over momentarily. "Maybe your father will help out with the dress..."

I let her chatter on, happy to see her so animated, but wishing she'd show some normal parental concern. She never questioned my decision, no one ever asked me if I was sure. Another decision I was making on my own. I sometimes wished I had parents as my friends did, parents who would interfere just a little in my life. I resented having all this responsibility.

During the next week, while Roger was away, I began to accept what was happening. I was going to be someone's wife! Suddenly, my aimless life had meaning and purpose. I would finally have a real home and a husband. I never thought about any of the realities of being married or even of getting married. I didn't even think about the actual wedding until Roger's mother came over early one morning after John had gone out.

Mrs. Gordon was younger than Mom, around forty, with blonde hair piled high on her head. She bustled into Mom and John's house, anxious to discuss wedding plans. I had only met her once before and had never said more than two words to her. She was an attractive, pleasant woman.

"Well, Mrs. Bennett," she said, "Are you ready for a wedding? Roger says we have to do this all as quickly as possible."

I felt a little embarrassed at Roger's anxiousness.

Mom smiled. "Would you like a coffee or a tea, Mrs. Gordon?"

"Oh no, I just had one, and please call me Betty."

"Okay, and call me Millie."

There was an uncomfortable pause broken by Mrs. Gordon.

"Millie, would you be able to help with the wedding?"

"Well..." Mom looked at me.

I felt awkward and pulled my eyes away from hers.

Mrs. Gordon looked from Mom to me.

"Well, if you can't, you can't."

"I'm sorry, it's just that John has been laid off for a year, and I do some babysitting but it's not much ... but Barbara's father might be in a better position to help."

With these words, I looked up at Mom. "But I haven't even told him about us getting married; he hardly even knows Roger."

"Oh, that's okay, I'm sure he'll help you out."

"Well Barbara, maybe we should go over and see him."

"Now?" I blurted out. I didn't want to go to Dad's. I felt uncomfortable, but I didn't know how to get out of this situation.

"Yeah, come on, you can show me where it is," Mrs. Gordon said as she moved towards the door.

"What will I say to him?" I resented Mrs. Gordon's pushiness.

"Don't worry, I'll do the talking."

I looked at Mom, wishing she would say something that would stop us from going to Dad's.

Mrs. Gordon and I went straight to Dad's. Verna answered the door. She looked the same, with short red hair and her bullfrog-like chin.

"He's asleep," she said, opening the door and her eyes wider when she saw Mrs. Gordon.

Verna disappeared to wake Dad, leaving us in the dining room. I became acutely aware of how old the furniture was and how dark the house was. The sun shone through the living room window, lighting up the cigarette-smoky air.

Verna had already had quite a few; the ashtray on the dining room table was full. I briefly thought of my visit to Roger's house in Tecumseh, a suburb of Windsor, a house with brightly colored rooms and a colored television, and a backyard pool. But Mrs. Gordon didn't seem uncomfortable; she seemed unaware of her surroundings.

"I used to live on this street," she said smiling. "I think it was four or five houses down."

"You used to live around here?" I was shocked and relieved. That explained why she didn't seem condescending.

"Yeah, I haven't always been so rich," she joked and pushed my arm affectionately.

Suddenly, Dad appeared, still buttoning up his shirt. His hair was mussed, and the look on his face was not pleasant, only adding to my already awkward feelings. I felt small, yet I understood how Dad must feel, how surprised he must be.

As Mrs. Gordon spoke, I looked at the floor.

"... so, we were wondering if you would pay for half the wedding."

I squirmed inwardly, waiting for Dad's response. I didn't have to wait long.

"*No*," came the flat reply. "I'm sorry, I can't." He gave no explanation or excuses.

I almost felt relief, as if I deserved this for not approaching him and telling him in a different manner.

Mrs. Gordon did not question him.

"I understand, Mr. Bennett," she said pleasantly. "I'm sorry to bother you. But I do hope you will come to the wedding. Barbara will let you know the details. Goodbye now."

As I went to follow her, unable to meet Dad's eyes, he tapped me on the shoulder.

"Barbara, if you come back on Friday, I will give you some money for your dress."

I nodded.

When I went back, he gave me twenty-five dollars.

"I won't be coming to the wedding," he said, not looking at me.

I didn't say anything. I was hurt and confused—after all, he had gone to Mary's wedding a year earlier. I suspected he was angry because of Mrs. Gordon coming over. I fumbled with the catch on my shoulder bag to put the money away.

"Next week I'll give you some more money for a veil."

I never went back. I paid for my veil with the money I had saved. Mrs. Gordon made all the arrangements. She never consulted me or asked my opinion or Roger's.

Mom had to go down to City Hall with me because I was underage. She signed the form giving her consent as if signing a birthday card. I went through the motions, not realizing what I was doing. To me, getting married seemed right at this moment; I never gave a thought to tomorrow or having kids or what I would do with myself once I was married. After all, I could get a divorce if I wasn't happy. Mom and Dad had, and we'd all survived, hadn't we?

On November 14, 1970, Roger and I were married in Chalmers United Church in Windsor. We invited only immediate family to the church. The reception was at a banquet hall. About fifty people attended, mostly from the Gordons' side, which seemed fair since they had paid for everything. But Mom and John, Mary and Gary, and Lyle and Julie were there. Unfortunately, Jeanne, who had just given birth to her fourth child, was sick with hepatitis. I kept hoping Dad would come, but he didn't show up.

We couldn't afford a honeymoon, but we did go to a nearby motel for the night.

As I drifted off into a restless sleep, I slowly pulled away from Roger's arms. The closeness was smothering.

The next morning, I woke up early and rushed into the bathroom to put my makeup on. I couldn't let Roger see me as I was.

We went to Roger's parents' house for breakfast, anxious to get home to Toronto, to the apartment Roger had rented for us.

We attached the box spring and mattress that Roger's sister had given us onto the top of the old '56 Chevrolet Roger had bought for fifty dollars, which only lasted a few weeks before it broke down; we couldn't afford to get it fixed. We packed our wedding gifts into the back seat and headed for our new home. I had never been to Toronto before, except driving through to go to training school in Lindsay. I was looking forward to the big city and living in my apartment with my new husband. I never gave a second thought to leaving my family or if I would ever see them again.

This was the beginning of a new chapter in my life, and the long-buried effects of my childhood trauma were getting ready to surface.

Chapter 14

I looked around the apartment critically, duster in hand, surveying my efforts. I wished the windows let in more light—we had two rooms in part of the basement of a ranch-style house with only well windows that did little to brighten the apartment.

Aside from the bed we had brought with us, our furnishings consisted of a table, two chairs, and a chest of drawers that had already been there, and an old sofa that had been sitting on the other side of the basement, which the landlord agreed to rent us for five dollars a month. Roger's father had refused Roger's request to use his Sears card to charge a television, which sent Roger into a rage about how unfair it was that his father wouldn't help him out, and I came to realize how much friction there was between them. We ended up renting a colour TV for seven dollars a month.

With the pictures I had hung up and the odds and ends our mothers had given us, the apartment looked almost cozy. I straightened one of the doilies I'd made in training school and flopped down onto the sofa. I'd spent the entire morning cleaning the apartment from floor to ceiling, as I did every morning.

There was nothing else to do but wait for Roger to come home. He was working in the shipping department of a factory in a small community on the outskirts of Toronto. The Chev had broken down just after we'd moved here, and since we had no money to get it fixed, Roger had to hitchhike to and from work each day—about twenty miles from our neighbourhood in Downsview. He left early in the morning and didn't get back till late. The previous week, after almost a month of standing out in the cold weather each day, Roger's toenails had fallen off from frostbite — he didn't have the proper boots, and all his socks had holes in them. I didn't know how to darn, so I cut up some old face clothes and sewed pieces into the holes in his socks.

I made my lunch and turned on the TV. I thought about how Grandma and Grandpa used to sit and watch soap operas while eating their lunch every day. I wished Roger were here—it wasn't the same with just one person. I didn't know anyone else in Toronto. Restlessly, I got up and turned off the TV. I thought about going for a walk. With no functional windows, I could never tell what it was like outside, but it was probably cold and grey. The thought of going out in it wasn't appealing, but at least it would pass the time. I got my coat on and looked at the clock; if I stayed out long enough, the mail would be here when I got back.

Outside, it was cold and windy—December in Toronto seemed greyer and windier than in Windsor. I didn't have anywhere to go. The apartment was in the suburbs, and there were no shopping malls near—even if I did have money to spend, which I didn't. Downsview was an Italian neighbourhood. Even the signs in the grocery stores were in Italian as well as English. The foreign signs made me feel even more homesick. With nowhere to go and the wind blowing right through my winter coat, I was back home within minutes. The mail hadn't arrived yet.

The day dragged on. At six o'clock, I started dinner. I didn't know the first thing about cooking, but with a couple of cheap cookbooks I'd bought in the grocery store, I was trying out the simplest recipes I could find. Roger was so hungry by the time he got home that anything would have tasted good to him. I always had his dinner ready and waiting for him when he got home from work, including dessert—nothing elaborate, just a pudding or Jello. I believed this is what good women did.

It was eight o'clock when Roger finally arrived home.

"Payday today," he said as he came in the door. We'd been here a month, and he was to be paid every two weeks, but since the first two weeks' pay was held back, this was his first pay.

He took the cheque out of his wallet, signed the back, and solemnly handed it over to me. "Here Barbara, you do whatever you want with this."

I looked at him in a panic. "I don't know what to do with it; you take care of it."

"No, Barbara, I'm no good with money. I know you would be much better."

I felt overwhelmed. I had never budgeted money before, except for the brief time in my apartment, and I wasn't very good at it then. We both realized Roger's pay cheques would have to be spent carefully if we were to pay for our rent, food, and other expenses. While I served up dinner, I thought about how I would have to open an account and budget Roger's cheques over the month. I felt frustrated at my inexperience. How did people know what to do?

Roger plopped himself down in front of the TV after dinner, while I cleared the table. I began to fill up the sink with hot, soapy water.

"C'mere Barbara."

I dried my hands and went to him. "Shouldn't I do the dishes?" I asked uncertainly.

"Naw, you can do that later." He stretched out a leg and drew me in closer, then pulled me down beside him on the couch to watch TV. All the while I was thinking about the dishes. A good wife should do the dishes right away—Grandma always had. Roger began kissing me. I responded, partly because I wanted to, and partly because I felt it was my duty.

"How about a coffee now, Barb?" Roger said, pushing himself off me a while later and looking quite satisfied.

I suppressed the faint feelings of resentment that rose at his asking me to do everything for him. That's what wives are supposed to do, I reminded myself as I filled up the small pot with water. At least that was what I remembered from watching "Leave it to Beaver" and "Ozzie and Harriet" as a kid.

It was during these first four months, while we were living in Toronto, that I thought I was really in love with Roger. Our struggles brought us closer together, and we became very dependent on each other. We spent every minute together. We never went anywhere except for the occasional weekend trip to Windsor.

One day, I tried baking a cake

"What's this?" Roger tapped the miserable, flat cake with his fork. It gave a thud. He howled and began drumming on it with two forks.

"Quit that," I said sharply. It had risen beautifully in the oven and then fallen flat while it cooled. It was stone hard.

"It's a great drum," he said, continuing his beat. "How did you know I always wanted to be a drummer?"

"Stop it." I felt a hot rush of anger and humiliation. "You try cooking a meal, then if you're such an expert."

"I already work all day—all you do is sit around here—you'd think you could at least learn to cook." His voice changed, not cajoling anymore, but intense and angry.

"I'm trying—you think it's easy?" Now the tears were smarting in my eyes.

"A lot easier than hitchhiking in the cold and working in a filthy dirty shop all day. All I ask for is a decent meal when I get home. Christ, Barbara, can't you do anything right?"

The tears spilled over, and I ran from the table into the bedroom. I couldn't stay here. I wanted to get away quickly. Roger hated me; I was useless. He'd send me away. I couldn't bear it if he sent me away. I had to leave before he had the chance. I didn't need anybody anyway.

I hauled out my suitcase from the closet. Roger came in after me.

"Barbara, what are you doing? Don't go, I was only kidding. We'll work it out!" he pleaded.

I ignored him and continued packing. I had to get away.

"Please, Barbara, I love you, don't leave me." Tears were rolling down his face. "Please, Barbara, please."

Looking at him brought tears to my eyes. No one had ever loved or wanted me like this before. I couldn't leave. He put his arms around me, and he held me tight. After a moment, he began to kiss me. I could taste salt on my lips as we fell onto the bed in each other's arms.

It was Christmas, and we had got a lift from Roger's friend Ron back to Windsor to stay with Roger's family for a couple of days.

Roger lifted our suitcase out of the trunk. "Thanks for the lift, Ron. See you next Monday. Let me know what time you want to go back."

He carried our bags up the front walk and I followed behind, the nervous feeling I'd had the whole way here suddenly intensifying. What if I said or did the wrong thing? I was always filled with anxiety, always fearful of not being liked or being rejected. I struggled with this feeling throughout my life. It didn't matter how many times I was reassured that I was liked, loved, or cared about. The fear of rejection hung like a cloud over my head.

"Welcome home, son." Betty kissed Roger and turned to me. "Welcome, Barbara. Merry Christmas." She held the door open for us and led the way upstairs to the spare room. "There's a fresh set of towels for each of you," she said, gesturing to the bed, "and the bathroom's just at the bottom of the stairs—you'll probably want to freshen up, Barbara." She smiled at me.

I nodded, unable to say anything. She was so kind.

I sat quietly at dinner, eating slowly and carefully, listening to Carl and Roger arguing.

"When *I* was growing up—" Carl turned to me. "I grew up in the depression when we didn't have very much. My mother died when I was a baby, and I learned quickly that you have to fight for what you want — there's no such thing as handouts. But try telling that to him—" He jerked his head in Roger's direction. Roger rolled his eyes at me across the table. I sat frozen in silence, not wanting to take sides, not wanting anyone to be mad at me.

After dinner, I helped Betty with the dishes, then tried to sneak upstairs to our room. Roger was in the living room watching TV with Gerry and David, his younger brothers. I could hear them talking loudly about the show they were watching. I wanted to avoid being involved in their conversation. I met Carl as I was about to go up the stairs.

"You married the wrong brother, Barbara," he said. "You should have married Gerry. Roger is weak; he'll never amount to anything."

I laughed, thinking it was a joke. To me Roger was wonderful. He worked every day and gave me his pay cheque. He shared everything with me. What more could there be? I shrugged off Carl's words and didn't mention them to Roger.

Despite the problems between Roger and Carl, I liked Carl. He was an interesting, humorous man who enjoyed being center stage. As I lay on the double bed listening to the voices downstairs, I thought how much Roger was like Carl. Carl's facial expressions and wild-looking eyes became an important part of his storytelling. Roger could easily repeat a story of his father's, duplicating the facial expressions exactly. I wondered, was I like Betty, or was I supposed to be like her? She naturally faded into the background while Carl told his jokes or funny stories, much like I did.

Roger's sister Belinda and her husband Mike and their young daughter arrived to spend Christmas Day with the family, and in the big noisy gathering, it was easy to slip into the background and just observe.

I called Mom and Dad and arranged for Roger and me to visit. I was nervous about going to Dad's. I hadn't seen him since before the wedding, and he'd met Roger only briefly.

Mom hugged me and gave me a cookbook for Christmas, a most welcome gift.

“I was a young bride once too.” She said with a smile. We talked easily and casually. Her make-up mirror and bag still stood on the kitchen table, and as usual, she looked periodically into the mirror while we talked.

"You sure have yourself a handsome husband there, Barbara."

Roger blushed and looked uncomfortable. I smiled, proud to have such a good-looking husband, happy that Mom approved. Roger put an arm around my shoulder. "I think I've got a pretty good-looking wife here."

John was sitting across from us, rolling a cigarette, not saying much, but he snickered nervously at Roger's compliment to me.

"I wish you two didn't live so far away." Mom said, changing the conversation to a sadder tone.

"Oh Mom, don't worry about it, we'll be down to see you often.”

I could have stayed visiting with Mom all day, but I could feel Roger getting edgy. We stopped in to see Jeanne and Ray. Jeanne was fully recuperated, and her youngest son was doing well. She mentioned that Lyle and Julie had moved out of Windsor to a small town. I didn't visit them. The next day, we went to see Dad.

"Dad, you remember Roger?"

"I think so, we met once when you picked up Barbara from visiting with us."

"Happy to see you again, sir," Roger said, shaking hands with Dad.

I felt so proud; Roger always knew the right things to say—he handled himself so well. I envied his seeming ease with people.

Verna sat in her rocking chair in the next room without saying a word. No one mentioned the wedding, although I sensed it was in the back of Dad's mind, the way it was in mine. The distance between Dad and me was unmistakable. I wasn't sure how I felt about him, but it wasn't the same love I felt for Mom. I never missed him, but I liked to spend time with him.

Roger and I had been talking about moving out of Toronto, it was too big and far from everyone, and he was getting tired of hitchhiking to and from work every day.

"I've been talking to my sister," he said at dinner one evening. "She's got friends in London, and they said there are lots of jobs there. She gave me their phone number. I think we should go see them. See how we like it there."

I felt indifferent. I was willing to go wherever Roger wanted.

We contacted the Smiths and arranged for them to pick us up at the train station the following weekend. They were very friendly and willing to show us around, and Roger and I immediately liked London. We moved in March, and within a week, Roger had found a job in a small factory as a forklift driver.

"Maybe I should find a job too," I suggested tentatively at dinner the day Roger found his job. The pay was less than he'd got in Toronto, and things would be even tighter.

"No, I don't want you working. I want you to stay home and look after me. My parents fought all the time cause Dad didn't want Mom working, but she wouldn't quit."

I didn't mind staying home. I had no skills or education to offer an employer anyway. Maybe Roger was right. Aunt Alice's words echoed in my head, "**Maybe you will make someone a good housewife someday.**" Was this my purpose in life? I could do this, I could be a good wife.

The first thing I did was send our new address to my family and to Irene, who had sent us a Christmas card with a note on it asking me to keep in touch. In Mom's last letter, she said that she and John had gotten married in a quiet ceremony at

City Hall. I couldn't believe she would marry him after all the problems they had. It seemed like a strange thing to do, but Mom did a lot of strange things.

We were renting a small furnished apartment in a fourplex in an older section of London. The owner of the building had several other buildings in the city and didn't pay much attention to the upkeep. However, we fixed up our place with paint and wallpaper and were happy with it. All the tenants were young couples just starting. We were happy and content for a while. Within months of moving to London, I noticed a change in Roger's personality. I wasn't exactly sure what it was, but I could feel a change.

It started when we began socializing with other couples we met in the building. I began to see a side of Roger I had never noticed before. He was very competitive. He tried to outdo others in conversations, in telling jokes, in everything. His job was the best, our apartment was the best, and I was the best-looking wife. He exaggerated facts and events to make himself look better or to make a story more interesting. When it looked as though people were doubtful of what he was saying, he would turn to me.

"Isn't that right, Barbara?"

I didn't know what to say. Roger looked me straight in the eye. His expression was scary.

"Oh come on, Barbara, you remember that!"

"Oh yeah." I was afraid to say anything else.

I soon became Roger's yes-man when we were with friends; my purpose was to back him up and support what he said. It didn't matter whether it was true or not; Roger made sure I knew what was expected of me. He did this without having to say a word— his eyes said it all.

Despite his competitive, exaggerating nature, Roger had a way of making people feel special. He seemed to have the ability to say what he knew a person wanted to hear. One of our neighbours, a lady of about 45, was a little overweight, and when Roger would see her, he'd say, "Oh Linda, you're looking good today, have you lost weight?"

Her face would beam. "Oh, you're just saying that."

I envied Roger's ease with which he talked to people, and he made friends easily. If it hadn't been for him, we wouldn't have had any friends, since I was still very withdrawn and didn't care about having friends. The only visitors we had were Roger's parents, who came a couple of times, and Irene. She had been in town for a meeting and stopped in to see how we were doing.

As Roger and I grew closer over the months, I felt I could trust him more—although I never completely trusted anyone—and I began sharing my past with him. When I came to tell him what happened at the Belanger's I could remember only vague details, but it was enough to enrage Roger. He became aggressive and violent, kicking and throwing things around the apartment. I had never seen him like this before.

"He can't get away with that, you have to tell his wife, he has to pay for what he did."

I was frightened.

"You must call them, Barbara, right now."

"I can't! I can't!" I burst into tears and ran into the bedroom, wishing I hadn't told him.

Roger came after me, even angrier and more, angry and aggressive. "You must tell his wife, write her a letter then!"

He was confusing me. I wasn't sure if he was angry with me or with Uncle George. When we went to bed, the conversation was fresh in my mind. I tried to push the image out of my mind of myself lying across the bed wearing my pink housecoat. I hated pink housecoats and would never wear one. I tossed and turned all night. How could I write Aunt Alice? What would I say? The idea of it filled me with embarrassment and shame. But maybe Roger is right, I thought. Maybe Aunt Alice should know. Maybe he is doing this to someone else, maybe they have other girls living there. But if I do this, Uncle George will hate me. But I guess it won't matter, I'll probably never see him again anyway. I have a home now; I'll never need to live with them again. Conflicting thoughts ran around and around in my brain.

I woke up with dark circles under my eyes and dragged myself out of bed at seven to fix Roger's lunch. He didn't eat breakfast but took an enormous lunch to compensate.

"I'll write it," I said in a low voice as I handed him his neatly packed brown paper bag.

Roger nodded as if there were no question that I wouldn't have and hastily kissed me goodbye.

The letter was difficult to write. I started and stopped many times before finally mailing it off. I mailed it before Roger came home, not wanting to show it to him. I just wanted to be rid of it.

Each day I waited patiently, thinking I would hear something from Aunt Alice. Roger kept urging me to call, and after two weeks of still not hearing anything, I gave in.

Aunt Alice's voice was distraught. "Barbara, why would you write me such a horrible letter? We were always good to you. Was it because you want money from us, or because you were not a virgin when you got married and had to tell your husband a story?"

"No! No!" I cried. "It's all true, ask Uncle George, ask him."

"I already have Barbara, and he said you are a liar."

There was a pause, and then I heard, "Hello, this is George Belanger."

I handed the receiver to Roger. I couldn't speak to Uncle George.

Roger shouted into the receiver. "You are a slime ball, and if I were you, I'd watch myself very carefully. There might be somebody waiting for you around the next corner!" Roger's face was filled with rage as he banged the receiver down.

I felt scared yet somehow pleased that he had defended me.

Whenever we could save a little extra money, we took the train to Windsor and stayed with Roger's parents. Once we arrived, we borrowed Roger's mother's car to visit Mom. I never heard from anyone else in the family. I missed Mary and knew we were growing apart. Gary didn't seem to want her visiting her family.

It was the beginning of June, and we were saving money for the July 1st weekend. The weather was supposed to be hot and sunny, and we were looking forward to spending the weekend sitting around Roger's parents' swimming pool.

Betty picked us up at the train station on Friday night. The house was full of people, none of whom I knew. I assumed they were friends of Roger's sister and brothers, who were also home for the weekend. We went through the house to the backyard. Someone immediately offered us a beer. I shook my head. We hadn't drunk any alcohol since our wedding. But Roger took the offered beer, avoiding my eyes.

I could see the alcohol begin to affect him almost immediately. His voice became louder, drawing attention to himself and me, who was beside him. I felt uncomfortable and pulled myself away. I felt scared that something was going to happen. I was taken aback by the strong aversion I felt to seeing that beer bottle in Roger's hand. An aversion to the alcohol itself, accompanied by a feeling of loss of control.

Roger joined the others, who were getting rowdy and throwing each other in the pool. I tried to stay out of the way, standing around the side of the change house. The guys were making obscene remarks. Embarrassed, I tried not to listen.

I hated it so much when people were drunk—it scared me. I remembered when Mom and John came home after being out drinking. There was always a big fight. I was sure something awful was going to happen. Carl and Betty were nowhere to be seen. Roger was talking to Gerry's friends, people he had known when he lived at home.

"Let's go for a walk, Roger," I said, trying to get him away.

"Oh, come on, Barbara, don't be a party pooper." He looked at me with a drunk, unfocused stare

I backed away and watched as he started fooling around with the other girls. I could feel the adrenalin rushing through my body as jealousy and anger rose in me. I went to Roger a couple of times again. His words were slurred, his stance unsteady.

Finally, I said in a loud voice: "I'm leaving, I'm going to Mom's—good-bye!"

I went into the house to get my things, hoping Roger would come in and stop me. I tried to think of how I was going to get to the other side of town. I grabbed my small overnight bag and started walking down the street, hoping I was going in the right direction.

Suddenly, I heard footsteps behind me. I turned and saw Roger coming a short distance away. I began to run in the other direction.

He called out. "Barbara, I want to talk to you."

I kept going.

"Wait! Wait!" He was right behind me now. He seemed to have sobered up a bit.

I kept walking, but more slowly.

Roger caught up to me. "Why are you doing this? What is wrong with you?"

I didn't reply. I felt overwhelmed with anger. I felt betrayed and rejected as if he'd done something horrible to me.

He grabbed my arm. "Answer me."

I pulled away.

He grabbed me again. "I'm sorry, okay?"

I looked into his half-drunken face. "I don't care if you are sorry; I've had it with you. I'm leaving."

At that moment, his whole face changed. "You are not going anywhere! Now come back with me!"

"I'm not going back with you!" I replied with such determination that I was surprised at the sound of my voice.

As I walked away, I passed a small kitten at the side of the road.

Roger's voice came from behind me. "If you don't turn around right now and come back to the house with me, I am going to kill this kitten."

I turned to look at him. He had picked up the kitten and was holding it with one hand around its chest. Of course, I didn't believe him. I kept walking.

"I mean it, Barbara, do you hear it squealing?"

I turned around. The kitten was squirming frantically in Roger's grip.

"Put the cat down!" I screamed at him. "Put it down!"

"Then you're coming back with me, right?" His voice was scary, and I knew he was hurting the kitten.

"Yes, I'll come back with you," I sneered at him.

He gave me a confident smile and put the kitten down. It fell over to one side and just lay there.

"You've killed it, you've killed it!" I screamed and reached for the kitten. It struggled to its feet and crawled away towards the big open field. "Eight lives left," I thought in the back of my mind.

Reluctantly, I walked back to the house with Roger, who put his arm around me. I was repulsed by his touch, but I was more scared to let him see my fear, so I didn't move away.

For the remainder of the weekend, I was quiet and kept my distance from him. I didn't know what bizarre thing he might do next. Roger was especially attentive, making sure my every need was taken care of.

On the train home, I felt more relaxed and tried to talk to him about what had happened. I wanted the truth—I wanted to understand why Roger had done that to the kitten.

"Roger, can we talk about the fight?"

Roger sat in stony silence, looking straight ahead.

"Please Roger, talk to me."

> He turned suddenly and grabbed my face with one hand, squeezing as hard as he could. "Shut up, I don't want to talk about this anymore." He spoke through gritted teeth.

I tried to pull his hand from my face. He was squeezing so tight my teeth were cutting into the insides of my cheeks. When he finally let go, I was so scared I didn't move or say anything for the rest of the trip.

This incident was the beginning of Roger's violence. If I expressed any unhappiness with the way our life was going, maybe because I wanted a job or wanted to go to school, we would fight, and the fights usually ended with me threatening to leave, my only way of dealing with conflict. I knew Roger wouldn't let me go. He would panic and hit me. It seemed to be the only way he knew how to control me. Neither of us knew how to deal with conflict.

The violence became much more than squeezing my face. I had black eyes, I had my head split open from being hit on the soap dish in the bathroom, and, most commonly, I had a bruised neck from Roger trying to strangle me. He would only let my throat go when I couldn't breathe, and he could see my face was red.

In a way, when he hit me, I knew I had the upper hand because he would feel so bad, he would do anything for me for months after. The next day when he saw the marks, he left on me he would cry. "Oh Barbara, I'm so sorry, how could I do that to you? Please forgive me."

Each time I believed him. I needed so much to believe that he loved me. To prevent his anger, I gave in to everything he wanted, and sometimes there would be months when these fights didn't happen.

After we had been in London for about six months, Roger got another job, at a warehousing company, and was finally making a decent wage. We were able to buy our own furniture and move into a bigger apartment. Roger even agreed to let me babysit as long as I did it at home.

We had discussed having children and decided we were not ready yet. However, Roger told all our friends that we had decided not to have children. One evening, when we came home after an evening of playing cards at a neighbour's, I got up my courage to ask him about it.

"Roger," I said gently, "why are you telling everyone we're not going to have any children?"

"Oh, I just said that so people won't keep asking us when are we going to have children," he replied nonchalantly.

"But when you say that everyone looks at us like we are weird or something."

"Just never mind, I'll handle this my way."

I felt extremely frustrated. I hated the way he took control and tried to run my life. There was growing resentment in me. I felt suppressed. I began to wonder who I really was—was I just playing a role, was this all there was?

I began to spend time at the library. I wasn't sure what I was looking for, but I felt something was missing. There was something I didn't understand about life, about my childhood, about Roger and me, about relationships.

A short time later, my doctor wanted me to go off my birth control pills for a while. I began using a diaphragm and soon after became pregnant.

I anxiously waited for Roger to come home from work, rehearsing how I would tell him. What would he say? I wasn't even sure how I felt. Part of me was happy, but I wasn't concerned with my feelings—they weren't important. Roger's were.

As he sat down for dinner, I could feel my heart pounding.

"Roger, I went to the doctor today."

He looked at me, almost startled. I was sure he knew what I was going to say.

"I'm pregnant."

He continued eating, with no response.

"Didn't you use your diaphragm?"

"Yes, but I guess it didn't work."

"I thought we talked about this and decided we weren't going to have any kids."

"Well, I'm sorry, it just happened," I said defensively. I hated myself. I had let him down; now our life was ruined, and our plans were over. I knew it was my fault; I always messed up. Although I was scared, I felt thrilled to be pregnant, but I kept my feelings hidden.

"You should have been careful!" Roger screamed.

"I *was* being careful!" I screamed back, my anger boiling to the surface.

Our fight ended with both of us in tears, wondering what we were going to do with a baby. Neither of us knew the first thing about babies.

I wrote Mom a letter and told her about my pregnancy. She wrote back saying she was happy if we were happy. She added that she was moving out of John's house and filing for divorce. I thought they had finally resolved their problems, but marriage seemed to make matters worse. I wished Roger and I hadn't got married, I wished we had just lived together, maybe we wouldn't be fighting so much. Mom's divorce only reinforced my feelings that marriages didn't work, and that people were better off living together. Then you just moved out; you didn't have to go through a divorce.

My pregnancy progressed without complications. I was due in February. As my stomach grew, I realized there was a growing human being inside of me. I began to feel an attachment to this wonderful movement. But I also felt scared and insecure. I didn't know how to care for a baby. What if I couldn't be a mother? What if I were like Mom? What if the baby didn't like me? I added pregnancy and being a mother to my list of things I didn't know how to do. I spent more time at the library reading everything I could find on pregnancy and taking care of babies.

I also discovered a world of things I didn't know about or had never heard of. I read all kinds of books—history, biography, psychology—anything and everything. As I read, I couldn't believe how much I had missed. My life had consisted only of a struggle to survive. I never thought about trees or animals. My thoughts went to Dad, who always pointed out squirrels scurrying up trees, or a brightly colored cardinal sitting on a branch. This was the only thought I had ever given to nature.

Eventually, I got to the point where I could finish a book in a day. Reading started me thinking about myself, my parents, and my childhood. For the first time, I realized I'd had a traumatic childhood. I learned my insecurities and feelings of inadequacy might have come from my upbringing. Feelings that I was never quite good enough, that I was somehow different, that I was somehow responsible for my parents being the way they were, that I had somehow instigated Uncle George and John to do the things they did. What was it about me that was so horrible that would provoke people to hurt me this way? I began to think of the child growing inside of me, and how I wanted to raise that child.

When Roger came home after work, I couldn't wait to tell him what I had learned that day. "Roger, did you know it's very important for a child to feel safe, to feel loved? They say they can even hear things while they are still in the womb, they can feel if their mother is upset?"

"You shouldn't believe everything you read, Barbara."

"I don't, but it makes me think about things I never thought about before."

"Most books are garbage; somebody writes them hoping lots of simple-minded people will buy them and make them rich."

I ignored him.

I also discovered that if I wrote down my feelings, I could deal with them better. I wrote down my feelings but quickly disposed of the pages afterwards, for fear someone would read my innermost thoughts.

As I gained knowledge, I also gained inner strength. I became more aware of the world around me; I felt as if my mind was opening. But although my mind was opening my personality was not. I was still very withdrawn. I had no friends of my own. There were other couples that Roger and I played cards with or went to the movies with, but they never really became my friends. I could spend an entire evening with Roger and another couple and not utter a word. This never seemed to bother Roger. As long as all eyes were on him, he was happy.

As my pregnancy and my reading progressed, Roger seemed to act differently toward me. He wasn't as affectionate; he seemed to pull back. When he was angry, he called me a fat bastard. I became ashamed of my growing stomach—I was about six months pregnant by then. We argued more often, but something in me was beginning to rebel. I didn't want to be treated as if I were a possession of Roger's. I was separate from him; I would soon have another life that was dependent on me, another person I would have to be strong for.

My newfound strength was fragile. An angry word from Roger would send me back to my insecure self again.

"Roger, I think we should go to parenting classes to learn how to be good parents."

"I'm not going to no classes. My parents raised me just fine, and I can raise my child just fine."

"But Roger, it can't hurt anything. I'd really like to go."

"No, I said we don't need to go."

"Well fine, then, I'm going by myself."

"Oh yeah, you're going to go just to make me look bad, right?"

"No, I just want to go. I'm really scared, I don't know how to take care of the baby."

"I said we're not going, and that means you. I'll show you how to take care of the baby, just ask me what you don't know."

"Oh, you're going to tell me how to care for a baby, *sure thing*."

At the sight of Roger's angry red face rushing toward me, I ran into the bedroom.

"Barbara, I'm not finished with you yet!"

He threw open the bedroom door. The look in his eyes filled me with terror. I crawled across the bed, trying to get as far away from him as I could. He reached across the bed, grabbing my wrist and pulling me across the bed towards him.

"Please, Roger! *Please, the baby*! Let me go, please!"

He reached for my mouth as he always did. He squeezed until I tasted blood. He pushed me back hard against the wall. I slid down the wall, wishing I could make myself disappear.

I sat on the floor, clutching my stomach, tears streaming down my face as Roger stood in front of me. The hatred inside of me for him was almost overwhelming. "You've killed my baby. I can't feel it move anymore. You are a murderer!"

He reached down and pulled me roughly to my feet. Then he looked into my eyes and spat at me. He threw me hard onto the bed.

Somewhere I summoned the strength to scream at him. "I hate you! You are a pig! I hope you die!" There was nothing left to lose anyway. I was sure my baby was dead now; I didn't care what he did to me.

Roger didn't say anything; he didn't even turn around. After he had left the room, I sat on the side of the bed holding my stomach. I waited and waited for my baby to move.

Minutes later, Roger came back into the bedroom holding a butcher knife. My heart stopped, and I sat paralyzed in fear.

Roger calmly handed the knife to me, handle first. "Here Barbara, kill me, stab me. I am no good." He was kneeling in front of me, tears rolling down his face.

"Come on do it, I deserve it."

I looked at the knife in my hand, then at the pathetic figure in front of me. I knew I was not capable of doing what he asked. I dropped the knife to the floor and retreated into the bathroom, locking the door behind me. The only thing that mattered to me was my baby.

I sat on the toilet very still and very quietly until I finally felt my baby move.

Roger pleaded for my forgiveness, and I gave it to him. I believed I loved him, and I wanted desperately for my baby to have a mother and father, a real family.

I never told anyone the way Roger treated me. Even when I went to Windsor with a black eye, Mrs. Gordon asked me what happened.

"We were fooling around, and I accidentally hit her in the eye," Roger answered for me.

"I bet," Betty said as she searched my eyes for the truth.

That year, I didn't feel up to the long drive to Windsor for Christmas, so we stayed home and had a quiet Christmas together. We talked about names for the baby and settled on Clinton for a boy and Lisa for a girl. We also talked about the possibility that the baby might not be born normal. I was surprised by Roger's reaction.

"I don't want a mongoloid or a deformed baby. We'd leave him in the hospital and just tell everyone that the baby was born dead."

I didn't say anything, and he didn't ask me how I thought or felt. His decision was the way it would be. I resented the way he seemed to have control over my baby.

Two weeks after Christmas, I went to the doctor for my check-up. He was concerned that the baby was so small, and I was so close to my due date.

"I'm going to make an appointment for you to go to the hospital on Monday to have an amniocentesis. It's nothing to worry about, it's just routine, but we want to make sure."

Roger was convinced this meant something was wrong with the baby. I had my own private fears, but I didn't speak these to Roger.

On the Saturday night before I was to go to the hospital for the test, Roger and I were watching TV, and I began having pains. I tried to ignore them, but they got worse throughout the evening.

"Roger, I think you'd better take me to the hospital."

I could see that Roger was about to wave my suggestion aside, but something in my face must have stopped him. He went for the car keys without a word.

At the hospital, they examined me and said I was in the first stages of labour. Sunday and Monday, I kept going in and out of labour. Roger was frantic with worry; he barely left the hospital the whole time I was there. Finally, on Tuesday morning, the doctor decided to induce labour.

On January 29th, 1974, at 1:47 pm, I gave birth to a beautiful, perfectly normal five-pound, thirteen-ounce baby girl. When they wheeled us out of the delivery room, I could see the relief on Roger's face.

He glanced at the baby, then grabbed my hand and kissed my forehead. "I was so worried about you; I love you so much."

I could see in his eyes that he meant what he was saying. But I was hurt that he just gave Lisa just a passing glance.

Chapter 15

I rushed around trying to get things ready for Lisa's bath before she began screaming again. Roger was at work, and I found bathing her at this time helped her to relax. She was an anxious, colicky baby. Having no family near and no friends, Roger and I found it difficult caring for her, although I was becoming more comfortable

I filled the small plastic tub with warm water, anxious not to make it too warm or too cold. I carefully carried it into the kitchen, setting it on the table.

Lisa was in her sitter, which I had carefully placed on the floor so she wouldn't fall off the sofa where I usually kept it. She was so fragile to me; I was so afraid I'd do the wrong thing.

She was whimpering, getting ready to let out a scream.

"Lisa's going to have a nice bath, yes she is."

I thought of Mom and wondered how she could have sent her kids away. I had been three years old the first time she sent me to live with the Belanger's. I felt an intense anger rush through my body.

In all the books I'd read on taking care of babies, the strongest message was that babies need to feel secure. As I took off Lisa's undershirt and diapers, I talked to her constantly. "You are the prettiest baby in the world, your mommy and daddy are going to take good care of you."

As I said these words, I knew Lisa needed both her parents—I wanted her to have both her parents. I wanted her to feel a father's love, something I had missed. Roger and I must never get a divorce; we must not do that to our baby.

The minute I stopped talking to Lisa, she began to squirm and whine. I considered singing, but that wasn't one of my strong points. Whenever I sang along with songs on the radio, Roger always made it clear I was ruining the song. Her eyes followed my voice. She trusted me so much that I promised myself I would never let her down. I loved the feel of her soft skin when I rubbed baby oil all over her after her bath. When she looked into my eyes, my heart melted, and I knew I would always care for my sweet, precious baby. She brought a feeling of love to my heart that I had never experienced before. I attempted to share how I felt with Roger, but he didn't seem to understand.

I was usually so exhausted after these baths I found myself relieved to put Lisa down for a nap for a couple of hours, until her next feeding time.

My realization that divorce was no longer a way out for me made me feel insecure that I would lose Roger, although I never discussed any of this with him. What if he found someone better? And I knew there were better women than me out there. What if some girl fell in love with Roger and took him away from Lisa and me—what would I do? I was afraid of ending up like Mom and having to give my child away to people like the Belanger's. I tried harder to get along with Roger and did whatever he asked of me. I cooked him special meals and had sex whenever he wanted, in whatever way he wanted.

But there was also growing anger inside me, a resentment towards Roger. I was short with him and cutting during arguments. I felt trapped. I had trapped myself in this marriage.

Roger egged on my jealousy and insecurity. I was even jealous of the girls on television. What if Roger met them and left me? His favourite was Joey Heatherton. I hated hearing her name on TV or seeing her Serta mattress commercials.

"Wow, I'd like to try that mattress out with her." Roger always looked at me to make sure I would react.

"I don't think she wants you," I sneered.

"Sure she does. I bet if I met her, she'd run off with me like that." Roger snapped his fingers in the air.

At this point, I would storm over and turn off the television. He would turn it back on, and I would turn it off. We would begin pushing and shoving. I would scream and yell, and Roger would grab my mouth to shut me up, and more times than not Lisa would wake up screaming. I rushed to her, feeling incredibly guilty.

In the evening, when Roger was working the night shift, and Lisa was sleeping, I envied Roger for being out working. I wished I could go somewhere. I wished I had friends. I put Lisa down for the night around nine o'clock and waited for Roger to come home. By midnight, I was desperate for someone to talk to. I wanted so much to see another adult's face. If Roger was ten or fifteen minutes late, I went into a rage.

"Where were you?" I screamed the minute he walked through the door.

"I just had to finish up a few things at work. Why, what time is it?"

"You were supposed to be home fifteen minutes ago," I roared.

A funny smile appeared on Roger's face as if he were hiding something. "Oh, come on, let's see that big smile," he said, rubbing his finger under my chin.

Angrily, I pushed his hand away. "Leave me alone."

"So where do you think I was anyway, having a quickie in the bathroom with Joanne?" Joanne was the secretary at work who Roger teased me about daily.

"You pig, I hate you! *I hate you*!" I ran into the bathroom, locked the door behind me, and sat on the toilet crying. This wasn't going to work. I was going to have to leave. If I didn't, he was going to find someone, I knew it.

"Barbara, get out of there now!"

"Leave me alone."

Roger began banging on the door. "I'll break this door now if you don't open it."

"I don't care what you do. I hate you; I hate you; I hate you!"

In a panic I heard the lock break, and backed into the end of the bathtub, screaming as Roger rushed in. "Don't touch me. Don't touch me!"

"I've had it with you, get out of there now!" Roger's face was a frightening red, his eyes black with anger.

I didn't move.

He grabbed me by my hair and pulled me up.

"Please Roger don't, please."

He grasped my head and banged it back and forth, back and forth, onto the ceramic soap dish. I felt a pulsing sensation in my head. I was terrified.

"Please, Roger, you're right. I promise I'll never do this again. Just let me go."

"Are you sure? You're not going to start again when I stop are you?"

"No, I won't. I promise."

Roger let go.

As I pulled myself out of the bathtub, my head felt lightheaded, and my body felt stiff all over. I went into Lisa's room. She was stirring, but not fully awake. "I'm so sorry, Lisa. I'll try not to make Daddy hit me anymore."

It became a familiar pattern in our marriage. When we were in the car, Roger loved to make comments about the girls walking down the street.

"Look at the boobs on that one. I'd sure like to get her in the sack."

I could feel my heart pounding.

"Gee Barbara, if you looked like that, I'd never leave you."

My heart sank. I knew he was right. I wasn't good enough for him. Why had he married me? There were far more attractive women than I. Anger was the only way I knew how to cover up my feelings. "Will you shut up! I can't stand it anymore! How would you like it if I did that, if I looked at every guy on the street?"

"Oh, it's just fun. You have no sense of humour. Sometimes I think you need help. You really should talk to someone about this problem of yours."

My tension increased in trying to care for Lisa, who was hyper and very vocal. She seemed to sense I was tense and became even more nervous.

When her screaming started, I was out of bed like a shot, stumbling into her room. I picked her up, but she kept on screaming. I didn't know what to do. The medicine the doctor had given for the colic didn't seem to help.

"For Christ's sake, shut her up," growled Roger from the other room.

"I can't!"

Agitated, I paced up and down the room, rocking Lisa in my arms, completely at a loss as to what to do.

Abruptly, Lisa stopped screaming. She held her breath until she turned bright purple. I went into a panic.

"Roger," I screamed, "she's doing it again—do something!"

I could hear Roger cursing as he got out of bed; he tore into the room and grabbed Lisa from my arms. Startled, Lisa let out her breath and began to wail again.

Roger handed her back to me. "Can't you even take care of your own baby?"

Another thing I couldn't do — I couldn't be a good mother. I was going to be like Mom, I knew it.

At six, pale and exhausted from lack of sleep, I got up to give Lisa her early morning feeding, leaving Roger to sleep. Now that he was working the afternoon shift, Roger was able to see more of Lisa, since she was awake most of the day. When Lisa was quiet, he was good with her, holding her and rocking her to sleep. It gave me at least a short break.

But the breaks weren't long enough. By the time Roger came home at midnight, I was exhausted. Unfortunately, Roger was usually wound up from work and not ready to go to bed yet.

"Roger, please. Let's go to bed."

"I'm not tired yet—make me another piece of toast."

I slammed a plate down in front of him. "I'm going to bed."

"No, you're not. I want you here."

Night after night of staying up till one or two, in addition to my interrupted sleep from getting up with Lisa every few hours, was taking its toll. I was edgy and short-tempered. Roger and I were constantly at each other.

One evening after a particularly loud fight, we were both startled into silence by a loud knock on the door. Roger motioned me to stay out of sight.

"Are you Mr. Gordon?" I heard a deep male voice say. "We've received some complaints from the neighbours about the noise. We just want to check that everything is okay."

"Oh we were just fooling around," Roger said.

"Can we speak to your wife?"

"Oh yeah, sure — Barb."

I came out from behind the door. Two big police officers stood at the door.

"Are you alright, Miss?" one of them asked, obviously aware of my red eyes.

"Oh yeah, I'm fine, we were just fooling around."

Roger and I were quiet after they left. We were embarrassed, knowing the neighbours had heard. I hated myself for letting things get so far. "Roger, we have to try to stop this fighting, it's not good for us or the baby."

"I know, Barbara, you're right. I'm sorry, I'll try not to lose my temper again."

I found it hard not to be tired and edgy. I wanted to talk to someone. I wanted so much for this fighting to stop. We hadn't fought for a few weeks, but I still felt I had to talk to someone. On a routine visit to the doctor, I discussed my nervousness with him. He wrote me a prescription for Valium. I was apprehensive about taking tranquilizers. I thought of Mom's suicide attempt and remembered her always taking pills. Without filling the prescription, I went home to talk it over with Roger first.

Roger shrugged. "If you need them, you need them. Don't worry, you won't get addicted."

He was right; the doctor wouldn't have prescribed them if he didn't feel I needed them. I began taking them and immediately felt some relief; things didn't bother me as much. After about a month I had calmed down and was better able to cope. I quickly became dependent on tranquilizers to relieve my stress. If I became the least bit anxious, I took a Valium.

It was March, and Lisa was about two months old. We still hadn't taken her to Windsor to see our families, although Roger's family had come up once to see her. I talked to Mom occasionally on the phone and talked to Dad a couple of times. Our car, which we had bought from our last income tax refund, was old and I didn't want to get stranded on the highway with a baby. We had felt that by my birthday in April, my 21st, we would be able to go down to visit everyone.

One evening, while I was bathing Lisa, the phone rang. Roger picked it up."

"Oh hi, Mom."

There was a long silence, then Roger said something about the hospital. My thoughts went back to months earlier when Roger's family had come up to see Lisa. Carl had pulled me aside and told me he'd had a chest X-ray and that they'd found a shadow on his lung. I didn't know what to say. I didn't know what a shadow meant. I could see from Carl's expression, which always revealed what he was feeling, that he was worried, but not knowing how serious it was, I hadn't given it a second thought until now. I listened to Roger on the phone.

"When is he going to the hospital? So he'll be out the next day. Okay Mom, we'll be down on Saturday."

Roger put the receiver down.

"What is it Roger?" I could see the concern on his face.

"It's my dad. He has a shadow on his lung and a lump on his shoulder. The doctor is going to take the lump off and see what it is."

"Oh I'm sure it's nothing," I said.

Roger nodded in agreement.

Carl was diagnosed with lung cancer. We all knew that hardly anyone survived lung cancer. Although no one said the word "terminal" out loud.

We went to Windsor every other weekend. Roger wanted to see his father as much as he could. It was difficult packing up Lisa and bringing her to Windsor so often. She was uncomfortable anywhere but at home. She screamed frantically when I tried to put her down in a strange crib for a nap. Nothing I did would reassure her. She gave in only when she was overtaken by total exhaustion.

As Carl became sicker and sicker, he became less tolerant of Lisa's screaming, and our weekends became increasingly stressful for everyone. I offered to stay home, but as usual, Roger wanted me at his side. This went on for six months.

Last weekend we saw Carl was Father's Day. Roger's sister Belinda was over, with her family.

Roger and I hadn't known what to buy him—we'd settled on a shirt and tie. I knew Roger wasn't comfortable with the gift, but we didn't know what else to get. When we walked in the door, Carl was sitting at the kitchen table looking older even than he had two weeks earlier. His ankles were so swollen that he could not move without intense pain. His hair had fallen out, and he was skin and bones.

As he sat nodding off to sleep at the table, I felt for him. I could see the pain he was suffering—although I seemed to be the only one who could see it. The rest of the family carried on as if everything was normal.

Roger went over to him, the gift in hand. "Here, Dad, happy Father's Day. I hope you like it—I didn't know what to get you."

"Yes, it's hard to know what to buy for a dying man," Carl mumbled as he tore the wrapping paper off.

The room became still for a moment. I was sure Belinda was going to burst into tears. I felt relieved at the statement and held some admiration for Carl for being able to admit to what was happening since no one else would. Maybe that's why he'd said it, to snap the others into reality.

Carl and Betty owned some land that they planned on selling when Carl retired. He had been intending to retire when he was 57, one year away. Betty was going to continue working for a few more years since she was only 43. In his last days, Carl told Betty he wanted the children each to have a piece of the land since there would be insurance money for Betty. Anxious to fulfil Carl's last wishes, Betty told the kids she would give them each a plot of land or its equivalent in cash.

Belinda chose the land, and the boys chose money, which was $20,000 each. Betty was to hold the money for them until they needed it. That way she would be able to invest it and collect the interest.

After the funeral, Roger's behavior changed. He became angrier and more hostile, unable to accept his father's death.

"This shouldn't have happened to me. I don't deserve this. I'm too young to lose my father."

Nothing I could say would console him. He became angry at the least provocation.

"Maybe we should get away for a while, Roger," I suggested tentatively a week or so later. I was weary from his ranting. To my surprise, he agreed.

"But what about Lisa?"

Roger shrugged. "Your Mom can come and look after her or something."

I felt guilty leaving Lisa, but the thought of getting away filled me with relief. I called Mom, who said she would be happy to come up and spend a few days with Lisa.

My spirits were light as we set off. But Niagara Falls brought no relief. The entire four days we were away, we argued about everything and nothing. Roger was tense. He couldn't relax. He was getting terrible headaches. He continued nonstop about the injustice of his father's death.

After we arrived back home, I invited Mom to stay on and visit with us for a couple of days. We offered to drive her home the following weekend, when I had planned on finally bringing Lisa to see Dad. With Carl's sickness, I hadn't been able to get there, but Dad had been very understanding about it.

Roger didn't try to control his anger in front of Mom. He ranted and raved about the death of his father, about his poor mother who was now alone. He went on and on.

I tried to calm him. "Leave me alone, you don't know what it's like for me. I never got to show my dad what I could be, show him I wasn't what he thought I was. You've still got your father."

Mom sat quietly on the sofa, as usual, not contributing. I wished she would say something. Why didn't she know what to say?

"I understand, Roger," I said wearily, "but lots of people lose their fathers, and your father was in such pain, don't you think he's better off where he is?"

"No I don't."

"Fine, then. Act like a baby, I don't care."

On the second day we were home from Niagara Falls. Roger went raging out of the house around seven in the evening.

As the door slammed, I burst into tears. Mom came and put her arm around me. "Don't worry, dear, he'll be back; he's just going through a hard time right now. He's young, and he's lost his father; give him time."

"He won't let me help him; he just pushes me away. Now I don't know where he is—he's probably going to find someone else. He'll probably never come home."

"I know it's hard, dear. It was hard for me too," she sighed. "It's not easy being married. Your father used to get paid on Fridays and spend his entire pay cheque in the hotels before he came home. Grandma and Grandpa used to bring us food just so we could eat."

I'd heard this before and wondered what this had to do with Roger and me anyway.

She continued. "It wasn't just that, either. It would have been okay if he'd been more loving and affectionate. Do you know, your father never kissed me while we had sex."

I wished she wouldn't tell me this. I could never imagine my parents in the same room, let alone in the same bed.

"He just got on top of me, and it was finished two minutes later. He never told me he loved me, nothing." I thought how typical this conversation was of Mom, always thinking about herself.

"Please, Mom, I'm not interested."

"Well, I just thought that now you were old enough to understand some things."

Her words were wearing on me. I hated it when she talked about Dad. I hated it when she felt sorry for herself. Something about her presence made me angry. I was feeling things about her I had never felt before.

I exploded. "Mom, what do you know about anything, sending your kids away to live with strangers! I could never let Lisa live away from me." I could feel my body filling with anger. My heart was pounding, my hands were shaking. I was frightened. I had never been really angry at Mom before.

Nervously, she began fidgeting with her hands in her lap.

"Why didn't you take us and go live with Grandma and Grandpa as they wanted?" I was shouting.

Mom looked cautiously at me, and her eyes filled with tears. I knew this outburst was the last thing she expected from me. I was the daughter who unconditionally loved her. I had always put her on a pedestal and was willing to accept her for what she was. I didn't care anymore. I was too angry.

She began speaking, barely above a whisper, her eyes downcast, only briefly looking up to be sure I was listening.

"I didn't want my children to be raised by my parents. Nor could I spend the rest of my life living with them. I wanted my children to be able to have freedom. I wanted them to learn to make up their own minds. I didn't want them to miss everything I had missed. Your grandmother wouldn't let me go to a movie or dances. Your father was the only boy I ever went out with. And when I became pregnant, your grandmother called up Daddy's mother and told her that her son had better marry me. I felt awful. I could hardly face your father." Tears were falling onto her shaking hands.

"Once I found myself alone, I realized that I couldn't take care of you children by myself. I tried, but I wasn't strong enough. I'm sorry. I felt bad that Mary did end up living with Grandma and Grandpa most of her life, but they loved her so much. As for you, the Belanger's wanted you. I knew I could never give you what they could. Jeanne was always closer to her father. And Lyle, well he was old enough to decide what he wanted for himself."

Mom covered her face with her hands, her shoulders jerking uncontrollably.

I waited, feeling nothing. Within minutes, she composed herself and continued. I listened carefully, watching the agitated movements of her hands and the tears streaming down her face. I didn't feel sorry, I felt anger.

"Mom, all I ever wanted was to be with you. I didn't care what I had as long as I could be with you." I sighed.

Then, before I could stop myself, I said, "Do you know what George Belanger did to me?" I blurted out what I could remember of the story.

Mom cried harder.

I couldn't stop. The words just kept coming. "Do you know what it was like locked away in a training school at twelve years old? I felt like I was the worst person in the world. I felt so bad, so disgusting. Now I spend my days wondering if my husband will come home at night, or if he will find someone better. I wonder if I'm taking care of my baby properly.

When I talk to some of the other mothers, I don't see them worrying about everything as I do. Other women's husbands come home late, and they don't go crazy like I do. Deep inside I feel there must be something despicable inside of me, and when people see it they will hate me. They will want to get rid of me as you, my loving mother, did."

I was shouting at her. I felt only hate for her. It was as if a lifetime of anger was erupting. I could not stop it, nor did I want to. My desire to hurt her was overwhelming. I wanted her to take my pain away. I wanted her to pay. I had an almost overpowering desire to grab her by the shoulders and shake her like a rag doll. The feeling was so strong I realized I had to get away from her. I ran into the bathroom, locking the door behind me. I sat down on the floor and cried. I wished Roger were home.

Suddenly, I heard Mom's voice speaking in low tones. I wondered who she was talking to. I pressed my ear to the door and listened.

"Can you come and pick me up? I'm at Barbara's in London." Mom gave whoever was on the phone directions. I heard a rap on the bathroom door.

"Barbara, I'm leaving. A friend is coming down from Windsor to pick me up; he'll be here soon."

After I calmed down, I went in to check on Lisa. She had slept through it. I felt a stab of guilt. Screaming and yelling were a part of her life. Today was no different from any other day for her. I grabbed a sheet and blanket and went into the living room to make up a bed on the couch. I didn't want to sleep in our bed without Roger. Mom was sitting in the chair beside the sofa. It was close to midnight.

"You don't have to go home," I said, not even turning to look at her as I spread a sheet on the couch.

"I think it would be best if I left, dear."

I lay down on the sofa with my back to her.

It seemed like an eternity until there was a light tapping on the door. I didn't move. I didn't want to say goodbye to Mom. I didn't know how to. I pretended I was asleep. Mom leaned over and kissed my face. She gently rubbed my forehead as she had done so many times when I was younger. This time, her touch didn't make things better.

After the door closed behind her, I got up quickly and peeked out the window. I was surprised to see it was John who had come to pick her up. I felt a hollowness inside — partly because of Mom, but partly also because of Roger. My head was filled with visions of where he was, and with whom. I felt a brief stab of pain that was quickly consumed by an even more intense rush of anger.

I raced into the bedroom. I dragged out the suitcase and began pulling Roger's clothes off hangers and out of drawers and stuffing them into it. I was sure he was with another girl, maybe it was Joanne. I hefted the suitcase over to the door and placed it in the hall, locking the door behind me. I knew Roger had left his key behind and couldn't get in.

I spent the rest of the night lying on the sofa, wondering what I was going to do with my life. I went into Lisa's room and stood by her crib. She was my reason for living; she was my life now.

"It's just us now," I whispered. I felt so connected to her. "I'll never let anything happen to you. You'll never have a life like I had. I'll make sure of that."

Someone was knocking loudly on the door. I glanced at the clock. It was seven a.m. The night's events came rushing back. He was only coming home now. He must have been with another girl; he must have met one in a bar somewhere. I hated him; I didn't want him back now or ever.

"Barbara, let me in, come on!" He kept on pounding.

I didn't move or say anything. He kept knocking for about ten minutes. By now the neighbours were shouting for him to be quiet. Eventually, the knocking stopped.

Minutes later, the phone rang. I picked it up.

"Barb, why the hell didn't you open the door? And why is my suitcase outside?"

"Because I want you out! I don't ever want you to come back ever."

"What are you talking about?"

"Go back to your girlfriends!" I screamed.

"What girlfriend? I was at a guy's house; you remember John Brett from work. I was there, call and ask him if you don't believe me."

"I don't care. I'm sick and tired of you. I'm sick and tired of arguing."

"You'll regret this Barbara, I'm the only one who ever loved you; you'll miss me." There was a click as he hung up.

Roger rented a small furnished apartment down the street. I missed him terribly. I had lived with him for almost five years, longer than I had lived with anyone else in my life. I also had very little money and no skills to find a proper paying job. Lisa was crawling, getting ready to walk. When I looked at her, I felt guilty. I wanted so much for her to have a normal family. I wanted her to have a father; I had promised her she would have a normal life. Within two months, Roger and I were back together.

This time I attempted to put conditions on his coming back. Roger agreed to everything. He promised he would not hit me anymore. My part of the bargain was that I would not be jealous; I would trust him. A tall order, but I wanted things to work. I was sure now everything would be alright, we would be a normal, happy family now.

And at first, things were fine. Roger and I were very careful and considerate of each other. We tried to control our anger, each giving in rather than arguing.

About six weeks after Roger moved back in, the phone rang around midnight one Friday night. Sleepily, I groped for the phone.

"Barbara? It's Ray."

Hearing his voice, I was instantly awake. For him to call me, something was wrong. I sat up and turned on the light. Roger groaned and pulled the covers over his head.

"I'm afraid your father's had an accident," John was saying. "He fell down the stairs and hit his head. He's been taken to the hospital."

"Oh my God, is he alright?"

"Well," he hesitated. "He's in pretty bad shape. He's unconscious, and they think it could be pretty serious."

"Which hospital is it? I'll be there as soon as I can." I hung up and shook Roger.

"Roger, wake up, get dressed. My Dad has had an accident, I have to go to the hospital."

Roger sat up in bed, looked into my eyes, and said, very coolly, "I have to work in the morning, I can't go anywhere."

I thought he hadn't heard me right. "Did you hear me? My dad has had a bad accident. Call work, tell them this is an emergency."

"I can't do that, Barbara." He turned over and went back to sleep.

I paced the floor in bewilderment. I had to get to Dad. I thought back to weeks ago when I had talked to him on the phone. I had promised to bring Lisa down to see him. I called the train station. No trains were leaving until nine o'clock in the morning. Feeling completely helpless, I paced and paced. Finally, I lay down on the couch, tossing and turning until morning.

After Roger left for work without saying a word, I called Jeanne. Dad was the same.

"I'm taking the train; I should be there around noon."

"Okay, we'll be at Lyle's—call when you get in, and we'll come and get you."

Next, I went to a neighbour to arrange for her to look after Lisa until Roger got home.

I was gathering up Lisa's things into a bag to take next door when I heard the key in the door, and Roger walked in. I looked at him in stunned surprise.

"I got off early, get ready. I'll take you to see your dad." I didn't question him; I wasn't in the mood for an argument.

On the drive down, a bird flew into the front of our car. I had heard that this was an omen of death. My skin became covered with goosebumps. We arrived at Lyle's house just before noon. As soon as I walked through the door, I knew Dad was gone. I dropped down into a nearby chair. There were no tears. Dad was 57 years old.

All through the funeral service, I remained dry-eyed and numb. Roger gave the impression of a concerned husband throughout the funeral. He never left my side.

At the end of the service, a screen was pulled around the coffin to give the immediate family some privacy to go in and pay their last respects. Verna went in first, then we each went in alone.

When my turn came, I bent over the open coffin and kissed Dad's cheek, just as he had mine so many times. I stood quietly, hoping he could hear my thoughts. "I'm sorry for all the things we were not able to do, and all the times we didn't share. I love you, Daddy. Goodbye."

Then the tears finally fled, relieving my pain.

I hadn't noticed Mary at the service until I walked out of the room, and she was on her way in. I was surprised to see she was very pregnant. She kept her distance from everyone. Gary was with her and seemed very protective of her. She didn't seem to shed any tears for the father she hardly knew.

Once at home, Roger's concern abruptly disappeared. His callous words screamed through my mind.

"I'm glad this happened to you; now you know how I felt."

I turned sharply towards him. "You are a selfish, sick person."

He grabbed my face, but he wasn't fast enough. I locked myself and Lisa in the bathroom. I knew he wouldn't try to break the door in, as we had just replaced the lock from the last fight.

Chapter 16

Days before Christmas, I was standing in line at the drug counter waiting for a prescription to be filled, and I began to feel strange. Suddenly, I felt incredibly warm. I pulled my scarf away from my neck. It didn't seem to help. My forehead and upper lip were perspiring. I unbuttoned my long winter coat, wishing the line ahead of me would move more quickly.

The prescription was for Lisa. She was two years old and seemed to be constantly on antibiotics for tonsillitis. When I spoke to the doctor about taking her tonsils out, he said they weren't bad enough.

My heart was thumping hard in my chest. I felt my whole body break into a sweat. Fear travelled through me—what was happening? I felt lightheaded. Was I going to faint right here in the middle of Woolco Department Store?

I wanted to run and find Roger, who was somewhere in the store with Lisa. I was next in line, I forced myself to wait, fighting the feeling that I was going to have a heart attack, or something awful was going to happen to me.

"That'll be $17.59, please." The woman's voice sounded as if it were coming through a tunnel. I rummaged through my purse for my wallet.

"Are you alright?" I could see the woman's eyes searching mine.

"Yes, I'm fine, it's just so warm in here."

I was frightened—other people could see something was wrong. I had to get out of here now. I handed the cashier a twenty-dollar bill, shoved my change in my purse, and turned quickly, running straight into Roger and Lisa.

"Come on let's go!" I pleaded. They followed.

"What's wrong with you?" Roger barked, pulling the car door shut.

"I just want to go home; I don't feel very good."

Once I was inside the house, I felt fine. I put the incident out of my mind until a couple of weeks later, when I went out to do Christmas shopping. I had the same sensations, only worse this time. I was sure I was going crazy. I couldn't pay for the things I'd wanted. I dropped the toys and ran out of the store.

These episodes increased in intensity over the next few weeks. Every time I left the house, I had one of these attacks. Even going for a ride in the car, I felt like I was going crazy. I had to insist that Roger take me home. I had to stop doing the grocery shopping. I couldn't go out of the house. I wrote Roger long lists of what groceries to get.

"I hate doing this alone. Why don't you come with me, Barb?"

"I can't, I have to do the laundry."

Each week, I made up another excuse for why I couldn't go shopping or for a drive. I bought Lisa's clothes through the Simpson-Sears catalogue and convinced Roger that I preferred to do the shopping this way. I wasn't even able to take Lisa out of the house for a walk. If I went too far away, I would get one of these attacks.

Finally, I knew I had to go to the doctor. I was sure I had something seriously wrong with me, like a brain tumour or some other equally horrible illness. I made an appointment.

"Oh, it's just anxiety," Doctor Marnier said as if he were diagnosing a headache.

"Why would I have this? And what is it anyway?" I was totally confused.

"Oh, nerves can bring on anxiety attacks. Have you had any changes in your life lately, or any extra stress or problems?"

"Well... I've never had a problem with nerves before." I didn't want to believe there was anything mentally wrong with me. I'd always been so strong. I'd survived everything, Uncle George, training school, this couldn't be happening now.

"I'll write you another prescription for Valium. This time I want you to take three a day and try to relax."

I went home and thought about what the doctor had asked, "Had I had any changes or extra stress in my life?"

Two years earlier, Roger had quit his job and gone into the bathtub refinishing business with his brother, Gerry. Gerry had moved in with us and was sleeping on the sofa. The only good thing about Gerry living with us was that Roger hardly ever hit me.

The business was stressful, both financially and emotionally. Roger and Gerry knew nothing about refinishing bathtubs, and they had borrowed a large amount of money from the bank. To keep overhead low, they were running the business out of our home. Our family life all but disappeared, with people constantly coming and going. Roger and I had very little time alone together, and we did nothing as a family with Lisa. The little sense of security I had begun to feel with Roger was fading fast.

Even during meals, Roger and Gerry talked nonstop about the business and how they could make more money. If Lisa or I tried to speak, we were hushed up. I could see a change in Lisa. She would curl up in a chair and suck her thumb incessantly. Her behaviour was forcing me to see that this was no kind of life. I had to do something, but I didn't know what. Roger and Gerry teased her constantly, urging her to repeat obscenities or rude sentences. They thought it was funny to see a little girl swearing. I grabbed Lisa away from them, only to be mocked by Roger.

"See, baby, your mother doesn't want you to have any fun," Roger said, reaching out his hands toward Lisa. She turned away from me and went to him.

Frustrated, I stormed to our bedroom. I curled up on the bed, wishing I knew what to do and how to make things better. My hope of having a normal, happy family life was fading. I had always been able to look ahead and see a ray of hope, even as a child, I hoped for the day when I would grow up. I was sure my life would be better when I was an adult. Now I wondered if I was destined to live a chaotic existence. Maybe I would never find the happiness that people on TV did.

By late 1976, things began to look a little better financially. We took cash from the company for a down payment on a house and bought a side split in the suburbs. Gerry found his own one-bedroom apartment. I was cautiously hopeful that now we could be a normal family.

For the next while we became that family. The three of us went for walks, visited the zoo, and even took Lisa roller skating. I could feel a closeness again. I was finally able to sleep through the night without worrying about what would happen the next day.

Our reprieve was short-lived. By February 1977, the business took a turn for the worse and was almost to the point of bankruptcy. I could see Roger changing due to the effects of stress. He seemed to be acting the way he had after his father had died. He spent hours in front of the TV turning the remote control from station to station. When he wanted to talk to someone and Gerry wasn't around, he called me.

"Barb! C'mere and sit with me."

I dreaded hearing his voice. I knew he wanted me to sit beside him so he could talk non-stop about a new business idea, or how special he was, or how he could do things no one else could do.

"Did you hear me?" he shouted upstairs again when I didn't come down immediately.

"Yes, I'm just cleaning the bathroom."

"Never mind that stuff, come on and spend time with me."

We spent so much time together that I felt smothered. He was always home, and Gerry was usually there too. I dragged myself downstairs and sat beside him.

"What took you so long?"

I could see he was agitated by his dilated eyes and rapidly shaking leg.

"Roger, I do have other things to do," I said impatiently, not caring if he was angry.

"I have something important to tell you. Something that will help us get out of our financial problems."

I listened with little enthusiasm. I'd heard many of his plans before and didn't place faith in any of them. I wondered about the prescription the doctor had given him for his headaches. Maybe he was taking too many. Maybe that's why his thinking was sometimes odd or confused.

"Barb, listen, don't say anything until I'm finished. There is a way that we can have whatever we want in this life." He was talking almost maniacally. I looked at him with confusion.

"Don't look at me like that—it's supposed to work. All we have to do is write up a contract that states when we die, our souls will go to the devil, and we sign our names in our own blood." His voice was desperate. I'd never heard of this kind of stuff. I thought maybe he was joking; he couldn't be serious.

"Where did you hear of this?" I asked, searching his eyes for the truth.

"Never mind. Are you going to do it with me or not?" I could see he was serious about this.

"No, that's weird. What if it works, and when we die, we'll have to live in hell forever?" I didn't believe him, but I thought maybe this would jolt him into reality.

"Who cares, we'll be dead. But at least we'll have had money and success in this life."

"No, I can't do it, it's crazy."

"It's not crazy, you're just being selfish," Roger shouted at me. "You only care about yourself. What about me? I want to have something in this life." He stormed out of the house, punching a hole in the wall on his way out.

I later found a brass plate to hang over the hole. This was the first hole in our new house.

I picked up Lisa and took her to the backyard and pushed her on her swing. I was afraid to argue with Roger. I didn't know what was happening to him. I looked at the pills the doctor had prescribed. If they were to help me deal with extra stress and changes in my life...

They did control the episodes, though I hated to admit it. I hated being dependent on anything. I hated the way they made me feel numb and sleepy. I tried to talk it over with Roger, but he was indifferent. "If you need them, you need them, so what."

I felt like this was one more thing that was in control of my life. I didn't know what these anxiety attacks were and why they were happening to me. When I asked the doctor how long I would have to take Valium, he said as long as it was necessary, or until I learned how to relax. Relax—I didn't know how to relax.

One day, I popped two extra Valium and went to the library looking for answers. Books had helped me through my pregnancy; maybe they would help me again. I went to the psychology section.

A title caught my eye—*The Power of Positive Thinking*, by Norman Vincent Peale. I noticed there were quite a few books on this topic by him and other authors. I picked up a couple of the books and read the jackets. The words I read were new to me.

There were also books about how to stop being a victim, how to stop feeling guilty, and how to get control of your life. I was amazed to read that people could control events in their lives. They could do this just by thinking a different way. I checked books out of the library. I couldn't wait to get home to read.

When I found Lisa and Roger in the mall, I couldn't contain my enthusiasm. "Let's go, I've got some great books for us to read."

Roger gave me a funny look.

"Are you back to that stuff again?"

I found the strength to ignore his words.

As I began to read about people who had overcome incredible situations, I became excited. I read about people with nervous problems, self-esteem problems, and confidence problems, who had all learned to manage these problems more effectively by telling themselves they could. By feeding yourself positive thoughts, you could learn to feel positive. I read about a person who lifted a car with his bare hands to save another person who was trapped underneath. I read about a mother who couldn't swim, but when her child fell into the water and was drowning, she jumped in and saved her. I wondered where this power came from, this strength to overcome incredible odds. I read about people who had overcome situations much worse than mine just by believing and having faith and hope.

I came to the end of one of Norman Vincent Peale's books, and a new feeling spread through me, both an excitement and a kind of stillness. I *can* take control. I don't have to be a victim. It was an incredible revelation. I had always thought that life dealt each person a certain hand and we could only accept it. This is what I had seen my parents do.

I tried to share my joy with Roger.

"I don't believe in that bull shit."

"Oh come on, Roger, at least read the book. Listen, just let me read you this one part."

"No, nothing ever works out for me, and there is no stupid book that is going to change that. I told you what we must do to have what we want. If you don't do it with me, I'll do it myself." I didn't care; he could do it if he wanted, but I wasn't going to. I left the room and never again talked to Roger about it. I never knew if he did it or not.

I didn't want to give up trying to get Roger to read the books, even though he became angry with me each time I brought it up, and I was forced to stop. But I didn't stop reading and believing.

I read every book I could find on anxiety and panic attacks and learned there was a name for what I had — agoraphobia. I tried to teach myself how to relax by releasing the muscles in my body one by one. I also tried to see the good in myself. I knew to do this I had to learn to love myself.

I read *Your Erroneous Zones* by Wayne Dyer. I learned how to take charge of myself, how to break free from my past, and how to let go of my anger. I learned how to stop feeling that everything that happened was my fault. I was determined to overcome. I practiced positive thinking every moment of the day. I was amazed at how it really did work. I felt as if a whole new dimension of life had been opened for me.

However, I found this was a difficult process. When my anxiety attacks became overpowering, sometimes it seemed easier to take a Valium than to take the time to change my thinking. I fought this and forced myself to try harder and harder. Sometimes when I was out walking and felt my heart speeding up, I told myself, "Relax, nothing is going to happen, you don't need a Valium, you can do it." More and more often, I tried to replace a Valium with a positive thought. I tried to find the strength within me rather than from outside. I felt myself become stronger and more confident.

I found a strong religious message running through Norman Vincent Peale's books. I was not a religious person, nor was I opposed to it. I believed the message of the books would have been the same with or without religion. I always knew there was a higher power; I just hadn't put a name to it.

Gerry came over one day. He looked happier than he had for a long time.

"Let's sell the business," he said. "We know it is going under, so let's sell and get some money while we still can." He was elated, and Roger quickly joined in his enthusiasm.

We put the company up for sale. Within two months, it had sold. We received a small down payment, with the rest to be paid in five months.

After the company was gone, our lives calmed down considerably. We were able to think about other things. My thoughts went to Mom. I hadn't heard from her for quite a while. I had seen her only a few times since that outburst four years earlier, and the visits had been strained and uncomfortable. I thought about all the reading I had done about repressed or uncontrolled anger and how it can destroy people. Since I'd had that outburst with Mom, my anger towards her surfaced easily. I wondered if she was afraid of it and if that was why she didn't write or call.

"I'm so angry that you never write me," I wrote in a letter. "It seems if I don't write or call, we wouldn't have a relationship. Do you want me to forget that I have a mother?"

She wrote back:

January 17, 1978

Windsor, Ontario

Dearest Barbara Anne,

CAN I COME HOME NOW?

I mailed Lisa's birthday card today on my way to work. When I got home from work I got your letter from the mailbox. You will never know how happy it made me. I pray every night that I will hear from you dear.

Please do not try and forget me. I know I did not do everything right in my life but I did love you. No day goes by that I don't think about you and wish I was closer. Time is going very fast. I will be 60 years this year I hope I live for a long time though and try to make up for what I didn't do.

I would really like to see where you live and visit with you all. I certainly will try. I have had a very hard year. I could not do anything for Christmas this year it was just impossible I couldn't even buy any Christmas cards.

You say for me to tell you how I feel about this letter you wrote. Dear I know how you must feel and I wish I could live it over. You are absolutely right please forgive me if you can. Some day you will know how I cared for all my children. I have a letter to be read when the Lord calls me. You will know then how I loved you all in different ways. I have my will out and it will be read.

I wanted to call you just to talk to you on my Birthday but I couldn't even pay my phone bill at that time.

I hope my writing isn't too bad but my hand is shaky after working all day and coming home and sewing. But I wanted to answer your letter right away so you would not worry.

I wish I didn't have to work at all just do my sewing. You see by the time I pay my rent I don't have anything left out of my welfare cheque. I have to pay hydro and phone and eat a little so you see I have to work.

Honey I tried to call you on New Year's Eve but I couldn't get through to you.

Now I guess this is all for now and always remember I do love you Barbara. I missed you so much when you went so far away after you got married.

Would you love Lisa and kiss her for me. I remember when I babysat her, and held her on my lap here in this kitchen the last time you dropped in. Please say Hi to Roger for me. With this letter goes all my love to you all.

Forever your Mom

Reading this letter, my anger evaporated. She was asking my forgiveness, and I found I could give it without reservation. Thinking about things from her point of view, I began to understand she also had her demons to fight, and maybe she wasn't as strong as another person might have been. When I thought about it this way, I could see she hadn't intentionally tried to hurt her children or ruin our lives. I could see she was living in her own private hell. I never felt anger towards her again.

The money we received as a deposit on the company was almost gone by the time the balance was due. We were anxiously awaiting the day when the balance would be paid.

But that day did not come. The new owners refused to pay the balance owing, and we didn't have the resources to fight them.

Roger became more depressed. It was harder and harder to talk to him. He acted like he was drunk all the time. He slurred his words and kept tripping and falling. I couldn't figure out what was wrong.

Then I found the bottles. Bottles and bottles of pills were hidden throughout the house—in drawers, coat pockets, even under the seat in the car. The bottles had different doctors' names on them.

At first, I couldn't figure out what was going on. I confronted Roger, and he confessed. He had a series of doctors writing him prescriptions. He would simultaneously renew the prescriptions at different drug stores. Each doctor was not aware of the other. This way he always had a steady supply of pills to keep him eternally high.

He seemed almost proud of himself for being able to pull this off. I wondered why he wanted to feel high all the time. He reminded me of Mom and Dad, who also wanted to feel this way. I hated the feeling of being drunk, and out of control.

As our financial situation worsened, Roger asked his mother for his $20,000 inheritance. She wrote him a cheque. This gave Roger more time to stay home and avoid looking for work.

I resented him being home. Why didn't he work like other men? Why did he think he was so special?

I saw an ad in a magazine for a correspondence course. It was perfect — I would not have to leave home. I always hoped to go back to school. I didn't feel confident enough to go away from home to attend school. I was only able to be away from home for short periods before I could feel an anxiety attack coming back. But I was confident I was going to fight until I won control over my own life once and for all.

I began distancing myself from Roger. I wanted to be alone. I didn't want to be connected to him. I did not want him to be dependent on me. I wanted to stand on my own. I don't think he noticed; he seemed to be in another world most of the time. I spent my time with Lisa.

One hot, hazy summer afternoon, Lisa was outside playing with one of the neighbourhood children. Roger came out and sat on the porch. I stood at the door behind them. Lisa and Jennifer were playing with their dolls.

"Jennifer, come on over here and see me," Roger called.

Jennifer and Lisa both looked up from their dolls.

"Come here and sit on my lap."

"I will, Daddy," Lisa said as she came rushing toward him.

He put up his hand to stop her. "No, I want Jennifer."

Jennifer smiled and came rushing to Roger and jumped on his lap. He put his arm around Jennifer while keeping Lisa at a distance.

"Jennifer is my girl today," Roger said.

"I'm your girl. I'm your girl." Lisa pushed and shoved her way trying to reach her dad. She tried to pull Jennifer off Roger. Roger seemed to be enjoying Lisa's crying and protests.

I yanked open the screen door. "What are you doing?" I yelled at Roger.

I reached down and picked up a screaming Lisa. I took her into the house. I tried to be affectionate, but she wanted to get back outside to make sure no one was stealing her father away.

No matter how often or how hard I tried to explain to Roger that this hurt Lisa, he wouldn't stop.

"What do you know about right and wrong with the family you came from?" he said sarcastically.

"A lot more than you do," I yelled back in anger.

Sometimes he gave Lisa's friends money in front of her. He wouldn't give Lisa anything unless she could prove how much she loved him. She had to hug and kiss him and say nice things to him. Roger said his father had done this to his brother and him, and it was just fun. To me it wasn't fun, it was mean and hurtful. I knew what he was doing was not "just fun." It made me angry and frustrated, but there was nothing I could do to stop him. I decided I would never have another child with Roger. He had not talked of wanting another child anyway although it had been in my mind.

I knew the inheritance money wasn't going to last forever. Several times I tentatively suggested that Roger find work.

"Maybe you should look for a job, and we could put some of the inheritance money on the mortgage."

His reaction was always the same. "I'm a businessman. I can't work for anyone. Another idea will come to me soon."

He bought various gadgets to fill the void in his life. One day he came home with a $1,000 camera. The next week, he bought a complete set of darkroom equipment. Three months later, he was bored again.

This time, he started reading about Hitler and the concentration camps. He even compared himself to Hitler and convinced himself he had the same charisma. He was sure he could make people follow him in the same way. He was becoming scary.

CAN I COME HOME NOW?

I was awakened early one morning by the sound of the phone ringing. I sleepily spoke into the receiver.

"Barb, this is Jeanne."

I sat up in bed. I knew it must be bad news from the tone of her voice.

"Mom has had a heart attack, and they don't know if she is going to make it."

Chapter 17

On May 25th, 1979, Mom died — two months after her first heart attack. She hadn't recovered completely from the first when she had another. As a last resort, the doctors operated to put in a pacemaker, although her chances of surviving even the operation were slim. She did survive, but her heart was so badly damaged it would not respond to the electrical currents sent out by the pacemaker. There was nothing more the doctors could do; they said her arteries were as blocked as those of a ninety-year-old woman. Mom was sixty years old.

None of my family had offered to put us up in Windsor for the three days of the wake and funeral, and Roger's mother was now living in Arizona, so we rented a hotel room. During the day, we left Lisa with Jeanne's fifteen-year-old daughter, Kim.

The hotel room seemed barren and unwelcoming when we returned from the funeral home the first night. The day had been exhausting from sitting in an airless room, and I was feeling numb and headachy.

Roger turned on the TV and flopped on the bed. "God, I hate funerals."

The sounds of people talking in ordinary tones on the TV and the artificial laughter jarred my own painful feelings. I wished I could talk to Roger, but he was distant; I knew I couldn't talk to him about Mom. The person I knew I could talk to was Irene. I had been thinking about her since we'd arrived. I hadn't seen her for a while, but even though I didn't talk to her that often, I always knew she was there if I needed her. I dialled her number.

"Irene, I'm in Windsor... My mom has died."

"I'll come and see you tomorrow evening," she said. Just hearing her familiar, sympathetic voice made me feel a little better.

The next evening, after another numbing day at the funeral home Roger, Lisa, and I were watching TV in the room when I heard a knock at the door. Irene and I hugged. I felt comforted.

"Did you get to see much of your mother before she died?" Irene asked.

I nodded. "A little. She was transferred to the University Hospital in London to do some tests they couldn't do in Windsor, and I got to see her every day for a couple of weeks. I brought Lisa most days, too, so Lisa got to know her a little." I was silent for a minute, sad, even a bit angry, that Lisa would now never get to know her grandmother, never have a normal relationship with her. Mom got to know Mary's two children in the last few years. Mary and Gary were now divorced." I added, "She lived next door to Mary for a while." I stopped again.

"Well, at least the good Lord gave your mother the last two months to make peace with her children," Irene said. I wondered how she could find anything positive in this situation. We chatted about The Inn; she glowed when she told me about the changes and improvements she was able to make. Also, she spoke of "her girls" and the hurdles they had overcome. I felt good that she was still helping other girls in the way that she had once helped me.

Mom left us a letter along with her will. There was a short note attached to the front of the letter. After the funeral, we all went to Lyle's house, and we were each given this letter to take into a private room off the kitchen to read.

Oct /74

I do want a small ceremony just friends and family and I do want to be cremated and my ashes spread over Daddy's grave.

This is all I ask any of you children my last wishes, I hope you will grant me this.

As Always Mom

I do want this letter read to all of you so you will know how much and how very dearly I loved you all in my way.

Reading this I was stunned. I couldn't believe she wanted to be buried with Dad. After all these years of separation, she still loved him.

The letter had been started in 1974 and added to and amended over the next few years.

Oct 7/74

This is my letter to you my children:

The grandchildren always meant so much to me, when you have them you will understand what I mean.

I would like these things as my last requests; to be laid out in my wedding dress with the beads I wore, also I want to look like the picture you will find in this letter. I do not want my diamond ring on, it is for Kim my oldest granddaughter.

Do not feel bad or shed too many tears, I was around long enough for you all to show me how much you loved me. I sat alone so many times in my life and missed you and wished you would come over just for a few minutes, but do not feel bad, it must have been the way you wanted it.

I am not taking sides but in the last few years, Jeanne has been very loving and thoughtful to me and I have been very grateful for this.

She made many mistakes but she always told me, "Mom as we get older we will change too."

You see I didn't want to wait, I wanted your love while I was with you, and just to see you and the grandchildren once in a while.

I have enjoyed going to Barbara and Rogers' they were wonderful to me, and I wanted so much to have them back while I was alive.

I do not let a day go by that I do not think of Mary Rose. She is my daughter who I bore and loved and missed and wanted so very dearly to love her children. As of today I have not seen her for months. I wish they would, as I mentioned, just drop in.

I wish things were different with Lyle and me, it has been over a year this past June that we have not spoken. I do know why, because I went back to John, but where have I to go.

John and I do not yet see eye to eye, and very seldom speak, I just sew and stay home alone. I wish we were a family. I know I am not perfect but I have always tried to be a loving Mom. I am always so happy when I am with any of you. I never wanted to be a burden to any of you, and I have never tried to interfere, I just wanted to be near you. That's why when Lyle told me never to bother him and I never will until he wants me to, but that wound will never heal.

Lyle was very special in my life no matter what he's done or said I'll always look up to him, my only son, and through him his father, who I have always loved will live again.

If there is any money in the bank Lyle can have it.

There are bonds for the three girls this is the very best I can do. I hope I live long enough to pay for them.

This is the way things stand as I write this letter but we never know, as time goes by I will add what I can. If my cat is still around at the time Lyle can take Tuna as I know he loves animals.

As for John, I have nothing he would want if he lives longer than me, only a few memories that weren't so bad. I only wish things had gone along O.K. and everyone had got along better, life is short at its' longest.

If the T.V. is still working sell it and split the money.

Jeanne, take all my business in my dresser drawer and do what you want with it, it will be interesting for you and Lyle, the things I have kept.

There is however some "in memory" if you would like to have one made of me dear children. The literature is all there and what you are supposed to do to get them finished.

This will be all I will say, I am putting this away now until the time you will need it.

Hope you all have happy memories of me.

Your Mom

It is now Feb 28, 1976 a few more lines to add. Things are wonderful now, I am by myself and you all come and see me. Lyle and Julie come so often and it makes my life complete, they are doing all the time for me. My prayers are answered, only that I would be happy if I could see and be close to Mary Rose, before my time would come. I wish I would see Barbara Anne more often. Barbara is the only one I held to feed while I tried to do my work. I missed her so when she went so far away and got married so young but she is very happy.

March 21/77

I have changed my will as of this date, it had to be because of circumstances which I will not go into between Jeanne and myself.

Now it is Wednesday April 19/78. I am going today to my Lawyers and have everything left to Lyle and he can do with it what he sees fit.

Jeanne does not come and see me, it leaves me no alternative. My plans were not to be like this but this is the way it has to be.

Forever Mom

These were mom's last words. The finality of it hit me in the pit of my stomach. I'd always had a fear of losing Mom, and when I briefly allowed myself to think of her dying, I'd shake my head to get the thought out of my mind. Now it was reality, I couldn't erase it. I was never going to have a mother like everyone else. Lisa was never going to have a grandmother who looked and acted like other grandmothers. Mom was never going to be happy; she would never have what she wanted out of life. The picture I carried in my mind of Mom sitting at the kitchen table in John's house, crying, with the shades pulled tightly down in the middle of summer, would never change. She would always wear that sad face. What a wasted life.

The days and weeks that followed were filled with sadness. My sense of loss was overwhelming. The thought that I could never feel her touch again devastated me. My dreams were overflowing with thoughts of her. Everything I did seemed to remind me of her. I felt alone and empty. It seemed as if I'd spent my whole life trying to win her love. I somehow thought that if I could do this, my life would be complete in a way. Now she was gone, and I wasn't sure if I ever did win her love, or if it was even possible.

Roger was angry with the way I was moping around the house. He couldn't understand my feelings for Mom because I hadn't seen her that much. He thought I should be able to just turn off my feelings for her.

"What are you crying about? She was no good for nothing. She never did anything for you in your whole life." I felt such hate for him at that moment. I hated hearing his heartless words.

Every day life was still carrying on. Roger had started another business, this time a manufacturing company whose major products were cleaning products. He financed this by putting a second mortgage on the house. I hardly paid any attention, hardly cared; I was so consumed with grief.

When I failed to show enthusiasm for his business ideas, Roger became even more demanding.

"Barbara, this has got to stop! Lisa and I need you to take care of us. Just forget about her, she was nothing but a drunk anyway."

To him, she was a drunk. To me, she was my mother.

That summer, we met our neighbours—an Italian family with two boys. The older one, Steve, was 22 and taking Computer Science at the university. Tom was 16 and going to high school. We began playing cards with them. As the summer progressed, we looked forward to these get-togethers more and more; they were a much-welcomed distraction. We hooked up lights around the pool we had installed with Roger's inheritance. We would sit outside around the pool playing cards until the early hours of the morning.

Roger was calm and well-behaved at first. I was relieved but watched him warily, and sure enough, as he relaxed and got to know everyone, he let his mask fall. Within weeks, he was obnoxious and self-centred. If I happened to be winning, he would get mad and throw the dice at me or say something rude. He had to be the best at everything; he couldn't stand to lose.

"Gee, Barb, it's too bad you haven't got the brains to win this game without cheating, eh?"

The others looked uncertain when he talked like this, unsure if it was a joke or an insult.

"Yeah, I guess I must have taken lessons from you." I tried to laugh it off, tried to hide my anger.

"You haven't got half the brains I've got. Besides, there are only two places where women belong. Isn't that right Steve? The kitchen and the bedroom."

A silence fell over the game board. Steve looked embarrassed. I felt my face go red. I didn't know what to say. I felt raging anger inside, new anger. Roger's cutting remarks and put-downs weren't new, but I felt a new intolerance. How dare he talk to me that way? Somehow, this change had something to do with Mom's death. Her death brought home sharply that I was alone in the world. I had always felt alone, but now I was alone. I had no parents; the rest of my family was all so distant. I could no longer dream I would one day have a family like everyone else— that dream was over. But along with this aloneness came a strength, a drive, I could sense in myself. I wasn't quite sure what I was supposed to do with it yet. So the anger boiled inside me, and I kept silent, feeling as though I were waiting for something.

The new business was descending deeper and deeper into debt, but Roger wouldn't go out and work. He wanted to stay home and hire other people to do the work. This made the expenses horrendous. His being at home all the time also meant we never had a break from each other. We argued constantly. His rambling became worse. He would say nothing that made any sense, and he was constantly repeating himself. I assumed he was pretty drugged up by now. I had given up trying to help him with that problem a long time ago.

I found Tom and Steve a pleasant distraction. Steve was only three years younger than me, and I felt a connection to him. Tom was a mature 16-year-old whom I enjoyed talking to. Their lives seemed so simple and uncomplicated. I envied the fact that they seemed to have what I had been striving for—a simple, normal life.

I enrolled in another correspondence course—this time in commercial art as I'd always had an interest in drawing. Within a short time, I received a diploma in commercial art, and along with it a crucial sense of accomplishment and a desire for more.

One night, I woke up abruptly. I looked at the clock; 4 o'clock. Roger still hadn't come to bed, but this wasn't unusual. He usually stayed up till the early hours of the morning watching TV and then slept all day.

I sat up. A darkened image was sitting on the end of the bed. A familiar figure. I wasn't afraid.

"Mom?" I called softly.

"Yes dear, it's Mom."

She came closer and I buried my head in her shoulder. I cried so hard the dark fabric of her clothes got soaking wet.

"I'm okay, dear. I like what I'm doing here. Please don't cry anymore for me, I am happy."

"Oh Mom, I miss you...."

The next thing I knew, Roger was standing beside the bed. My arms were empty and my face was wet.

"Who were you talking to?"

I hesitated. I didn't want him to make a joke of it. I decided not to say anything.

In the following days, slowly, I began to feel alive again. I thought of Mom's wasted life, and I vowed to myself not to repeat her mistakes. I wanted to live, to learn. When I tried to share this with Roger, he immediately put me down. I sensed he felt threatened. I was becoming increasingly aware that something was missing in our marriage, something wasn't right. I wanted someone to talk to about something other than getting rich. I wanted someone to talk with me, not at me. I didn't want to be teased or belittled.

My life seemed to have a purpose now that it never had before. Maybe that purpose was just to live a happy life, to be a happy person. It had been ten years since I'd met Roger, and I had changed from the 17-year-old he met. He still saw me as that scared little girl who had no confidence and was just thankful to find somebody to love her. I wasn't that girl anymore. I wasn't sure yet who I was, but I knew I was changing.

One afternoon, while Roger was busy making phone calls, I wandered over to Steve's house. I needed a break from the house. Roger's presence at home all the time was smothering, and I was tired of hearing his voice arguing with clients on the phone. Steve invited me in. We sat in the living room and talked; his mother joined us. She was a plump Italian lady who was constantly trying to fatten me up. Steve resembled her. He had the same open smile and big dark eyes.

"You should enrol in a night course," he said.

The thought of university intimidated me. I shook my head, feeling shy.

"You could do it. I'll bring home a school calendar for you to look through, okay?"

He was so encouraging I couldn't say no. He made me feel like I could do anything. I went home, full of confidence and excitement. Roger was just hanging up the phone when I told him that Steve was bringing me a calendar from university. Roger just laughed.

"You're too old to go to school. Besides, the university is full of smart, rich kids. I don't think you'd like it, Barb."

My confidence sank through the floor. He was right. Who was I to be thinking about going to university?

When Steve brought over the school calendar, I took it reluctantly, but his enthusiasm as he showed me how to understand it rekindled my confidence, and I forced myself to look through it. There were courses on psychology, sociology, and English. The descriptions made me hungry to be there, to learn all these things I had no idea about. I could do this; I could go to school. I didn't care what Roger said; I was going to find a way to get an education.

In all the books I'd read, the same message ran through them all: You can change your thinking. You can become a survivor instead of a victim, just by believing in yourself. I could control my own life; I didn't have to turn it over to Roger or anyone else. I was becoming a survivor. My anxiety attacks were almost gone, and I hardly ever had to take Valium anymore. I could feel Roger's frustration as he realized he was losing his hold on me.

> One day I went downstairs to find him in tears. I sat down beside him; I felt for him. "What's wrong?" I asked gently touching his arm.

"I don't know, everything is getting to me. You don't love me, we're in debt, and I've spent my inheritance. Nothing ever works out."

I felt such compassion for him; he looked like a wounded child. He needed me, and I now knew I was the stronger of the two of us.

"Roger, you've got to see someone, you've got to stop feeling this way."

He looked defiant. "I'm not going to see no shrink."

I didn't say anything more, I just sat with him until he seemed alright.

I got an odd feeling in the pit of my stomach. Although we were growing apart, I still cared for him. Occasionally, I could see glimpses of the old Roger whom I had fallen in love with—the Roger who was light-hearted and generous. I remembered when he used to make me laugh so hard that I was sure my sides would burst. I wished I could believe in him as I had then, but I'd grown too much; I would never be that Barbara again. And Roger needed somebody like that Barbara, not the one I was becoming.

One afternoon Roger told me he had a life insurance agent coming over that evening.

"What for?" I asked.

"Well, I don't have any life insurance, and I should get some; you never know what could happen." He gave me a strange smile and walked away.

My stomach got that panicky feeling again.

Once he got the insurance policy, he began saying strange things

"If anything happens to me while I'm out, there is money for you, Barb, take care of Lisa and yourself," he said one evening before he left the house. His words terrified me. I sat anxiously, waiting for him to come back. My mind was filled with visions of him lying in a ditch somewhere or in a burning car. Time seemed to crawl. As it got later and later, I ran to the window every time I heard the sound of a car. Finally, I saw the reflection of the headlights in the window as the car pulled into the driveway. Relief spread through me when he walked in the door. I rushed to him and put my arms around him and cried. This occurred repeatedly. I lived in fear that something was going to happen to him.

Lisa was a ray of sunshine in my days. She brought home brightly colored paintings from school and went into a long dialogue about what each picture was. Roger and I still shared these moments, laughing at her descriptions and praising her artistic talent. I hung the pictures on the refrigerator until the next set came to replace them.

As our marriage and business fell apart, Roger became even more depressed and angry.

"I can't stand it, Barbara. Nothing ever works out for me. My whole life has been a waste."

“No Roger, don’t think that way. Things will get better.” I tried to reassure him, but I wasn’t sure things would get better.

He would go into detail describing which bridge he was going to drive off. He said I would be better off without him. I could pay all the debts off, and I would still have a good bank account. I tried to be confident that the business would pick up soon.

"Don't give up, we've come so far. Besides we can always sell it like we did the other one. Then you can do something else, start over again."

I kept urging him to talk to someone, even our family doctor-anyone.

He finally agreed to see our doctor. I tried to be as supportive as I could. After Roger's visit, our family doctor made an appointment for him to see a psychiatrist. Roger was not pleased with seeing a "shrink" but he went.

After his second visit, he came home with a prescription for Lithium and a diagnosis of manic-depression. I was proud of how well he seemed to have handled it. He was to begin taking medication and come back in three weeks.

Since manic-depression was something I'd never heard of, I went to the library and looked in the medical section. I found a medical dictionary and thumbed through the 'M's. "Manic-depressive - of a mental disorder with alternating bouts of excitement and depression." That certainly described Roger. As with my self-diagnosed "agoraphobia", it was a relief to know it had a name and that it was manageable. I was sure with the medication things would be all right now.

In the meantime, Roger decided to give up the business. "I've been thinking about it. I want to be a real estate agent. They make piles of money, Barb, and I'd still be on my own, but it's way more secure."

I was wary, but it did sound better than what he was doing. "Don't you have to take a course for that?" I asked.

Roger nodded. "I looked into that too. It's six weeks. Nothing to it."

I hadn't made any definite plans for going back to school myself, but it didn't seem likely we could both do it. But there was no question in my mind Roger's career had to take priority now. There would be time for me later. I wasn't going to give up. I didn't say any of this to Roger, just kept encouraging him and supporting him.

The business sold quickly, and although we didn't make a profit, we did get out of debt. Our lives seemed to be back on track.

The medication was helping Roger. He was calmer than I had ever seen him. He seemed to be on an even keel most of the time. For the first time in years, I could sit down and talk to my husband without being yelled at or having things thrown at me. I felt hopeful our marriage would work now.

As with all drugs, Lithium had its side effects. I thought the side effects would be a small price to pay for the obvious benefits, but Roger didn't feel the same way. He didn't like the mild tremors in his hands or the occasional muscle spasms. He also didn't like the way people commented on how different he was. I tried to reassure him.

He went back to the psychiatrist for a couple more visits. He was also receiving counselling. However, he wasn't happy with what he was learning about himself. After each meeting, he came home yelling and screaming.

"That guy's crazy. He doesn't know what he's talking about."

I tried to be more supportive of Roger reassuring him that it may take some time to be able to deal with all this new information. Although I knew I could not make him help himself. That would be up to him.

Roger enrolled in a six-week real estate course. I helped him study. The course required concentration, and this was much more difficult than he had expected. He blamed his inability to concentrate on the Lithium and quit taking it.

Within two weeks he was obnoxious, moody, and short-tempered again. I dealt with this in the only way I knew how - by withdrawing. My withdrawal made Roger increasingly insecure. The more I ignored him the harder he tried to control me and strip away any self-confidence I was building.

Since Roger didn't want to help himself, I could feel myself becoming more and more hostile toward him. I had to learn to help myself, why couldn't he do it, too?

Despite this, we still had sex every night. I did it as a duty, although I was resentful and didn't enjoy it. I'm not sure Roger enjoyed it either. I began to imagine myself leaving him — where would I go, what would I do?

For years I had been thankful just to have someone who wanted me. All I had ever wanted was to have a family and a home. But now the price I had to pay was becoming too high.

Meanwhile, Steve was still trying to convince me to take a couple of university courses, but I was still hesitant. Partly because of Roger and partly because I didn't have the confidence that I could do it. Steve and I were becoming good friends. We philosophized about different issues. We discussed things I had never even thought about before. He seemed so different from Roger. There was a peacefulness about him that made me feel safe with him, almost like I was someone else - not this person stuck in an unhappy marriage, with a husband who was struggling to keep his sanity.

Roger would overhear Steve and me talking while we were sitting on the porch or out in the backyard, and later when we were alone, he would comment that what we were talking about didn't matter anyway.

"The only thing that matters Barb, is being rich. If you got money, people treat you better."

As time went on, I found myself more and more attracted to Steve. I had never really met a person who was so "normal." He was calm and easy-going. When we talked, he didn't find my views stupid or unimportant like Roger always had. For the first time, I felt like a person, not a possession - not somebody to be pushed around.

I found myself waiting for Steve to come over to our house. I realized I had come to rely on hearing his encouraging words. I felt guilty about it, yet I also felt good about being able to talk to someone who was not stoned or ready to attack me if I said the wrong word.

Lately, Lisa had been missing school with frequent bouts of tonsillitis. Finally, after I insisted that something had to be done, the doctor made an appointment for her to go into the hospital to have them removed.

Roger and I waited with Lisa until they came to wheel her away to the operating room. She looked so small in the white hospital gown on the big bed. She held onto my hand tightly, trying to smile. Roger kissed her brow, and she was gone. Afterward, Roger and I wandered down to the waiting room. It was empty with a depressing air about it, as if too much bad news had been told in it. Roger and I sat beside each other, magazines open in our laps, not speaking. I thought about Steve. I almost wished he were with me rather than Roger. It was so much easier to talk to Steve. I felt I needed to be honest with Roger and tell him how I felt.

"Roger, I need to talk to you about something."

He looked at me. I knew he would be hurt by what I was going to say, but I needed to say it.

"It's Steve, we've become close. I'm sure you noticed."

Roger's face changed; he seemed almost afraid of what I would say next.

"I feel more than I should for him," I said, tears rolling down my face.

"Oh, come on, you're joking right?" Roger said with a nervous laugh.

I shook my head.

There was silence.

After what seemed like an eternity, Roger tried to make light of the situation.

"You're just infatuated. If you got to know him, you'd be bored to tears. Besides, he's just a short little Italian guy."

"How important are looks anyway?" I retorted, hating how he could only see the surface.

"Come on, Barbara, we are beautiful people. Looks are important to us."

His words stunned me. I never noticed how shallow he was. I wondered how I could have spent almost 10 years with this man and not been aware of this. I felt almost as if I had been sleepwalking for years and was suddenly awakened. Maybe I had wanted my marriage to work so badly that I turned a blind eye.

Before I could say anything, two men in white were wheeling Lisa past us on a stretcher. We went to her side. She was groggy but managed a slight smile. We spent the rest of the day with her in the ward.

At home, later that evening, I waited for Roger to bring up Steve, but he didn't. I wondered why I had told him about Steve. Was it to make him angry, or to make him treat me better, or was I falling in love with Steve?

A short time after this confession, our marriage became worse. The smallest thing would set either of us off. We argued constantly. Some evenings during dinner, we argued so aggressively that Lisa would leave the table. We wouldn't even realize she was gone. If I threatened to leave Roger, he would say I was probably planning on running off with Steve. I regretted telling him about my feelings for Steve.

I had begun reading again and lost myself in my books. I reread Norman Vincent Peale's books and began reading Shirley MacLaine's. She was quickly becoming my favourite author. I was discovering there was a wonderful world out there.

As our arguments escalated, they became extremely malicious.

"You're nothing but a druggy, you can't even hold a job and support your family!"

"At least I never screwed my aunt like you did to your uncle," he hollered one evening. So, he believed it was my fault. That was it. Anger flooded through me. Blindly, I ran at him, pounding his chest and hitting his arms. I felt him trying to get a grip on my arms, but I wrenched them away, pounding and hitting. All my anger seemed concentrated in my arms; I had never felt so strong. He hit me across the face and grabbed my throat. He squeezed until I couldn't breathe. I made my body go limp, hoping he would think I was dead and let me go. It worked; he released his grip.

"Barbara I am sorry, I'm sorry!"

I pulled away and lay on the bed crying, while he sat in the living room crying. Lisa had slept through it all.

Despite everything, Roger would still invite Steve over. While he was over Roger would watch us closely, almost studying us. I asked him why he kept doing this. He just smiled.

"Why don't we sell this house and move away and start over?" I pleaded.

"Why should we do that?"

"Please Roger, we need a fresh start. I hate feeling this way."

"Come on, Barb, I don't believe that bull shit about you and Steve. You're just trying to make me jealous. You just want to get back at me for something."

I sighed. My words were falling on deaf ears.

Despite everything, Roger finished his real estate course and passed. He listed a couple of houses. He was feeling pretty good about his new career.

One evening, I went to bed early but couldn't fall asleep. I tossed and turned endlessly. Finally, at about one o'clock, I got up and went downstairs to the recreation room where Roger was watching TV.

"I can't sleep," I said, dropping down onto the sofa. He looked at me rather oddly from the chair where he was sitting.

"What do you mean?"

"Just what I said. I can't sleep. I worry about things, and I can't sleep."

He looked toward me, still with a funny look on his face. "Yeah, I heard you walking around about an hour ago."

"Walking around?" I repeated, puzzled. "I was in bed trying to sleep, I wasn't walking around."

"That's what I thought you'd say. I don't want to upset you, Barbara, but you were up a while ago. You must have been walking in your sleep. You had this funny look on your face, and you wouldn't talk to me."

"What are you talking about?" My heart was pumping hard in my chest.

> "You tried to run out the back door in your nightgown," Roger said. "Luckily, I caught you just in time."

I could feel my heart racing, my hands trembling. Oh no, not again. A part of me had always believed Uncle George. Maybe he had been right all along, maybe it was all my fault.

I couldn't speak. Tears flooded down my face. Roger came and sat beside me and put his arm around me.

"Shsh, it's okay, I'll take care of you. No one else would ever put up with this, but I will. Don't worry, it'll be okay."

I leaned over and put my head on his shoulder. I felt comforted.

Chapter 18

The weeks following Roger telling me that I had been walking in my sleep were difficult. I was afraid to fall asleep for fear of what I might do. I had visions of going into Lisa's room and hurting her, walking outside naked, or doing other strange thing. If I did fall asleep, when I woke up, I questioned Roger.

"Did I do anything? Did I get up? Where did I go?" I would ask almost in a frenzy.

My days were spent being miserable and yelling at Lisa. More often than I cared to, I had been thinking about Uncle George. Considering what Roger had told me, I was forced to believe that Uncle George had been telling the truth. Now I knew what had happened was my fault. I tried to talk to Roger about it.

"Poor Uncle George. That must have been a terrible ordeal for him." I paused.

"I wonder what other things I've done that I don't know about."

Roger tried to comfort me.

"Don't worry, I'm sure you haven't done anything else. I told you that I would take care of you, didn't I? Now stop thinking about that stuff."

"I can't stop thinking about it. I want to see someone. There has to be a way to stop this sleepwalking once and for all."

"Oh, come on Barb, it only happened once."

"Maybe it's happened other times, and you don't know about it."

Roger began to get very frustrated if I talked about getting outside help. He did everything but order me not to talk to anyone. His reaction made me suspicious. I wondered why he wouldn't want me to get help. I finally confronted him. He immediately began to cry.

"Please don't hate me, Barbara. I didn't mean to hurt you."

"What's wrong?" I was confused.

"You didn't walk in your sleep. I've never seen you walk in your sleep in the entire ten years we've been married."

"Are you saying you were lying?"

"Yes. I said it so you would think there was something wrong with you Barb. I was scared you would leave me."

I swallowed hard.

"You were so cold and distant with me. I thought you would run off with Steve. Please forgive me."

I felt cold inside. I looked at this pitiful man begging my forgiveness and felt nothing. I got up and walked outside to where Lisa was playing with her friends. I pulled her aside.

"Sweetheart, I'm sorry that I've been yelling at you so much lately."

"That's okay, Mom. "She hugged me quickly and went back to her friends.

I sat on the grass watching Lisa and her little playmates. They were playing house. I never remember playing house.

Although I was upset by Roger's admission, another part of me was somewhat relieved. Everything was as I had originally believed. I felt able to cope. Things were familiar again. If I had not walked in my sleep throughout my marriage, I felt confident that I wouldn't start now. As for what happened with Uncle George, I just pushed it away to the part of my mind where it had always been.

I heard the door slam behind me. I turned, and Roger was walking towards me. I moved closer to the children so he would not have an opportunity to talk to me. He picked up on my state of mind. He abruptly turned and walked back to the house.

I was successful at avoiding Roger that entire Saturday night. I did some reading, and then I went to bed early and slept as I'd never slept before.

Sunday morning, I got up and made bacon and eggs like I did every Sunday morning. Roger tried to be cheerful. I avoided eye contact. After breakfast, Lisa went out to play. I sat down at the table across from Roger.

"Roger, I want you to leave."

He laughed nervously.

"I'm serious. I want you to leave today."

"Why should I leave? You leave!"

"It's better for Lisa if you leave; it will be less disruptive."

"How can you be so cold Barb? We made love two days ago, and now you are telling me to leave."

"Yeah, well a lot has happened in the last two days."

We argued until Roger realized I was serious. He went up to pack.

I was amazed at my strength. I was totally in control. I felt Roger had left me no choice. I pushed any feelings I had aside. My sanity had to be my most important consideration. I had to get away from Roger. I did not want to play his games anymore.

I called Lisa into the house. When I told her Roger was leaving, she took it well. But I had the feeling she didn't understand the full impact. Roger came downstairs with a suitcase.

"Are you sure about this?" He said his eyes were black with rage. I sensed he knew not to push me. This was a part of me Roger had never seen. I wondered if this had been the part of me that had helped me to survive throughout my life.

"Yes, I'm sure," I said. I showed no emotion. I was in control outwardly, but inside, I was crying. There was a side of Roger I would miss, a part I would always love. But I didn't want to go through life his way. And I knew if I didn't do exactly as he wanted, my life would be full of arguments and violence.

In July 1980, Roger and I separated. We sold the house and paid our debts. There was little money left, and we split it between us. I stiffened my back and went on to start a new life.

Steve became a very supportive friend to me. He helped me find an apartment, and then helped Lisa and me move from the house to our new apartment. He taught me to drive, and I bought an old 1974 Ford Maverick for $750.

Once all the basics were done, I had to get down to reality. I had a little bit of money in the bank, but I had no job and no skills. I hadn't worked for 10 years, and I had a grade 8 education. Having a 6-year-old daughter to support and care for left no alternative but to do something pretty quickly. Roger paid $200 child support and $1 alimony a month. Not much, but it was a start.

The only thing I was sure of was that I wanted Lisa and me to have as normal and as happy a life as possible. Lisa was my main concern. I talked to her about the separation and impending divorce. I explained to her that it wasn't her fault. I assured her that she would still have both her parents. I told her I would always love her and would never abandon her. I think I said those words more for my childhood insecurities than for Lisa. I remember as a child feeling so neglected by my mother. When I was convinced Lisa was happy and had adjusted, I put more of my time into other parts of my life.

I went out daily following up on ads for jobs in the newspaper. I was always met with the same responses.

"I'm sorry, Mrs. Gordon, you have no experience."

"I'm sorry you are not qualified."

Steve dropped over regularly to see how Lisa and I were doing. My frustration was difficult to hide.

"I don't know what to do. I can't find work. I don't want to go on welfare. I want Lisa to have a better life."

"Now is the perfect time for you to go back to school."

I thought Steve was out of his mind.

"How can I go back to school when I have no money?"

"You can apply for student grants and loans."

Steve went on to explain how it worked. He even brought me the forms the next day. I filled them out, mailed them back, and waited. I was so thankful to have Steve.

Eventually, Steve and I became involved. It seemed like a natural progression. Although we both knew it was going to be a difficult relationship, we seemed unable to stop it. We were both at different stages of our lives. Steve was almost finished school and was planning on moving to Toronto in a few months. It was a dream of his; he had always spoken of living in Toronto. I was just beginning and not sure of what I wanted to do. We discussed the problems we would encounter and tried to keep a lid on our feelings.

Lisa visited Roger on weekends. We still argued when he called. It seemed to be a habit for us. He was living in a nearby apartment building and dating a wide variety of young women.

I was enjoying being on my own with Lisa. Although I had financial stress, I could easily live with it. Lisa and I did all kinds of things together and became close. She was so important to me. I wanted to make her life a happy one. Even though we didn't have a lot of money, I wanted her to remember a rich childhood. Rich with warmth, love, and security.

Within weeks, I received my acceptance forms from Fanshawe College, plus a notification from the Ontario Student Assistance Program (OSAP) stating how much money I would receive. I was accepted into the General Arts program in January 1981. Also, I was to receive $1200 in grant money and $1900 in loans. After figuring it all out, I knew I would have enough money to go to school and support Lisa and myself. I was happy. I called Steve. I was so lucky to have him believe in me. No one had ever believed in me as he had. That evening he brought a bottle of wine over, and we celebrated.

I was nervous and insecure as I began school. I wondered if I would be able to fit in with the younger students. My past experiences with school had not been good. I tried to put those memories behind me and start with a clean slate. Fortunately, I was able to do that.

In April I finished my first semester at college. I received four credits and an overall average of B. I felt confident and accomplished. I knew I wanted to continue in college. I wanted to go on and learn a skill and be able to support myself and Lisa. I decided on the Library Technician course. It was a two-year program that would enable me to work in a library. This career choice seemed to fit right in with my love of books and reading.

By the first of June, I learned I was accepted into the program. Also, my OSAP was approved for another school year. I was finally looking forward to each day. I was making decisions.

The only downside was that Steve was leaving. He had finished school and was offered a job in Toronto. The job was perfect, and Steve accepted it. Even though we kept in contact, Steve's leaving left a wide gap in my life.

While I was out of school for the summer, I babysat children. I needed to make money, but I also wanted to spend time with Lisa. I took the kids swimming, biking, and hiking. We played various outdoor games, like baseball and catch ball. We had a good summer, but by the time September rolled around, I was eager to get back to school.

I immersed myself in my schoolwork and took care of Lisa. I made friends at school. I became good friends with a neighbour I had babysat for during the summer who lived in the same apartment building. Beata and I shared our hopes and dreams. I learned to open up and trust more than I ever had in my life. I didn't date and was not interested in anyone. I had been asked out by a couple of fellows who lived in the building. I declined each time. I wasn't interested. I felt I was looking for something special, and I didn't see it in any of them.

When Roger learned of Steve's departure, he began coming into the apartment when he picked up Lisa. Before this, he would always sit in the parking lot and honk the horn for her. He was very friendly and kind to me.

"Barb, let's try it again. I'm off the drugs, my head is cleared up. I'm sorry for the mess I made of things."

I listened. I wanted to give him the benefit of the doubt.

"I make good money now. You don't have to work. You can quit going to that stupid school. We could have a good life together."

Even though I still had feelings for Roger, I knew it would never work between us. I was not the same girl he married 11 years earlier. I wasn't that insecure, confused girl who just wanted to belong somewhere, anywhere. I wasn't that same girl who always felt everything was her fault. I was a woman with a goal and a purpose. I wanted to be happy and fulfilled. I wanted to be the best I could be. The last thing I wanted to do was waste my life. I wanted to be able to look back on my life and know that I had been happy and was an active participant in my life.

With Roger, this would never be possible. When I tried to explain it to him, he refused to see the person I was now. He still clung to the image of that 17-year-old girl he married. I knew there was no hope for us.

Home was very important to me. But I didn't want a home so I could hide from the world. I wanted to create a home that would be warm and loving. A place where I could go to get the strength to go out into the world and strive for what I wanted. But mostly I still wanted Lisa to see a normal, happy family. A family that would be nurturing and supportive. I know this was a tall order, but I had the determination to wait for what I wanted.

Chapter 19

On July 17, 1982, I met Ed Godin who lived in the apartment down the hall from me. The following Tuesday we went out for dinner.

Ed took me to dinner and a nightclub. Since it was a Tuesday night, we didn't have to work our way through any crowds or long lines. We were both noticeably nervous. Almost immediately I sensed Ed was probably just as shy as I was.

During dinner, we learned about each other's pasts. Ed was 39, ten years older than me and had been separated for almost a year. He had three children, one boy in college and a boy and girl who lived with his ex-wife. He had a good job. I could see he had spent years building up his career.

As the evening progressed, we began to relax. I felt something different with Ed. Something I had never felt before. It felt right. Ed brought me home around 11:30. He kissed me gently on the cheek before rushing off to his apartment. I felt a sense of peace deep within. I knew we would see each other again.

Lisa woke me up the following morning, bursting with questions.

"How was your date? Are you going out with him again? What did you have for supper? Did you bring me anything?"

"Hold on a minute, I'm not even awake yet."

I got up, put my housecoat on, and plugged in the kettle. Lisa and I sat down at the table, and I told her all about our date. She understood as much as a six-year-old can. Her boundless enthusiasm put to rest any worries I had about her accepting another man into our lives. I now knew she was anxious to have a "real family" again.

Ed and I began to see more of each other. We always included Lisa in our plans. Our outings were family activities except when Lisa went to Roger's. On the weekends she was away, we would go out to dinner or a show.

Ed came over early one evening.

"I've got the day off work tomorrow, why don't we go on a picnic?"

"Yeah, let's Mom!" Lisa was so excited.

"I have to babysit Dorothy tomorrow."

Dorothy was Beata's daughter. I was babysitting her for the summer. I felt a little relieved to have an excuse not to go. I felt nervous and scared about going out of the city with someone I didn't know that well.

"So, we'll bring Dorothy with us."

I was surprised at Ed's lack of hesitation. I felt panicky; I could feel the anxiety growing inside. I was always fearful of new and unfamiliar situations.

"I don't have any money to buy stuff for a picnic."

"Mom, you just don't want to go."

"That's not true Lisa."

"Then why are you coming up with all these excuses? “Ed asked.

I looked at the ground. I could tell he was hurt. He must have believed I didn't want to go.

"You know I will pay for everything. I asked you and the girls to go, didn't I?"

"Yes but..."

"But nothing. Tell me the truth, do you want to go or not?"

I wanted to go, but I couldn't seem to control the thought that something horrible would happen. I didn't know Ed well enough. I held back tears. Part of me wanted to reach out, and a part of me wanted to crawl back into the safe cocoon in which I had surrounded myself.

"Yes, I want to go." I blurted out before I could think about it anymore.

"Yea we're going. I'm going to tell Dorothy." Lisa disappeared behind a slamming door.

Ed looked into my tear-filled eyes.

"What is it, Barbara? What are you scared of?"

"I don't know. I just feel that maybe I don't know you well enough."

"What do you think I'll do to you? Stop for a minute and think about us. We've seen each other for three weeks. Have I done anything wrong to you?"

"No."

"And I never will. I know terrible things have happened to you in your life but that's over now. I will never hurt you. You and Lisa are safe with me."

I could see how sincere Ed was. No one had ever said these words to me. No one except Ed ever seemed to know how safe I needed to feel.

Ed, Lisa, and I went out to the supermarket and bought all the ingredients. Early the next morning, we went to a beautiful place I had never been to before.

Rock Glen was a rock garden nestled in the countryside. It had waterfalls, a campground, and a large picnic area. Lisa and Dorothy immediately spotted the double water slide.

Ed was so good with the girls. He waited patiently while they went down the water slide again and again. I stayed in the background observing. I could feel myself relax. I was at peace. I wanted to hang on to this feeling forever and ever.

By the end of the day, everyone was tired. Our bellies were full of fried chicken, and we were sunburnt more than we should have been. The drive home was quiet. As I sat beside Ed, I knew that I could love this man. Ed had what I'd been looking for. He was quiet, undemanding, and willing to accept me with all my emotional baggage. I knew I could still be my own person with Ed. I never wanted to lose my newfound self again. Ed was steady, disciplined, and decent. Lisa and I would have a good life with him.

In March of 1983, eight months after we began dating, Ed and I moved in together. One year later, on my 31st birthday, we were married.

I had finally found my forever home.

Epilogue

I wish I could write that I lived happily ever after, but as always in life, there were some bumps along the road.

I struggle daily with anxiety and the feeling that I am not good enough. I believe these feelings will always haunt me. When your parents reject you, it's difficult to feel that you have any value in this world. I do not hate my parents; they had their issues. Their choices were the result of the difficulties in their own lives; Mary and I happened to be collateral damage. At the end of Mary's life, we had many long conversations. During one of our talks, Mary made a profound statement about our existence. "Barb, I don't know why we were even born; no one wanted us." My eyes welled up as that's exactly how I felt for most of my life. Mary and I shared a pain that is hard for others to understand.

I was already a broken and vulnerable little girl before Uncle George and John became a part of my life. I was the perfect victim for their evil desires. I had no strength to fight and nowhere to turn. I was much like a punching bag open for hits and always bouncing back for the next one.

Leaving my marriage and meeting Ed were turning points in my life. After meeting Ed, I continued to read books and become stronger. With Ed's encouragement, I went to university and received my BA in English. In my thirties, I attended a support group for incest survivors, and it made a world of difference in my life. I finally came to truly realize that what happened was not my fault. At that time in my life, my daughter was not with me. She was living with her father, and I am choosing not to go into the details of that situation.

My story is a difficult one to read, and many people will not be able to get through it. Others wonder why I would choose to share it. My story needs to be told for all the victims who are ready to give up. I am proof that you can become a survivor. With Ed's support and my strong desire to overcome, I was able to create a good life for myself and my daughter. When I think of Mary's question shortly before her death, about why we were born, I believe I was born to tell our story. Mary was never well enough mentally or physically to tell her story. What John did to her, and being sent to live away from the family, were events she could not reconcile in her mind. Although my grandparents loved her, she never felt she belonged, as my grandmother would always remind her that she wasn't theirs.

In 2019, and at the suggestion of a lawyer familiar with my case and other sexual abuse cases, I was urged to file a claim with the Criminal Injuries Compensation Board. I received the maximum award for pain and suffering because of the abuse from Uncle George and John. It gave me a sense of validation and closure for the first time in my life. As well, I have become involved in a Class Action Lawsuit that alleges that the Province of Ontario had been negligent in advising Crown Wards, who had experienced abuse, of their rights to civil claims and administrative remedies. This case is ongoing. Another form of vindication, I wasn't that *bad* girl who was sent to training school; it was the training school that was *bad*.

Updates

Lyle and Julie remained married until he died in 2015. My relationship with Lyle was pretty much nonexistent until two years before his death, when I received an email from his granddaughter. She had found me on Facebook and told me that Lyle had cancer. I got together with Jeanne, and we went to see Lyle in the hospital. The visit was as if no time had passed. We continued to visit with Lyle for the next two years until his death. I have no relationship with my brother's three children at present.

Jeanne and Ray have four children. They remained married until Ray died in 2019. Jeanne and I have retained a good relationship through the years. We didn't see each other a lot, but we always talked. We do not see eye to eye on my parents' role in our lives, but we were able to work around that.

Mary struggled through her life with a brain injury from the car accident and mental health issues. We grew apart, as Gary did not want to have a relationship with the family. Mary and Gary had two children, a boy and a girl, and divorced after seven years. Mary passed away in 2017. At the time of her death, Mary weighed 75 pounds and was completely mentally unstable. I received an award for a story I wrote about Mary's life. The story is published in my book "Glimpses in Time: A collection of memoirs and more."

Ed and I shared many years of happiness until he was diagnosed with terminal cancer in 2006. After months of chemotherapy and radiation, Ed died. My world fell apart.

He was my rock; he showed me what love was and convinced me that I was a person who was worthy of love. His death opened a floodgate of pain and memories from my past. I had to find my way without Ed's support. I will always miss him and be grateful for his presence in my life.

Lisa is happily married and a successful teacher. She has two children, twins—a boy and a girl. Her children are wonderful, successful, and do not carry any of the scars of their ancestors. I don't believe Lisa remembers her early life with her dad and me. Roger remarried and had another child. He passed away from Alzheimer's disease in 2025. Lisa and I have a very good relationship today.

My grandchildren are perfect and the best part of everyone. Finally, the cycle has been broken.

Eventually, I found happiness again after Ed's death, and in 2012, I married a wonderful man. I have published 7 books, and they can be found on my website: https://barbaragodin.ca. Follow my page for more information and updates.

Beyond the Pages: Thought-Provoking Memoir Book Club Questions

Key Questions for Discussion

1. **Author's Motivation**: What do you think motivated Barbara to share her life story? What impact do you think Barbara hoped to have on readers?

2. **Voice and Tone**: How did you respond to Barbara's "voice"? Was it engaging, sympathetic, or something else? **Truthfulness**: Were there any instances where you felt Barbara was not being truthful? How did you react to these sections?

3. **Personal Connection**: Which parts of Barbara's experience could you relate to? Did any specific moments resonate with your own life?

4. **Emotional Impact**: What feelings or emotions did this “Can I Come Home Now?” evoke for you? Did it make you laugh, cry, or reflect deeply?

5. **Comparative Analysis**: How does this memoir compare to others you have read? Is it similar in style or theme to any other memoirs?

6. **Writing Style**: Discuss Barbara's use of language and writing style. How does it contribute to the overall impact of the memoir?

7. **Lasting Impressions**: What do you think will be your lasting impression of the book? Would you recommend it to a friend? Why or why not?

8. **Author's Purpose**: What do you think Barbara's purpose was in writing this memoir? What message or theme do you think is most important?

8. **Future Reading**: After reading this memoir, do you want to explore more works by this author? Why or why not?

Additional Questions

CAN I COME HOME NOW?

- Was there a particular passage or line that stood out to you? Why did it resonate?
- How did your opinion of the author change as you read the memoir?
- If you could ask the author one question, what would it be?

Don't miss out!

Visit the website below and you can sign up to receive emails whenever Barbara Godin publishes a new book. There's no charge and no obligation.

https://books2read.com/r/B-A-EPYK-IGRBC

BOOKS 2 READ

Connecting independent readers to independent writers.

Also by Barbara Godin

Dear Barb: Answers to Your Everyday Questions
Glimpses in Time: A collection of memoirs and more
Dear Barb 2: Advice for Daily Life
Can I Come HOME Now?
Seasons of the Heart
Maya's Journey & Maria's Dream
Christmas Stories: Short Stories For Everyone

Watch for more at https://barbaragodin.ca.

About the Author

Barbara Godin is a bestselling author, poet, and advice columnist whose work resonates deeply with readers seeking hope, healing, and connection. Her memoir, Can I Come HOME Now?, a #1 Bestseller, chronicles her journey of overcoming abuse and neglect to reclaim her life, inspiring countless readers to rise above their own challenges. Barbara's latest poetry collection, Seasons of the Heart, captures the beauty and complexity of human emotion, while her Words of Wisdom series, drawn from her beloved "Dear Barb" columns, offers practical guidance and heartfelt insights. A graduate with a B.A. in English, Barbara's writing blends raw honesty with lyrical grace. When not crafting stories or advice, she enjoys walking, hiking, biking, and spending quiet moments with her cherished cat. Through her words, Barbara continues to touch hearts and illuminate the resilience of the human spirit.

Read more at https://barbaragodin.ca.

www.ingramcontent.com/pod-product-compliance
Lightning Source LLC
LaVergne TN
LVHW050525160826
845677LV00011B/1959

* 9 7 9 8 2 1 5 2 7 1 7 8 0 *